Science
Foundations

NEW EDITION

Biology

...artin

CAMBRIDGE
UNIVERSITY PRESS

D0336956

Series Editor	Bryan Milner
Biology Editor	Jean Martin
Authors	Jenny Burden
	Chris Christofi
	Geraint Evans
	Jean Martin
Consultants	Nigel Heslop
	Martyn Keeley
	Helen Norris
Author for Second Edition	Jean Martin

CAMBRIDGE UNIVERSITY PRESS

Cambridge, New York, Melbourne, Madrid, Cape Town, Singapore, São Paulo

Cambridge University Press
The Edinburgh Building, Cambridge CB2 2RU, UK

www.cambridge.org
Information on this title: www.cambridge.org/9780521010368

First edition published 1997
Second edition published 2001
6th printing 2005

Printed in Dubai by Oriental Press

Designed and produced by Gecko Limited, Bicester, Oxon

A catalogue record for this publication is available from the British Library

ISBN-13 978-0-521-01036-8 paperback
ISBN-10 0-521-01036-5 paperback

Contents

■ How to use this book   **6**

■ Humans as organisms

KS3A	What are our bodies built from?	8
1	What are cells like?	10
KS3B	Are you on a diet?	12
2	Why do we need to digest our food?	14
3	How do we digest food?	16
4	Your digestive system: what happens where?	18
5	More about your digestive system (extended in H1 and H4)	20
KS3C	Respiration and breathing	22
6	Why do you need energy?	24
7	How you get the oxygen you need (extended in H1 and H4)	26
8	Two types of respiration (extended in H2)	28
9	Exchange surfaces and diffusion (extended in H1 and H4)	30
10	The heart – a pump for blood	32
11	Know your blood vessels – you could save a life!	34
12	Your body's transport system	36
13	Dracula's dinner (extended in H3)	38
14	Invading microorganisms	40
I+E 15	What happens when microorganisms get into your body?	42
I+E 16	The spread of infection	44
I+E 17	Humans against microorganisms	46
H1	More about breathing	48
H2	More about respiration	50
H3	More about red blood cells	52
H4	More about exchanges	54

■ Maintenance of life

1	How are plants built?	56
2	The cell for the job!	58
3	How do plants get their food? (extended in H1)	60
4	Food factories – the leaves	62
5	What do plants make sugar from?	64
6	Limits to plant growth (extended in H1)	66
7	Water that plant! (extended in H3)	68
8	How do plants get the water they need? (extended in H2)	70
9	How do plants get the carbon dioxide they need? (extended in H2)	72
10	How do plants know which way to grow?	74
11	Controlling the way plants grow	76
12	Making sense – the nervous system	78
13	Eyes – your windows on the world (extended in H5)	80
14	Making decisions – coordination (extended in H6)	82
15	Keeping things the same inside your body (extended in H7)	84
16	Keeping your blood glucose concentration constant (extended in H7)	86
17	Cleaning blood and balancing water – your kidneys (extended in H8)	88

I+E 18 People and drugs _____ 90
     19 The dangers of sniffing solvents _____ 92
     20 What's your poison – alcohol? _____ 94
I+E 21 Legal but harmful – tobacco (extended in H4) _____ 96
I+E 22 Smoking and lung cancer _____ 98
     H1 Plant nutrition _____ 100
     H2 How dissolved substances get into plants _____ 102
     H3 Plant cells and water _____ 104
     H4 Carbon monoxide and your body _____ 105
     H5 Clear images _____ 106
     H6 More about coordination _____ 107
     H7 Homeostasis _____ 108
     H8 More about your kidneys _____ 110

■ Environment

KS3A Staying alive _____ 112
   1 Surviving in different places _____ 114
   2 Surviving in water and on land _____ 116
   3 Different places, different plants _____ 118
   4 Why weed the garden? _____ 120
   5 Competition between animals _____ 122
   6 Predators and their prey _____ 124
   7 Kill and be killed _____ 126
KS3B Food chains, webs and pyramids _____ 128
I+E 8 Energy for life (extended in H1 and H2) _____ 130
   9 Recycling minerals _____ 132
  10 Microorganisms – little rotters! (extended in H4) ___ 134
  11 Down the drain _____ 136
  12 The carbon cycle _____ 138
I+E 13 Sustainable development _____ 140
I+E 14 More people, more problems _____ 142
I+E 15 How humans have changed the landscape _____ 144
I+E 16 How humans affect water (extended in H5) _____ 146
I+E 17 How humans affect the air _____ 148
I+E 18 Are we changing the climate? (extended in H3) ____ 150
I+E H1 More about efficient food production _____ 152
I+E H2 Getting more food to the consumer _____ 154
I+E H3 More about climate change _____ 155
    H4 The nitrogen cycle _____ 156
I+E H5 When fertilisers are pollutants _____ 158

■ Inheritance and selection

   1 How a woman becomes pregnant _____ 160
I+E 2 Using hormones to control pregnancy (extended in H1) ___ 162
I+E 3 Who do you look like? _____ 164
   4 More about inheritance _____ 166
   5 Why are we all different? _____ 168
   6 Where are our genes? _____ 170
   7 Sexual reproduction (extended in H2) _____ 172
   8 What makes you male or female? _____ 174
   9 Reproducing without sex (extended in H2) _____ 176
  10 Some human genes (extended in H3 and H4) _____ 178
  11 Two disorders caused by recessive alleles (extended in H3) __ 180
  12 Mutation and change (extended in H5) _____ 182

KS3A Selective breeding _____ 184
13 Choosing the best of the bunch _____ 186
14 More about clones _____ 188
I+E 15 Cloning and selective breeding _____ 190
I+E 16 Genetic engineering _____ 192
I+E 17 Evolution (extended in H5) _____ 194
18 The mystery of fossils _____ 196
19 Some special fossils _____ 198
I+E 20 Three billion years of life _____ 200
I+E 21 Fossil detective stories _____ 202
I+E H1 Hormones and fertility _____ 204
H2 What happens when nuclei and cells divide? ___ 206
H3 More about inherited diseases _____ 208
I+E H4 DNA and the genetic code _____ 210
I+E H5 More about evolution and mutation _____ 212

■ Handling data   214

■ Revising for tests and examinations   217

■ How to write good answers in GCSE Science examinations   218

■ What you need to remember: completed passages   221

■ Glossary/index   229

■ Acknowledgements

8t, Runk/Schoenberger from Grant Heilman; 8b, Colorsport/ Andrew Cowie; 12, courtesy of The Vegetarian Society; 27, Blair Seitz/SPL; 28, 29, 50, Action Plus; 30, David Scharf/SPL; 32, John Radcliffe Hospital/SPL; 38t, 42r, 60b, Michael Brooke; 38b, 52, 56, 87, 170, 197tl, tr, 199bl, 182b, Biophoto Associates; 41, Secchi-Lecaque/Roussel-UCLAF/CNRI/SPL; 42l, Barry Dowsett/SPL; 44tr, Photo Images/Werner Reith; 44tl, 68t, 74, 97, 168, Graham Portlock/Pentaprism; 44c, Sinclair Stammers/SPL; 44b, 174, Biophoto Associates/SPL; 47, Jon Wilson/SPL; 55, G I Bernard/ www.osf.uk.com; 60l, r, 76, 120r, 184b, 185ct, Nigel Cattlin/Holt Studios International; 83, 89, Colorsport; 88, 149, Mike Wyndham Picture Collection; 91, 212t, ct, cb, b, Mary Evans Picture Library; 92, In Memory of Darren Robertson; 96, courtesy of United Phosphorus Limited/photo by Victoria Hyde; 99, *Report of the Royal College of Physicians, 1962 – Smoking and Health*/courtesy of the Royal College of Physicians, London; 101, 193b, Nigel Cattlin/Holt Studios International; 104, Ecoscene/Sally Morgan; 111tl, Peter Hendrie/Image Bank; 111tr, Mark Thompson/Allsport; 111bl, Steve Niedorf/Image Bank; 111br, Kenneth Redding/Image Bank; 114t, Bryan & Cherry Alexander; 114b, Harald Lange/BC; 118t, Geoff Kidd/A–Z; 118b, Phil Gates; 120l, c, 199tl, Photo Images/Werner Reith; 122t, Stephen Dalton/NHPA; 122b, J A L Cooke/ www.osf.uk.com; 123l, Niall Benvie/www.osf.uk.com; 123r, 145b, 185b, Malcolm Fife; 124t, Paul Beard; 124b, Anthony Bannister/ NHPA; 126, Bill Wood/NHPA; 127, Marty Stouffer/Animals Animals/ www.osf.uk.com 132t, Geoff DorÇ/BC; 132c, Dr Kari Lounatmaa/SPL; 132b, David Scharf/SPL; 140, Popperfoto/Reuters; 141b, Peter Dean/Agripictures; 142, Christopher Jones/Life File; 143, Ecoscene; 144, R A Beatty/Ecoscene; 145t, Keith Wheeler; 146t, 147, Nick Hawkes/Ecoscene; 146c, Alexandra Jones/Ecoscene; 146b, J Whitworth/ A–Z; 184t, Bob Gibbons/Holt Studios International; 153, Jay Freis/Image Bank; 154t, Roger G Howard; 154c, b, 205, Andrew Lambert;158bl, Ecoscene/Nick Hawkes; 158br, 206, 181b, Biophoto Associates; 159, Paul Glendell/Environmental Images; 162, Piers Morgan/Rex Features; 164, 210br, SPL; 180, courtesy of Cystic Fibrosis Trust; 182t, Chris Huxley/Caribbean Images; 182c, Dr J D A Delhanty; 185t, Michael Holford; 185c, Renee Lynn/Photo Researchers/www.osf.uk.com; 185cb, Duncan I McEwan; 186t, Ralph Reinhold/Animals Animals/www.osf.uk.com; 186c, Jane Burton/BC; 186b, 187, Gerard Lacz/NHPA; 190t, 190b, GeoScience Features Picture Library; 191r, Sarah Rowland/Holt Studios International; 191l, Chris Westwood/Environmental Images; 193t, Philippe Plailly/SPL; 194, David Fox/www.osf.uk.com; 195l, Jonathan P. Scott/Planet Earth Pictures; 195r, Thomas Dressler/ Planet Earth Pictures; 197br, A S Gould; 197bl, 200, Kevin Schafer/ NHPA; 197c, Dan Griggs/NHPA; 199tr, Maurice Nimmo/A–Z; 199ct, Sally Birch/www.osf.uk.com 199cb, Novosti/SPL; 199br, Derek Bromhall/www.osf.uk.com; 178l, 178r, John Walmsley; 181t, Dr Gopal Murti/SPL; 181c, Bill Longcore/SPL; 210t, Science Source/SPL;210bl, 210bcl, Ian Yeomans/Topham Picture Point; 210bcr, courtesy of the Nobel Foundation; 213t, Dr P Marazzi/SPL; 213c, Garry Watson/SPL; 213b, Manfred Kage/SPL

A–Z	= A–Z Botanical Collection Ltd
BC	= Bruce Coleman Ltd
NHPA	= Natural History Photographic Agency
www.osf.uk.com	= Oxford Scientific Films
SPL	= Science Photo Library

How to use this book

■ An introduction for students and their teachers

The four main sections of this book, *Humans as organisms*, *Maintenance of life*, *Environment* and *Inheritance and selection* contain three different types of material:

■ ideas from your previous studies of Science at Key Stage 3;

■ scientific ideas that all Key Stage 4 students are expected to know, whether they are entered for the Foundation Tier or the Higher Tier of GCSE Science tests and examinations;

■ scientific ideas that only candidates entered for the Higher Tier GCSE tests and examinations need to know.

■ Ideas from your previous science studies at Key Stage 3

You need to understand these ideas before you start on the new science for Key Stage 4.

But you will <u>not</u> be assessed <u>directly</u> on these Key Stage 3 ideas in GCSE Science tests and examinations.

Humans as organisms

KS3A Ideas you need from Key Stage 3 ← You will always see this heading

What are our bodies built from?

If the material takes up a whole page, or a double page spread, it will have a label like this.

Each time you are introduced to a new idea you will usually be asked a question. This is so you can make sure that you really understand the ideas. ← The answers to these questions are provided in the *Supplementary Materials*.

Because this material is not part of your GCSE syllabus, you will <u>not</u> be asked to produce a summary of the main ideas.

This material is always inside a purple border. →

Occasionally, the Key Stage 3 ideas will take up less than one whole page.

In such cases, the Key Stage 3 material will be included in a box at the start of the Key Stage 4 topic.

Ideas you need from Key Stage 3

■ Science that all Key Stage 4 students need to know

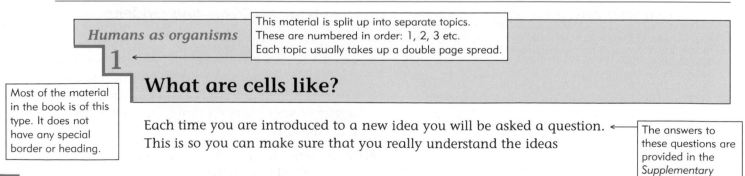

Humans as organisms

1

This material is split up into separate topics. These are numbered in order: 1, 2, 3 etc. Each topic usually takes up a double page spread.

What are cells like?

Most of the material in the book is of this type. It does not have any special border or heading.

Each time you are introduced to a new idea you will be asked a question. ← This is so you can make sure that you really understand the ideas

The answers to these questions are provided in the *Supplementary Materials*.

At the end of each topic you will find a section like this.

What you need to remember [Copy and complete using the **key words**]

You should keep your answers to these sections in a separate place.

They contain all the ideas you are expected to remember and understand in tests and examinations. So they are very useful for revision.

It is very important that these summaries are correct, so you should always check your summaries against those provided on pages 221–228 of this book.

At the bottom of some pages, you will find a note for Higher Tier students.

These ideas are extended, for Higher Tier students, in Humans as organisms H1 on pages 48–49.

■ Science that only Higher Tier students need to know

The material is split up into separate topics. These are labelled in order: H1, H2 etc.
Each topic takes up either a whole page or a double page spread.

Humans as organisms

H1 This extends *Humans as organisms* 7 for Higher Tier students

More about breathing

This material is always inside a brown border.

You will find questions in the text. Your answers to these questions will provide you with a summary of the ideas that you are expected to remember and understand for Higher Tier tests and examinations. You should keep them with your 'What you need to remember' summaries so you can use them for revision.

Because the answers to these questions are a summary of what is on the extension pages, no further answers are provided.

At the end of each topic you will find a section like this.

Using your knowledge

The questions in these sections are like many of the questions you will meet in Higher Tier tests and examinations. You have to use ideas from the topic to explain something new. You are not expected to remember the answers to these questions.

Answers to these questions are provided in the *Supplementary Materials*.

■ A note about practical work

Practical work, where you observe things and find out things for yourself, is an important part of Science. You will often see things in this book which you have yourself seen or done, but detailed instructions for practical work are not included. These will be provided separately by your teacher.

The *Supplementary Materials* contain many suggestions for practical activities.

■ A note about Ideas and Evidence

All GCSE Science syllabuses must now assess candidates' understanding of what the National Curriculum calls *Ideas and Evidence*. Those parts of this book which include material about this aspect of Science are indicated on the contents page like this:

I+E 15 What happens when microorganisms get into you body? _____ 42

What are our bodies built from?

Robert Hooke was the first person to see what plants and animals are made of. This was 300 years ago. He looked at parts of plants and animals using a microscope.

He found that both plants and animals are made up of lots of small bits like bricks in a wall.
He called these bits <u>cells</u>.

1 What is the basic unit of all animals and plants?

2 (a) Measure the length of <u>one</u> of the plant cells in the picture.

   (b) How long is the plant cell in real life?

3 Why do we need a microscope to see cells?

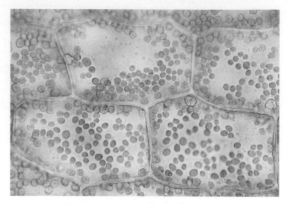

Photograph of plant leaf cells taken through a microscope. They are magnified 350 times.

■ **Tissues**

A <u>tissue</u> is a group of cells with the same shape and job. Different tissues do different jobs.

Muscle cells group together to form <u>muscular tissue</u>.

4 What does muscular tissue do?

5 What type of cells make up muscular tissue?

Muscle cells can <u>contract</u> or get shorter. The whole muscle then gets shorter, so it moves part of the body.

6 How does muscular tissue move food down the gullet?

This athlete is using muscular tissue to move her body.

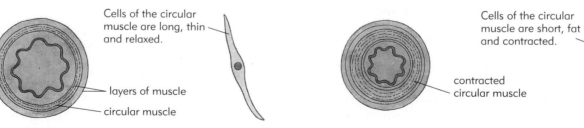

Cells of the circular muscle are long, thin and relaxed.

layers of muscle

circular muscle

Cells of the circular muscle are short, fat and contracted.

contracted circular muscle

When the circular muscles contract they squeeze the food along.

■ Other tissues have different jobs

Muscle cells are shaped so that the tissue can do its job. Other tissues in the body have different jobs, so their cells are different shapes.

7 Look at the picture. Draw the shapes of a muscle cell and a gland cell from the stomach. Remember to label them.

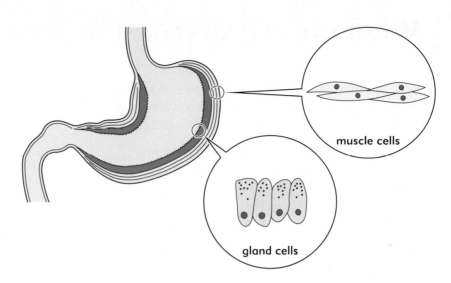

muscle cells

gland cells

The stomach is one of the organs of the digestive system. It contains glandular and muscular tissue.

Some of the organs in the digestive system contain glandular tissue. This makes digestive juices which help break down food. Other glandular tissues in the body make other useful juices. For example, sweat glands make sweat.

8 Copy and complete:

_____ tissue in the stomach churns the food around. Food is mixed with _____ juices made by the _____ tissue.

■ Organs and organ systems

Different tissues join together to make an organ. Several organs work together in an organ system. Each organ system in the body does particular jobs.

9 List six organs in the digestive system.

10 What are the jobs of the digestive system?

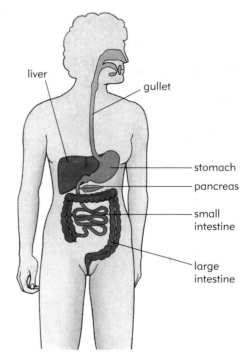

liver

gullet

stomach

pancreas

small intestine

large intestine

The human digestive system breaks down and absorbs food.

1

What are cells like?

Your body is made of billions of cells. Larger organisms like humans have more cells than smaller organisms like ants. Some organisms have only one cell.

Most animal cells have the same basic parts:

■ a **nucleus** which controls everything that happens in the cell;

■ **cytoplasm** where most of the cell's chemical reactions happen;

■ a cell **membrane** to control which substances pass in and out of the cell. It also holds the cell together.

1 Copy the table.
  Use the information above to complete it.

Cell part	What it does

All plant and animal cells have these same basic parts.

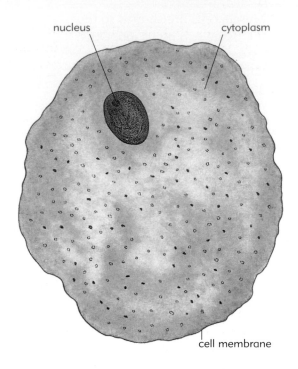

Parts of an animal cell.

■ Some cells look different

Cells may be different shapes and sizes but they still have a nucleus, cytoplasm and cell membrane. They may also have other parts so that they can do their jobs.

We say the cells are **specialised** to do their job.

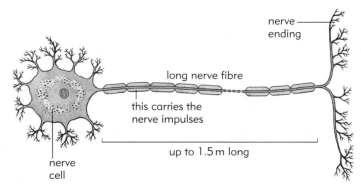

Nerve cells can carry signals (nerve impulses) between the brain and other parts of the body.

2 How is a nerve cell specialised to do its job?

3 How is a red blood cell specialised to do its job?

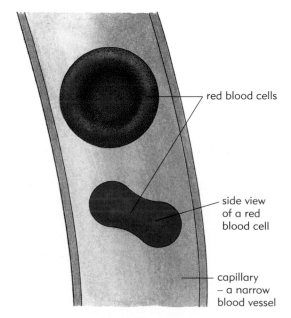

Red blood cells carry oxygen around the body. They are full of a substance that can combine with oxygen, but which also releases oxygen again.

■ Sperm cells have a tail

Look at the diagrams.

Sperm cells are placed in a woman's vagina.
From there they swim up the uterus and along the egg tube (oviduct). If they reach an egg cell in the oviduct they can fertilise it.

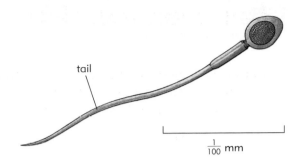

Sperm cells swim to fertilise an egg cell.

4 Copy the diagram of a human sperm cell.
Add these labels:

■ nucleus

■ cytoplasm

■ cell membrane.

5 What part of a sperm cell helps it reach the egg?

■ Cells that line the oviducts have hairs

Each oviduct is a tube which carries eggs from the ovary to the womb. Egg cells are released from an ovary and travel down an oviduct.
Each oviduct is lined with special cells.

These cells have tiny hairs which can move forwards and backwards.

6 Make a large copy of Cell X. Label the nucleus, cytoplasm and cell membrane.

7 Why do the cells lining an oviduct have tiny hairs on their surface?

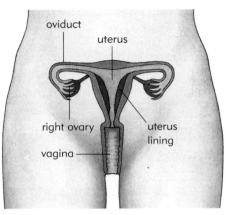

A woman's reproductive organs.

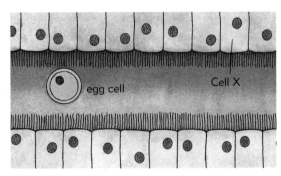

Inside an oviduct.

What you need to remember [Copy and complete using the **key words**]

What are our bodies built from?

Most human cells are made up of the same basic parts.

Cells have a _____ that controls everything which happens in the cell.

Most of the chemical reactions in a cell take place in the _____.

It is the cell _____ that controls the passage of substances in and out of the cell.

Cells that do a particular job are called _____ cells.

[You should be able to match specialised cells to the jobs that they do in tissues, organs or the whole organism when you are given information about the structure of cells.]

Are you on a diet?

■ What is a diet?

All the food you eat is your diet.

This means that everyone is on a diet, not just people trying to lose weight.

Things food can contain	What your body needs it for
carbohydrate	energy
protein	growth and replacing cells
fat	energy and making cell membranes
B vitamins	healthy cells

A healthy diet contains everything your body needs. It does not contain things that harm your body.

1 Write down <u>four</u> things that a healthy diet should contain.

2 Plan a simple snack lunch that would contain all these things.

The food that you eat for your lunch will also contain minerals, fibre, water and other vitamins that you need.

■ Different diets for different people

There are lots of ways of getting a healthy diet. Different people choose different types of food. Many people eat less red meat than they did. Vegetarians do not eat any meat at all.

3 Why do you think people become vegetarians?

4 A diet without meat can be healthier. Explain why.

5 Look at the diagrams above of the different types of food. What should vegetarians eat:

(a) to make sure they get enough protein?

(b) to make sure they get enough B vitamins?

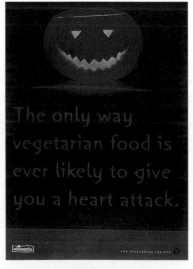

Eating too much animal fat may cause heart disease.

Where does your food go?

When you put your food into your mouth it is starting a journey through your <u>digestive system</u>. This journey will last up to three days. The job of your digestive system is to break down food so that it can pass into your blood.

Nine metres in three days

The tube which runs all through your body is much longer than you are. It can be up to nine metres long. You can see from the diagram that most of the tube is coiled up in the lower half of your body.

6 Copy and complete the diagram below.

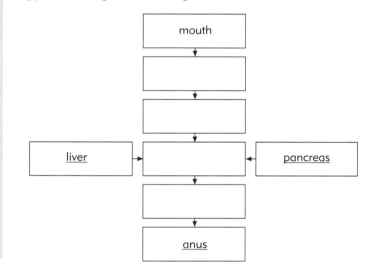

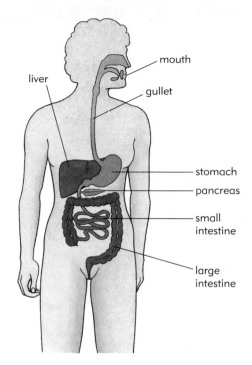

Your digestive system.

Absorbing digested food

Once your food has been <u>digested</u>, it passes through the lining of the small intestine into the bloodstream. When this happens, we say that the food is <u>absorbed</u>.

7 Copy and complete:

large food molecules $\longrightarrow$ small food molecules

(are not absorbed)   (are _____ into the _____.)

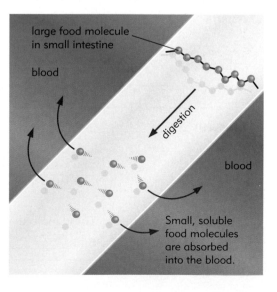

2

Why do we need to digest our food?

Most of the food we eat is made up of fairly large **molecules**. Starch, protein and fat are all made up of large molecules.

1 Name <u>two</u> foods that contain large starch molecules.

2 What sort of large molecules does butter contain?

Our bodies cannot use large molecules like starch. The large molecules cannot pass through the lining of our small intestines. This is because the large food molecules cannot dissolve. We say they are **insoluble**.

Large food molecules must be broken down into smaller ones that can dissolve. These molecules are **soluble** and can pass into the blood.

3 Copy and complete the sentence:

A substance which dissolves is called a _____ substance.

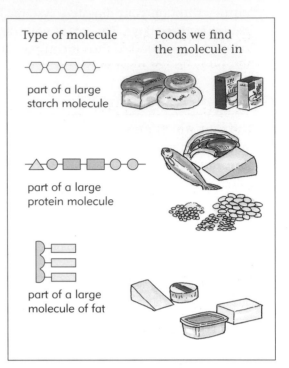

Type of molecule	Foods we find the molecule in
part of a large starch molecule	
part of a large protein molecule	
part of a large molecule of fat	

■ How do we break down large molecules?

Our bodies break down large food molecules into smaller ones. This breakdown is called **digestion**.

These small molecules dissolve and pass through the lining and into the bloodstream in the wall of the **small intestine**. The diagrams show you the small molecules that are made by digestion.

4 Copy and complete the table. Use the diagrams to help you.

Before digestion	After digestion
starch	glucose
protein	_____ _____
fat	_____ _____ and _____
These molecules are large and insoluble.	These molecules are _____ and _____.

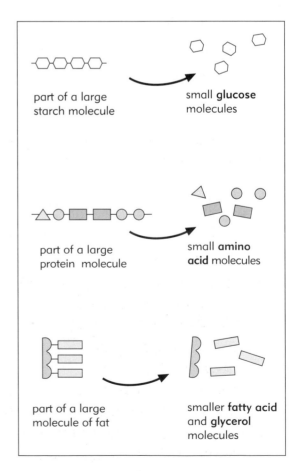

part of a large starch molecule → small **glucose** molecules

part of a large protein molecule → small **amino acid** molecules

part of a large molecule of fat → smaller **fatty acid** and **glycerol** molecules

5 Look at the picture of starch digestion. Then copy and complete the picture for the breakdown of protein.

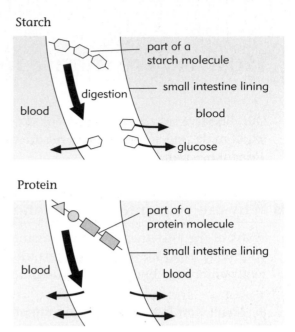

Starch

part of a starch molecule

small intestine lining

digestion

blood   blood

glucose

■ Is all food digested?

Vitamins do not need to be digested.

We cannot digest **fibre**. It makes up most of the undigested waste that we call **faeces**. This leaves the body via the **anus**.

6 Do you think vitamins are large or small molecules?

7 Do you think fibre molecules are large or small?

Protein

part of a protein molecule

small intestine lining

blood   blood

Only small, soluble molecules can pass through the lining into the blood.

■ Your body is like a tube

The diagram shows what happens to food as it passes through your digestive system.

8 Copy the diagram. Put the following sentences into the correct boxes on the diagram:

■ Small, soluble molecules pass into the blood.

■ Undigested waste leaves the anus.

■ Food enters your mouth.

■ Large molecules are digested.

There really is a tube all the way through your body. But it is more complicated than this diagram shows.

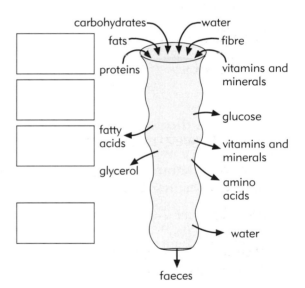

carbohydrates — water

fats — fibre

proteins — vitamins and minerals

glucose

fatty acids — vitamins and minerals

glycerol — amino acids

water

faeces

What you need to remember [Copy and complete using the **key words**]

Why do we need to digest our food?

Starch (a carbohydrate), proteins and fats are made of large _____.
They cannot dissolve so we say they are _____.
They are broken down into _____ molecules. They can then pass into the
bloodstream in the wall of the _____ _____.
Starch is broken down into _____.
Protein is broken down into _____ _____ molecules.
Fat is broken down into _____ _____ and _____ molecules.
Breaking down large food molecules is called _____.
_____ cannot be digested by humans. It makes up most of the undigested
waste that we call _____. This leaves the body via the _____.

15

3

How do we digest food?

Our digestive systems have to break down our food into small molecules so that we can absorb them. This takes several days.

■ Why are your intestines so long?

Think of the intestines as a tube passing through your body. Food moves through this tube, but it doesn't really enter your body until it is absorbed.

1 About how long is the human digestive system from the mouth to the anus?

2 Why do you think it has to be this long?

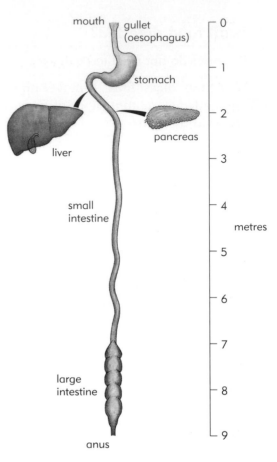

■ Enzymes digest our food

Our digestive systems contain glands. These glands produce substances called **enzymes**. Enzymes are catalysts. Catalysts make chemical reactions happen quickly and easily. Digestive enzymes help us to break down food more easily. Our bodies make lots of different digestive enzymes. Each enzyme breaks down a particular food. When an enzyme has broken down one food molecule, it can then break down another molecule of the same kind. It can do this over and over again. It makes the reaction happen without being used up.

3 Copy and complete the sentences to explain how enzymes break down fat.

First the enzyme snips off a _____ _____ molecule.

Then it does this _____ more times.

The fat molecule has then been digested into three _____ _____ molecules and a _____ molecule.

4 Why can a small amount of enzyme break down a large amount of food?

How you digest fat.

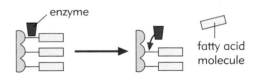

The enzyme snips off a fatty acid molecule.

Then it snips off another two.

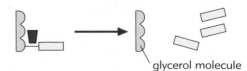

The same enzyme molecule can do this over and over again to more fat molecules.

It makes the reaction happen without being used up. We say it is a **catalyst**.

■ Different foods need different enzymes

■ Enzymes which break down fats are called **lipases**.

■ Enzymes which break down starch are called **amylases**.

■ Enzymes which break down proteins are called **proteases**.

Our bodies make several different enzymes in each of these groups.

5 Copy the table.

Put the words amylases, proteases and lipases above the correct arrows.
The first one has been done for you.

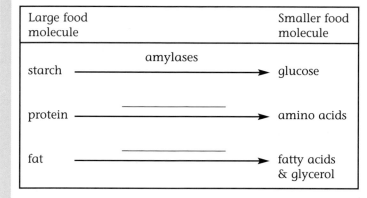

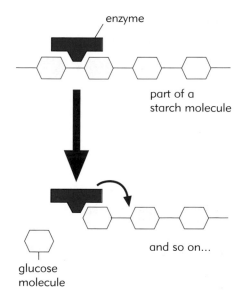

part of a starch molecule

glucose molecule

and so on...

How a starch molecule is digested.

6 Make a copy of the diagram.

Add more stages to show the part of the starch molecule being completely digested.

What you need to remember [Copy and complete using the **key words**]

How do we digest our food?

The breakdown of large food molecules into smaller ones is speeded up by _____.

An enzyme is a _____. It is not used up.

Enzymes that break down starch into sugars are called _____.

Enzymes that break down proteins into amino acids are called _____.

Enzymes that break down fats into fatty acids and glycerol are called _____.

4

Your digestive system: what happens where?

■ In your mouth

You start to digest your food as soon as you put it into your **mouth**. Your salivary **glands** produce saliva. Saliva contains amylase.

1 What sort of food does saliva digest?

2 How else does saliva help you to digest food? (Hint: think of eating a dry cracker!)

3 How does chewing food help digestion?

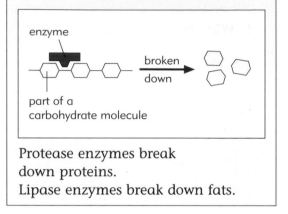

REMEMBER

Amylase is the enzyme that breaks down starch (a carbohydrate).

enzyme

part of a
carbohydrate molecule

broken
down

Protease enzymes break down proteins.
Lipase enzymes break down fats.

■ Down your gullet

Your gullet (or oesophagus) carries food from your mouth to your stomach. Muscles in the wall of your gullet squeeze the food along. It is a bit like pushing toothpaste all the way from the bottom of a nearly empty tube.

4 Copy and complete:

As _____ moves down the gullet, the next set of muscles push it a little further along. This is just like pushing _____ out of a tube.

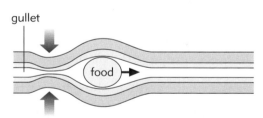

gullet

food

muscles squeeze

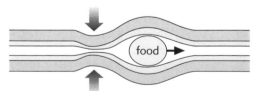

food

muscles squeeze
a bit further along

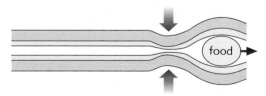

food

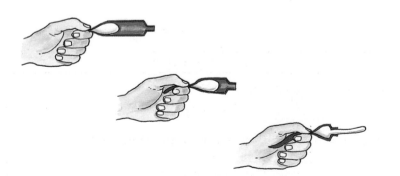

Pushing toothpaste from the bottom of a tube.
Food is moved along the intestines in the same way.

Muscles in the gullet wall squeeze the food along, section by section.

■ Next stop: your stomach

Your **stomach** is a bag of **muscle** tissue.
It churns up food for about three hours.

Your stomach has a lining of **glandular** tissue. This makes **hydrochloric** acid which kills most of the **bacteria** in food. The stomach lining also produces **enzymes**. These work best in acid conditions.

5 What <u>two</u> things does the glandular tissue of the stomach produce?

6 What part of your food starts being digested in the stomach?

7 Write down <u>two</u> reasons why your stomach produces hydrochloric acid.

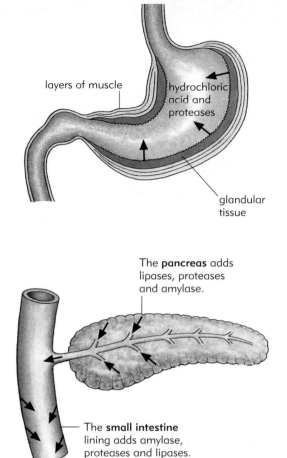

layers of muscle

hydrochloric acid and proteases

glandular tissue

The **pancreas** adds lipases, proteases and amylase.

■ Into the small intestine

Partly digested food leaves the stomach a little at a time. It goes into the small intestine. More enzymes are added from the pancreas and small intestine lining.

8 Which parts of food are digested in the small intestine?

9 How do you think food is moved along the intestine?

The **small intestine** lining adds amylase, proteases and lipases.

The pancreas and small intestine.

What you need to remember [Copy and complete using the **key words**]

Your digestive system: what happens where?

Enzymes are produced by _____ tissue.

_____ tissue moves food along the gullet and intestines and churns it up in the stomach.

_____ acid in the stomach kills _____.

The acid also makes the _____ in the stomach work better.

Type of food	Where it is digested	What makes the enzymes
starch	_____ and small intestine	salivary _____ , _____ and small intestine
protein	_____ and small intestine	stomach, pancreas and small intestine
fat	_____ _____	pancreas and small intestine

5 More about your digestive system

You make enzymes in your digestive glands.
Enzymes act as catalysts in the digestion of food.

1 Write down the names of <u>four</u> small molecules that are produced in digestion.

■ Your digestive glands don't just make enzymes

Protease enzymes in your stomach work best in **acid** conditions. So glands in your stomach lining produce hydrochloric acid. When the food from the stomach passes into the small intestines, it is still acidic.
The enzymes in your small intestines need alkaline conditions. Salts in bile neutralise the acid so these enzymes can work properly.

Bile also breaks fat down into tiny droplets of oil.
We say that bile **emulsifies** the fats. This increases the surface area for lipase enzymes to act on.

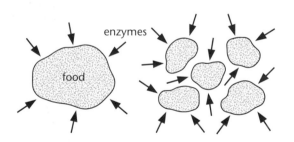

Enzymes break down food faster when the surface area of the food is large.

2 Copy and complete the sentences.

Bile is made in your _____ and stored in your _____ _____. It neutralises _____ from the stomach so that the enzymes in the small intestine can work well.
It also _____ fats. This increases the _____ _____ for _____ to act on.

3 What does the word 'emulsifies' mean?

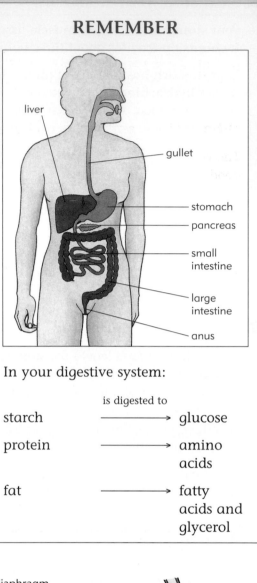

REMEMBER

In your digestive system:

	is digested to	
starch	⟶	glucose
protein	⟶	amino acids
fat	⟶	fatty acids and glycerol

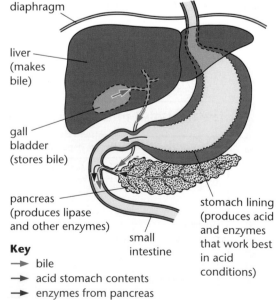

Key
→ bile
→ acid stomach contents
→ enzymes from pancreas

After digestion, what next?

After digestion the food molecules are small and soluble. They pass into the **bloodstream** in wall of the **small intestine**. The molecules of digested food are absorbed into the bloodstream, so we call this **absorption**.

What's the small intestine like?

The way that the small intestine is built makes it very good at absorbing food. It is long and the lining is very folded. This gives it a big surface area.

4 Copy and complete:

Food is absorbed in the _____ _____.
It has a very folded lining which gives it a bigger _____ _____. The bigger this surface is, the _____ food can be absorbed.

5 Why does the small intestine need a good blood supply?

Water must be absorbed

As well as solid food, our intestines have a lot of **water** in them.

6 Where does this water come from?

Our bodies must absorb water. If this doesn't happen our bodies will be short of water and we will be dehydrated. Also we will suffer from diarrhoea as too much water will leave the body in the faeces.

7 What part of your digestive system absorbs water?

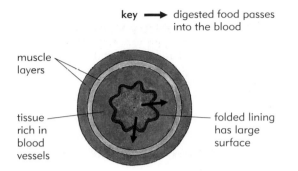

key ➡ digested food passes into the blood

muscle layers

tissue rich in blood vessels

folded lining has large surface

Section through the small intestine.

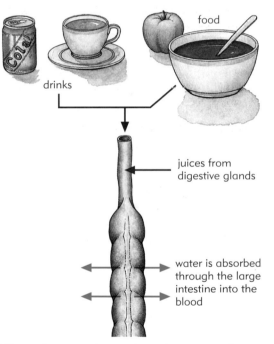

food

drinks

juices from digestive glands

water is absorbed through the large intestine into the blood

Where the water in our intestines comes from.

What you need to remember [Copy and complete using the **key words**]

More about your digestive system

The liver makes _____.
In the small intestine, bile:

■ neutralises _____. It provides the conditions that the enzymes need.

■ _____ fats. This increases the surface area for enzymes to work on.

Small soluble food molecules pass through the lining and into the _____ in the wall of the _____ intestine. We call this _____.
The large intestine absorbs _____ from the undigested food.

These ideas and ideas from Humans as organisms 7 are extended, for Higher Tier students, in Humans as organisms H1 and H4 on pages 48–49 and 54–55.

Respiration and breathing

■ Food is the body's fuel

Petrol is the fuel in a car. It burns to release energy. Glucose, a sugar which you get from your food, is your main fuel.

All the cells of your body obtain energy by respiring. Cells normally use oxygen to respire. You get oxygen from the air so we call this <u>aerobic respiration</u>.

1 Look at the diagram.
Then copy and complete the table.

In ＿＿＿＿＿ respiration our ＿＿＿＿＿...	
...use	...release
glucose	＿＿＿＿ ＿＿＿＿
＿＿＿＿	＿＿＿＿
	energy

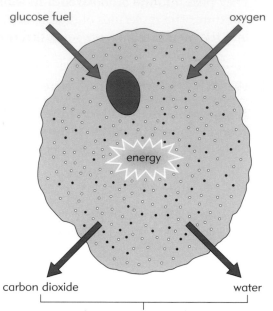

glucose fuel   oxygen

energy

carbon dioxide   water

these are waste products

■ How do we get the oxygen we need?

You get your oxygen when you breathe in. <u>Breathing</u> is just taking air in and out of your lungs. It is not the same as respiration.

When you breathe out, you get rid of a waste gas from your body.

2 Name the waste gas that you get rid of when you breathe out.

Air with lots of oxygen and hardly any carbon dioxide.

Air with less oxygen and more carbon dioxide.

<u>Gas exchange</u> happens in your lungs. So, the air you breathe in is not the same as the air you breathe out.

■ Where does the air go when you breathe in?

You breathe air into your <u>lungs</u>. The diagram shows where your lungs are in your body.

3 Copy and complete the following sentences.

Your lungs are in the upper part of your body.
This is called the _____ or the _____.
It is separated from the abdomen by the _____ muscle.
The thorax is surrounded by a cage of

_____.
This bony cage _____ the heart and lungs.

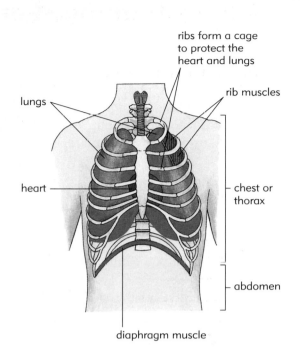

Where your lungs are.

The air you breathe in goes down a network of tubes.
It ends up in millions of tiny <u>air sacs</u>.
These are called <u>alveoli</u>.

4 Imagine you are an oxygen molecule near to someone's nose and the person breathes you in. Copy the flow diagram. Then complete it to show your journey to an alveolus.

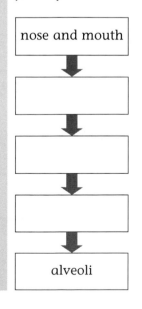

What your lungs are like.

6

Why do you need energy?

The food that you eat is the fuel that provides you with energy. When children rush about, some people say that they 'have a lot of energy'. One of the things you need energy for is to move about. You also need energy for warmth, and for growth and repair.

Bending the arm.

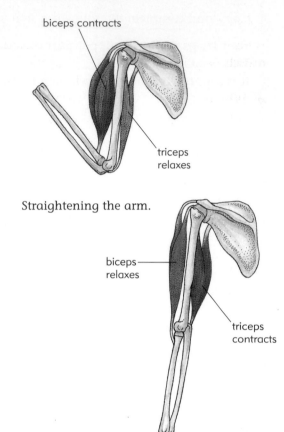

■ Energy for movement

When you **move**, your muscles contract. This means they get shorter and fatter. The diagram shows what happens when you bend and straighten your arm.

Straightening the arm.

1 Copy and complete the sentences:

When the arm bends, the _____ muscle contracts. When the arm straightens again, the _____ muscle contracts and the _____ muscle relaxes.

Muscles are made of muscle cells. Muscle cells need **energy** to contract. Some of the energy in muscles is released as heat.

2 Why do you get hot when you run?

■ Energy for warmth

Your normal body **temperature** is 37 °C. In the UK, the air around us is usually colder than this. The heat energy released in your cells is important for keeping you warm.

3 (a) What happens if your body temperature drops by 2 °C?

(b) What do we call this condition?

4 How much further does the body temperature need to fall before a person goes into a coma?

Body temperature (°C)	How does the body behave?
37	normal behaviour
35	shivering, body movements and speech become slow, drowsiness, start of hypothermia
30	goes into coma
28	breathing stops

We die if our body temperature falls too low. Most winters in Britain, 300 to 400 old people die of hypothermia.

It's cold, but gas is so expensive!

5 Why is it hard for old people to keep warm?

When we are cold we shiver. This is because our muscle cells contract.

6 Why do you think you shiver when you're cold?

■ Energy for growth and repair

Cells are mainly built up of **proteins**. We get our proteins from food. These proteins are broken down (digested) in our bodies into **amino acids**. Our cells then build the amino acids back up again into different proteins. The proteins are different because your cells join the amino acids together in different orders. The cells need **energy** to do this.

7 The diagram shows the breakdown of one protein. Draw a diagram to show the same amino acids built up into a <u>different</u> protein.

8 You eat protein in food like eggs or cheese. Your body uses this to make different protein in your muscle and skin. How does it do this?

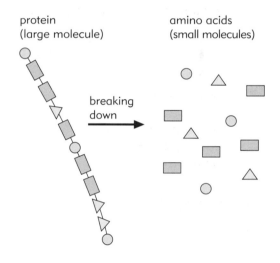

protein (large molecule)   amino acids (small molecules)

breaking down

What you need to remember [Copy and complete using the **key words**]

Why do you need energy?

Your muscles contract so that you can _____.

To do this, muscles need _____.

Some of the energy from food is used to keep your body at the same _____.

Cells are mainly built of _____.

Proteins themselves are built up of _____ _____.

This building up process also needs _____.

ROSEWARNE LEARNING CENTRE

How you get the oxygen you need

Breathing is taking <u>air</u> in and out of your lungs.
To make air move in, your ribcage moves outwards and
your diaphragm moves down. As you breathe out,
the opposite happens.

1 Copy and complete the table.

	Breathing in	**Breathing out**
ribcage		
diaphragm		arches up

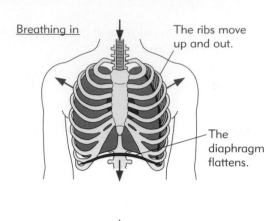

Breathing in — The ribs move up and out. — The diaphragm flattens.

■ What happens to air in your lungs?

When you breathe, you exchange stale air in your lungs
for fresh air. We call this **ventilation**.

The air that goes into your lungs ends up in millions of
tiny **alveoli**. Gases move between the air in the alveoli
and the **blood** in the capillaries around them. Each gas
moves from where it is in **high** concentration to where it
is in **low** concentration. We call this **diffusion**.

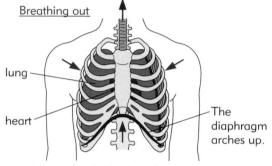

Breathing out — lung — heart — The diaphragm arches up.

We call the part of the body cavity
■ above the diaphragm the thorax
■ below the diaphragm the abdomen.

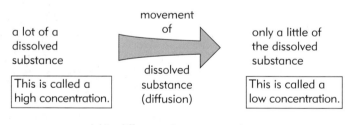

a lot of a dissolved substance

This is called a high concentration.

movement of dissolved substance (diffusion)

only a little of the dissolved substance

This is called a low concentration.

A big difference in concentration
means faster diffusion.

2 Copy and complete:

concentration
of oxygen in
_____

_____ ⟶

concentration
of oxygen
in _____

So, in the alveoli:

- the oxygen your body needs diffuses from the air into your blood;

- waste carbon dioxide from your body diffuses from your blood into the air.

3 Make a copy of the diagram. Draw and label arrows to show which gases diffuse into and out of the blood.

Oxygen travels in your blood to all the cells in your body.

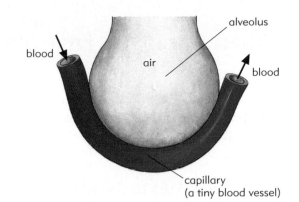

What happens inside an alveolus.

■ Is the air changed?

The table shows the differences between the air that you breathe in and the air you breathe out.

4 Describe these differences.

Gas	Air breathed in	Air breathed out
oxygen	21%	17%
carbon dioxide	almost zero	4%
nitrogen	79%	79%

■ How can breathed out air keep someone alive?

If you have a bad accident, you may stop breathing. You could die if you didn't get any oxygen for more than a few minutes.

Another person could save your life by breathing out into your lungs. This is called the kiss of life.

5 The kiss of life uses the air we breathe out. This can still help to keep someone alive. Explain why.

This person is using a model to practise the kiss of life.

What you need to remember [Copy and complete using the **key words**]

How you get the oxygen you need

You breathe air in and out of your lungs. This is _____.

Gases pass from where they are in _____ concentration to where they are in _____ concentration. We call this _____. So we say that oxygen diffuses into your _____ and carbon dioxide diffuses out.

This exchange of gases takes place in your _____.
Blood carries oxygen to your cells.

These ideas are extended, for Higher Tier students, in Humans as organisms H1 and H4 on pages 48–49 and 54–55.

8

Two types of respiration

Oxygen travels in your blood to all parts of your body. It diffuses from the blood in your capillaries to all the cells.

■ What happens to oxygen in your cells?

Think of **glucose** as a store of **energy**. Cells break down the glucose to release the energy. This is respiration.

Normally cells respire using **oxygen** from the air. When they use oxygen we call it aerobic **respiration**. Cells produce waste carbon dioxide and **water** when they respire in this way.

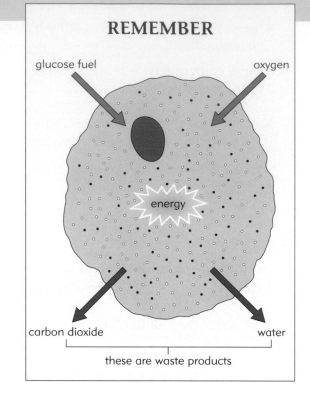

REMEMBER

glucose fuel   oxygen

energy

carbon dioxide   water

these are waste products

1 Copy and complete the word equation to show what happens in aerobic respiration.

respiration

_____ + oxygen ⟶ _____ _____ + water + ⟨energy⟩

Look at the picture of the athlete. He is a sprinter so he only runs short races. During a race, his heart and lungs work harder so that his blood carries more oxygen to his muscle cells.
They don't run out of oxygen.

2 During a short race the athlete's muscle cells get extra oxygen. Explain how this happens.

A sprinter pants and his heart beats faster during a race.

■ What happens if he doesn't get enough oxygen?

When the athlete trains, he does longer runs. At first his muscles get enough oxygen. Later his cells use oxygen faster than they can take it in. They have to respire without oxygen. We call this **anaerobic** respiration.

3 When do the athlete's muscle cells use anaerobic respiration?

4 Look at the word equation. Write down the name of the waste that is produced in anaerobic respiration.

glucose ⟶ **lactic acid** + energy

Lactic acid is a mild poison. So cells can use anaerobic respiration for a short time only. Later they use extra oxygen to get rid of the lactic acid.
We call the extra oxygen needed the **oxygen debt**.

5 Look at the picture. This marathon runner will not finish her race if she runs too fast. Explain why?

Lactic acid makes muscles ache and too tired to work. So marathon runners must run slowly enough to respire aerobically.

What you need to remember [Copy and complete using the **key words**]

Two types of respiration

Living cells release _____ from the sugar _____.
Normally _____ is used to do this.
This process is called aerobic _____.
It can be shown like this:

glucose + oxygen ⟶ carbon dioxide + _____ + energy

If cells don't get enough oxygen, they carry out _____ respiration.
It can be shown like this:

glucose ⟶ _____ _____ + energy

The amount of oxygen that cells need to get rid of the lactic acid is called
the _____ _____.

These ideas are extended, for Higher Tier students, in Humans as organisms H2 on pages 50–51.

9 Exchange surfaces and diffusion

■ How your cells get all the things they need

Humans are large organisms made from many millions of cells. Your small intestine and your lungs have a large **surface area** so that they can absorb all the dissolved food and oxygen that your cells need.

Your small intestine is where you absorb most of your food. It has a thin **moist** lining so that dissolved substances can pass through easily. Tiny folds in the intestine, called villi, contain lots of blood **capillaries**.

> 1 Look at the diagrams. Which structures provide a large surface area for absorption in
>
> (a) your lungs?
>
> (b) your small intestines?

The concentration of dissolved substances, such as glucose and amino acids, is higher inside the small intestine than in the capillaries in the villi. Dissolved substances always move from where there is a lot to where there is less. So glucose and amino acids move easily into the blood capillaries in the villi. This movement is called diffusion.

The greater the difference in concentration, the **faster** substances diffuse.

> 2 Copy the diagram of the villus.
> Complete the labels.

Because your blood circulates, the blood in the capillaries of your villi is constantly replaced. So the concentration of dissolved substances stays low.

> 3 If your blood didn't circulate what would happen to the rate of diffusion of dissolved food from your small intestine?

REMEMBER

Alveoli in your lungs:

■ provide a large surface area
■ have thin walls
■ have a moist lining
■ have a rich capillary supply.

The intestine lining is folded. The surface area is increased even more by microscopic 'folds' called villi.

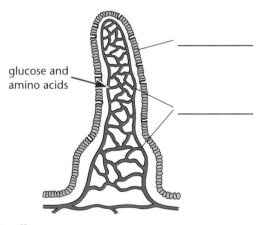

glucose and amino acids

A villus.

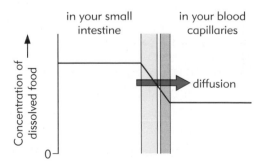

If your blood didn't circulate the concentration of dissolved food would quickly rise.

■ More about diffusion

Oxygen and carbon dioxide are exchanged in your alveoli. They are also exchanged between your blood and your body cells.

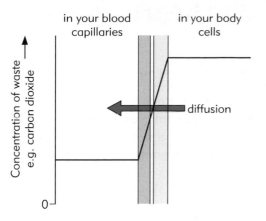

4 Look at the diagram.

   (a) Is the concentration of carbon dioxide higher in your cells or in your blood?

   (b) In which direction does carbon dioxide diffuse?

Dissolved particles and particles in gases move in all directions. So they spread out.

Look at the diagram.
There are more particles of carbon dioxide in the more concentrated solution. So more move from the cells into the blood than from the blood into the cells. We say that there is a net movement from the **higher** concentration in the cells to the **lower** concentration in the blood.

5 Copy and complete:

        net movement of particles

          (diffusion)
high   ――――――→   _____
concentration   concentration

   Substances _____ faster when there is a big difference in concentration.

Low concentration of carbon dioxide	High concentration of carbon dioxide
Fewer carbon dioxide molecules	More carbon dioxide molecules
More molecules of other substances	Fewer molecules of other substances

Key

○ carbon dioxide

· other particles (mainly water)

⟵ net movement of carbon dioxide in this direction (**diffusion**)

What you need to remember [Copy and complete using the **key words**]

Exchange surfaces and diffusion

Particles of a gas or a dissolved substance move in all directions. There is a net movement from a _____ concentration to a _____ concentration. This is called _____. A bigger difference in concentration makes diffusion _____. Organs which are specialised for exchanging materials are alike in many ways. They have:

■ an enormous _____ _____

■ thin walls

■ a _____ lining

■ a rich supply of blood _____.

These ideas are extended, for Higher Tier students, in Humans as organisms H1 and H4 on pages 48–49 and 54–55.

10

The heart – a pump for blood

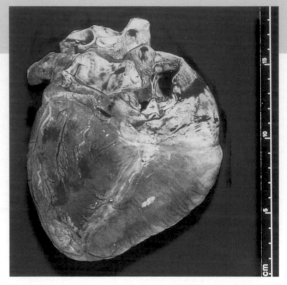

■ Why doesn't your heart ache?

Your heart pumps blood around your body. To do this, it beats about 70 times a minute. Imagine squeezing a tennis ball 70 times. The muscles in your hand would soon become tired and begin to ache. The walls of the heart are made of special **muscle** called cardiac muscle. It does not get tired.

1 Copy and complete the table.

Time	Number of heart beats
1 minute	70
1 hour	
1 day	

Your heart is about the size of your clenched fist.

You are looking at another person's heart. Diagrams of the heart are always drawn this way round.

■ Parts of the heart

As you can see from the diagram, the heart is made up of four chambers. The top two are thin walled chambers called atria. If we are talking about only one of these we call it an atrium. Below these are two larger, thick walled chambers. These are called ventricles.

2 Copy and complete the following sentences.

Blood comes into the right atrium from the head and body.

Blood goes from the right ventricle to the _____.

Blood comes into the left atrium from the _____.

Blood goes from the left ventricle to the _____.

3 The left ventricle has a thicker wall than the right ventricle. Why do you think this is?

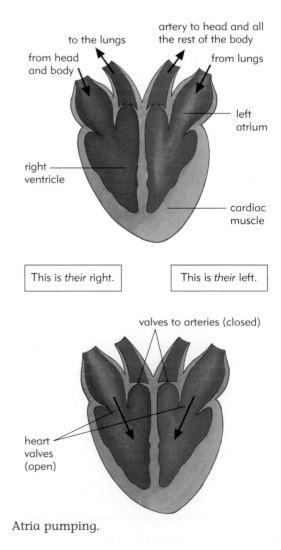

This is *their* right.　　This is *their* left.

Atria pumping.

■ How does the heart work ?

The atria contract. They squeeze the blood into the **ventricles**. The ventricles then contract.
They push the blood into the **arteries**.

The **valves** in the heart make sure that blood flows the right way.

4 Copy and complete the following sentences.

When the atria are pumping, the _____ valves are open and the _____ valves are closed. When the ventricles are pumping, the _____ valves are open and the _____ valves are closed.

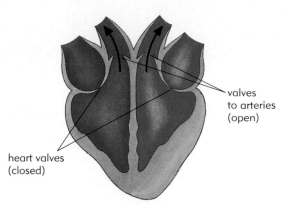

Ventricles pumping.

■ Why your heart is a double pump

5 Describe the path of your blood round your body. Start with this sentence.

■ Blood from your body, with little oxygen, goes into the right atrium of your heart.

Then use the following sentences. You will need to put them in the right order.

■ The blood is pumped through an artery to the lungs.

■ The blood goes into the left atrium of your heart.

■ The blood goes into the right ventricle of your heart.

■ The blood goes into the left ventricle of your heart.

■ The blood picks up oxygen and gets rid of carbon dioxide.

■ The blood is pumped through arteries to the rest of your body.

6 Copy and complete the following sentences.

This circulation makes sure that blood with plenty of oxygen goes to the _____. Blood with very little oxygen goes to the _____.

REMEMBER

In your lungs, your blood:

■ collects oxygen

■ gets rid of carbon dioxide.

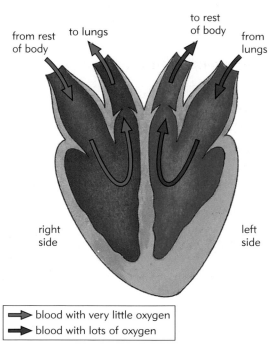

Each side of the heart is a separate pump.

What you need to remember [Copy and complete using the **key words**]

The heart – a pump for blood

Your heart wall is mainly _____ fibres.
When the atria contract, blood passes into the _____.
When the ventricles contract, blood is forced into _____.
The heart has _____ to stop the blood from flowing in the wrong direction.

11

Know your blood vessels – you could save a life!

You are the first at the scene of a road accident. Two people are hurt. One has blood spurting from a cut while the other has blood oozing from a cut.

1 Which one should you treat first? Give a reason for your answer.

■ How to stop blood spurting from a cut

To stop blood spurting from a cut, you need to know how blood travels round the body.

2 Use the information on the diagram to copy and complete the following sentences.

Arteries carry blood _____ the heart.

Veins carry blood _____ the heart.

Blood travels from arteries to veins through lots of tiny _____.

3 Blood spurts from a cut artery. It oozes slowly from a cut vein. Why do you think this is?

4 To stop blood spurting from a cut artery you must press on the side of the cut nearest to the heart. Explain why.

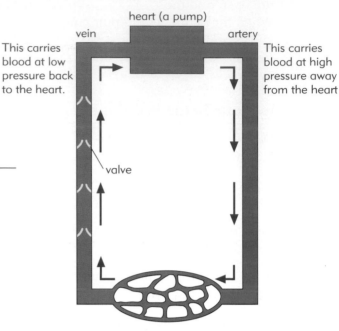

heart (a pump)

vein ... artery

This carries blood at low pressure back to the heart.

This carries blood at high pressure away from the heart

valve

There are lots of tiny blood vessels called **capillaries** in all organs.

■ Arteries and veins

Arteries have thick walls. This helps them withstand the high blood pressure caused by the pumping action of the heart. As the blood is forced into the arteries the walls stretch and then spring back.
We feel this as a pulse.

5 (a) Where can you feel your arteries stretching?

(b) Why should you use your fingers to take someone's pulse and not your thumb?

Blood goes back to the heart in **veins**. They have thin walls and contain **valves**.

6 What job do these valves do?

If an artery is near the surface of the skin you can feel a pulse at each heart beat. You can feel it in your neck, your wrist and your thumb.

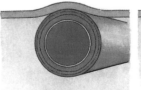

heart pumps
artery stretches

heart relaxes
artery goes back to original size

the blood flows forwards and pushes the valve open

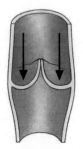

when the blood tries to flow backwards, the valve closes

The diagram shows a slice across (cross section) an artery, a vein and a capillary.

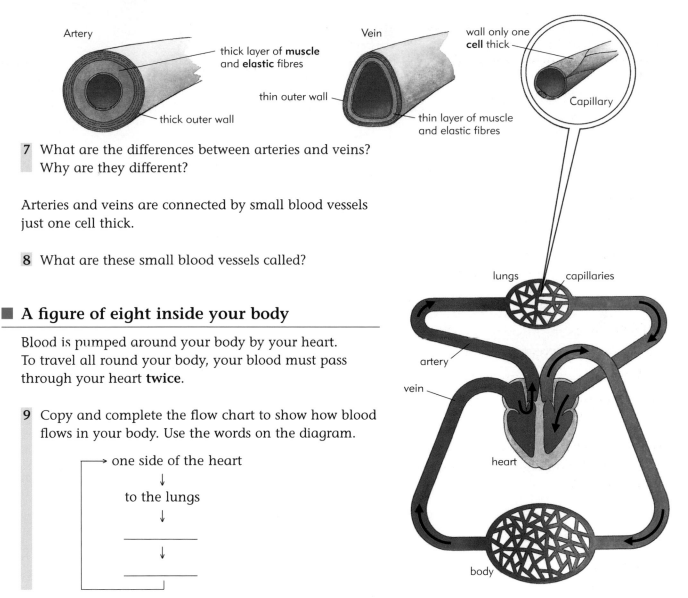

7 What are the differences between arteries and veins? Why are they different?

Arteries and veins are connected by small blood vessels just one cell thick.

8 What are these small blood vessels called?

■ A figure of eight inside your body

Blood is pumped around your body by your heart. To travel all round your body, your blood must pass through your heart **twice**.

9 Copy and complete the flow chart to show how blood flows in your body. Use the words on the diagram.

```
    ┌─→ one side of the heart
    │         ↓
    │    to the lungs
    │         ↓
    │    _____
    │         ↓
    │    _____
    └─────────┘
```

What you need to remember [Copy and complete using the key words]

Know your blood vessels – you could save a life!

Blood is carried away from the heart by _____ and back to the heart by _____. Small blood vessels called _____ join arteries and veins.
Arteries have thick walls of _____ and _____ fibres.
Veins have thinner walls and contain _____ which prevent the blood from flowing backwards. Capillaries are so small that their walls are only one _____ thick.
To travel all round your body, your blood must go through your heart _____ .

Your body's transport system

■ Blood picks things up and drops them off

Blood is the body's transport system. It travels around the body picking things up in some places and dropping them off in different places.

1 Look at the diagram.
Where are the following waste substances made:

(a) carbon dioxide?

(b) urea?

2 Write down <u>one</u> substance that blood takes to <u>all</u> body cells.

■ What is transported where?

- In the **lungs** the blood drops off waste carbon dioxide and picks up **oxygen**.

- The blood picks up dissolved food in the **small intestine**.

- The blood supplies dissolved **food** and **oxygen** to all the body cells. Muscle cells need a lot of food and oxygen when you are working hard.

- The blood carries away the **carbon dioxide** these cells produce.

- Blood picks up a waste substance called urea in the liver. It drops it off in the kidneys.

3 Copy and complete the table.
Use the sentences above to help you.

Organ	Main substance blood picks up	Main substance blood drops off
lung		
small intestine		
muscle		
kidney		
liver		

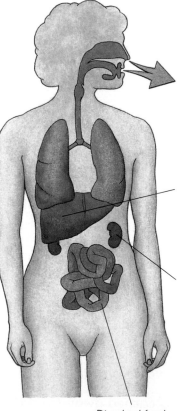

All the cells in the body make waste carbon dioxide. This carbon dioxide leaves the body through the lungs.

The liver makes a waste substance called urea when it breaks down amino acids.

The kidneys take urea out of the blood.

Dissolved food gets into the blood through the small intestine and it goes to all body cells.

■ How do things get into or out of your blood?

Inside the organs of your body, arteries divide to form **capillaries**. These are very narrow blood vessels with thin walls. There are lots and lots of capillaries. This means that every cell in the body is near to a capillary.

4 Make a big copy of the top diagram to show gases changing places in the lungs. Label each arrow with the words 'oxygen' or 'carbon dioxide'.

5 Copy the diagram of dissolved food getting into the blood from the small intestine. Complete the 'blood' labels with the words 'with little dissolved food' or 'with lots of dissolved food'.

6 Look at the bottom diagram. Then describe what happens. Start with this sentence:

■ Blood from an artery goes into a capillary.

Then write down the following sentences in the right order:

■ The liquid picks up carbon dioxide from the cells.

■ Some liquid from the plasma leaks out of the capillaries. It washes over the body cells.

■ The blood then flows on into a vein.

■ The liquid then seeps back into the capillaries again.

■ It gives up oxygen and dissolved food to the cells.

7 Capillaries make it easy for blood to give dissolved food and oxygen to cells and pick up carbon dioxide from cells. Write down <u>two</u> reasons for this.

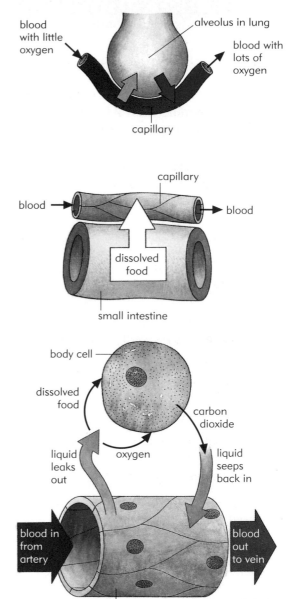

What you need to remember [Copy and complete using the **key words**]

Your transport system

Waste carbon dioxide leaves the blood and _____ enters the blood in the _____.

Blood picks up dissolved food in the _____ _____.

The cells in the organs and muscles receive _____ and dissolved _____ from the blood. They give out _____ _____ and other waste.

All of these substances pass in and out of very narrow blood vessels called _____.

13

Dracula's dinner

Your body contains about this much blood.

■ Replacing lost blood

Your body contains about 6 litres of blood.
If you lose more than 2 litres of this you could die.

1 How many cans of coke is the same volume as 6 litres of blood?

If you lost a lot of blood you could need a blood transfusion. You would be given blood from a donor. A blood donor can safely give about half a litre of blood at a time.

2 What fraction of their blood do blood donors give?

3 A person receiving blood usually needs blood from several donors. Why is this?

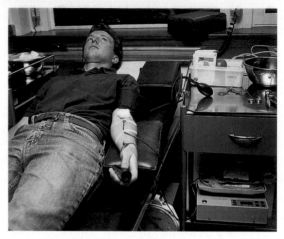

Each donor gives half a litre of blood.

■ Why is blood so important?

Blood is your body's transport system. It is made up of water, dissolved substances and blood cells. The water and dissolved substances are called plasma.
The diagram shows how much of each there are.

4 Copy and complete the table.

plasma	water	____%
	dissolved substances	5%
cells		____%

5 Look at the photograph below. Write down the names of the two kinds of cell in blood.

6 Why does blood look red?

Plasma carries dissolved substances. We say they are in solution. The cells are solid but float about in the plasma. We say the cells are in suspension. Some substances that plasma transports around your body in solution are:

■ carbon dioxide from body cells to the **lungs**;

■ digested foods from the **small intestines** to the body cells;

■ urea from the **liver** to the **kidneys**.

7 Write down <u>one</u> important job of your blood plasma.

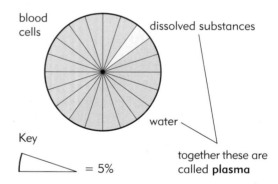

blood cells   dissolved substances

water

Key

⬗ = 5%

together these are called **plasma**

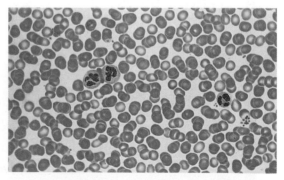

Blood seen through a microscope. **White** blood cells are stained purple so you can see them. Most of the cells are **red** blood cells. Blood also contains broken bits of cells called **platelets**.

■ What do different kinds of blood cells do?

Bacteria which get into your body can cause disease. White blood cells help to **defend** the body against disease. They can do this by **destroying** the bacteria.

When you cut yourself, platelets soon gather around the cut. The white cells which 'eat' bacteria also do this.

8 Write down <u>two</u> different ways that white blood cells can destroy bacteria.

9 Why do you think the white cells gather around a cut?

10 Copy and complete the table using the information in the diagram.
All the cells are drawn to the same scale.

Type of blood cell	What it does
white cell	destroys bacteria

largest

smallest

Blood cells

This type of white cell destroys bacteria by digesting them.

— nucleus

— partly digested bacterium

two types of white blood cell

This type of white cell makes substances called **antibodies** which destroy bacteria.

large nucleus

red blood cell
This cell has no nucleus. It carries **oxygen** around your body.

cell fragments with no nucleus

platelets
(these are bits of cells)
Platelets help blood to **clot** when we cut ourselves.

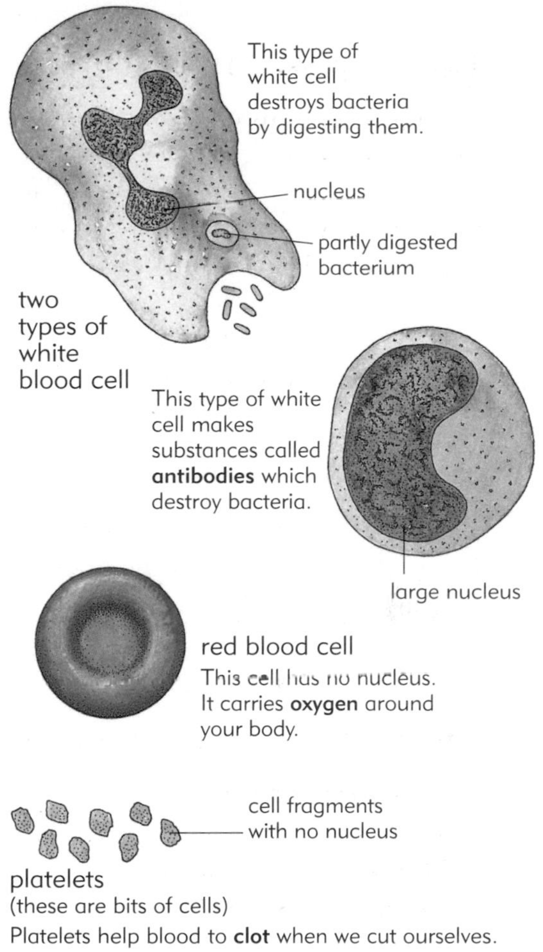

What you need to remember [Copy and complete using the **key words**]

Dracula's dinner

Blood is made of a liquid called _____. Blood also contains _____ cells, _____ cells and small bits of cells called _____ .

Red blood cells transport _____ from the lungs to other parts of the body.

Blood plasma carries many things around your body:
■ carbon dioxide from body cells to the_____ ;
■ digested foods from the _____ _____ to the body cells;
■ urea from the _____ to the _____ .

White blood cells help to _____ the body against disease. They do this by _____ bacteria or by producing _____ which destroy bacteria.

Platelets are bits of cells and have no nucleus. They help the blood to _____ at the site of a wound.

These ideas are extended, for Higher Tier students, in Humans as organisms H3 on pages 52–53.   39

14

Invading microorganisms

■ Small but dangerous

Very small living things are called microorganisms.

Microorganisms such as **bacteria** and **viruses** can get into your body. Some of them cause **disease**.
They can make you ill.

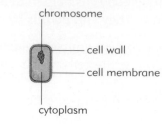

A bacterium.

■ Know your enemy

The cells of bacteria are even smaller than the cells of your body. The bacterium above is 2000 times larger than it is in life.

The plant and the animal cell are also 2000 times larger than in life.

1 Write down the parts which all three types of cell have.

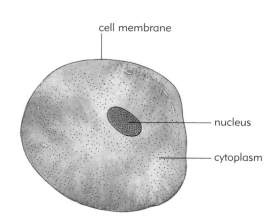

An animal cell.

All cells have genes inside them. These genes contain information which controls what happens in a cell.

The genes are contained in chromosomes.
Chromosomes are in the **nucleus** of animal and plant cells. The genes of a bacterium are not in a nucleus.

2 Write down <u>one</u> other difference between an animal cell and the cell of a bacterium.

■ Bacteria are everywhere

Like you, bacteria need food and water to survive.
Many of them need oxygen too. They grow best when it is warm. We find bacteria in places where there are all the things they need.

3 Write down <u>three</u> places where you would find bacteria.

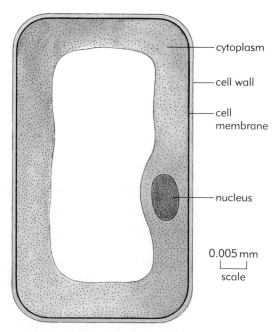

A plant cell.

■ You cannot escape

Your body is full of places where bacteria can live and reproduce.

4 Why is your body a good home for bacteria?

Millions of bacteria live between the cells of even the cleanest skin. Most of them do no harm, but some make you smell sweaty. Others can cause diseases such as sore throats and food poisoning.

5 Draw the shapes of <u>two</u> of the bacteria shown.

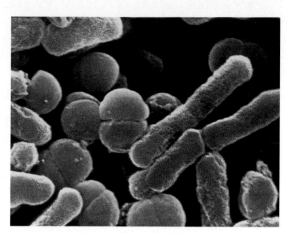
Bacteria that live in the human body.

■ What is the difference between bacteria and viruses?

Viruses are even smaller than bacteria. They are made of a few **genes** in a coat made of **protein**.

6 The picture below shows a bacterial cell infected by a virus. Which part of the virus goes into the cell?

Viruses cannot **reproduce** by themselves. They need to invade living cells and use the living cells to make more viruses. This **damages** the cells.

7 Why are viruses usually harmful?

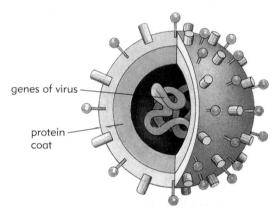
genes of virus

protein coat

A virus. This is about 300,000 times bigger than real life.

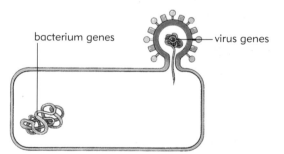
bacterium genes   virus genes

A virus infecting a bacterium.

What you need to remember [Copy and complete using the **key words**]

Invading microorganisms

Microorganisms such as _____ and _____ can get into your body and cause _____. The cells of bacteria have cytoplasm, cell membranes and cell walls, but the genes are not in a _____.
_____ are even smaller than bacteria. They have a few _____ in a _____ coat. They can only _____ inside living cells. This _____ the cells.

15 What happens when microorganisms get into your body?

■ Do microorganisms always make you ill?

Not all **microorganisms** make you ill. Many are easily destroyed by your white blood cells.
Others are harder to destroy.

When the numbers of microorganisms are small, you do not notice any effect. But microorganisms can breed very quickly. As their numbers get larger and they produce more toxins, you begin to feel ill. This may take a few hours, days or even weeks.

1 What kind of cell destroys microorganisms?

2 Jan's sister Carol caught scarlet fever. As soon as her mother knew Carol was **infected**, she kept the two girls apart. It was too late.
Jan became ill a week later.

   Why was it so long before Jan became ill?

3 What were the effects of the scarlet fever bacteria on the girls?

■ How do microorganisms cause these symptoms?

The pictures show how microorganisms can affect your body.

4 Your body temperature rises when you have an infection. Give <u>one</u> reason why.

5 You may also have a rash or a headache. Write down <u>one</u> possible cause for each of these symptoms.

I am hot
I feel sick
I have a rash

Carol describes her symptoms.

Your cells release more energy as heat.
You can't control your body temperature by sweating.

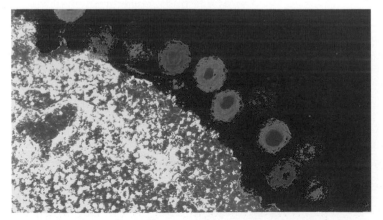

Viruses damage cells as they escape.

Toxic

Microorganisms make **toxins** (poisons).

How quickly can bacteria breed?

Bacteria reproduce by dividing into two. At human body temperature some can divide every 20 minutes.

6 Imagine you have eaten a pie with 50 bacteria in it. Copy the table and complete it to show the number of bacteria.

Time (mins)	Number of bacteria
0	50
20	
40	
60	

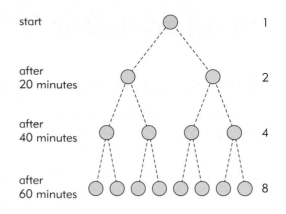

How can we prevent diseases spreading?

You should not keep food in a warm or dirty place. In such **unhygienic** conditions food can soon have enough bacteria in it to make you ill.

You can become ill with food poisoning within a few hours of eating infected food.

7 Look at the pictures. Explain <u>two</u> things you can do to make sure you do not get food poisoning.

Tuberculosis is a lung infection. It is caused by bacteria. In **overcrowded** conditions the bacteria easily spread from one person to another.

8 People are more likely to get tuberculosis if they live in overcrowded conditions. Why is this?

Microorganisms cannot breed quickly in cold conditions. They are killed when it gets very hot.

What you need to remember [Copy and complete using the **key words**]

What happens when microorganisms get into your body?

It takes large numbers of _____ to make you ill. They get into your body when you are in contact with an _____ person. Microorganisms reproduce rapidly inside your body. They make poisons (_____) which make you ill.

Large numbers of microorganisms are present in dirty or _____ conditions.

People living in _____ conditions are also more likely to take in microorganisms which cause infection.

[You need to be able to use evidence to explain how the conditions people live in and the way they behave affect the spread of disease.]

16

The spread of infection

'Coughs and sneezes spread diseases'

This old rhyme is true.
However, diseases are also spread in other ways.

1 The pictures show ways that diseases are spread.
Write a sentence about each one.

■ How do microorganisms get inside your body?

Some microorganisms get inside your body through wounds. Cuts, injections and animal bites can all let microorganisms in. Others get in through the thinner skin lining the natural 'openings' of your body.

2 Copy the table below.

How microorganisms get into your body	
Natural openings	Wounds
eyes	cuts

Use the diagram to help you to complete your table.

3 You need to wash your hands before you touch food. Why is this?

4 Germicides kill bacteria. Your doctor always wipes your skin with germicide before you have an injection. Why is this?

■ Skin – your first line of defence

Your body has ways of stopping microorganisms getting in. The cells of the outer layers of your **skin** are dead. They act like a barrier. However, there are some natural openings in the skin which can let bacteria in. For example, you get spots when bacteria infect pores in the skin.

5 Name the other kind of natural opening in skin.

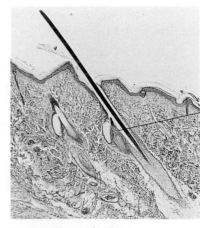

eyes
ears
nose
mouth (in food)
insect bites
pores in skin
infected needles
cuts
opening of reproductive system
dog bites
opening of urinary system

Where microorganisms get into your body.

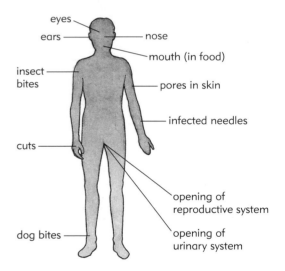

Each hair grows out of an opening called a hair follicle.

Section through skin.

■ What happens if your skin is broken?

Luckily your blood puts up another barrier when you cut yourself. Your blood dries up and goes hard. We say that it **clots**. Clotting starts as soon as the blood meets the air. It takes only a few minutes.

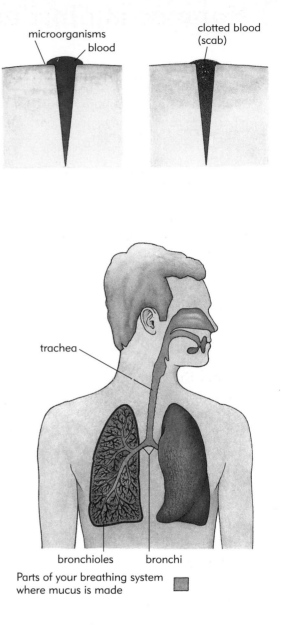

6 When blood clots, blood can no longer flow out through a cut. What cannot get in?

■ Fighting off the air-borne division

There are microorganisms in the air. These can get into the air passages to your lungs through your nose and mouth. Some of the microorganisms get trapped by the hairs and sticky mucus in your nose.
Mucus also traps dust.

7 It is more healthy to breathe in through your nose than your mouth. Why is this?

Mucus in your trachea and bronchi also **traps** microorganisms. This mucus is the phlegm which comes up into your mouth when you cough.

The cells in the air passsages have cilia. These are like little hairs. Smoking stops these cilia working, so if you smoke, microorganisms get into your lungs more easily.

8 Tuberculosis (TB) is caused by bacteria that infect your lungs. List the places where these bacteria could get trapped before they reach your lungs.

Parts of your breathing system where mucus is made

What you need to remember [Copy and complete using the **key words**]

The spread of infection

Your body has several ways of stopping microorganisms getting in.
Your _____ acts as a barrier.
Blood _____ to seal cuts.
The linings of the passages to the lungs make _____.
This is a sticky liquid which _____ microorganisms.

17

Humans against microorganisms

■ A case of whooping cough

Sharon has had whooping cough. Bacteria cause whooping cough. They spread easily through the air from one person to another.

1 Describe Sharon's illness. Use the chart to help you.

2 How could Sharon have caught the disease? Write down your idea in a few sentences.

Within a few weeks she was better.
Her body had destroyed the bacteria.

Day	5	10	15	20
runny nose, sneezing, feeling ill				feeling better
fever				
		very bad coughing fits		still coughing

What happened to Sharon.

■ How did Sharon's body destroy the bacteria?

The white cells in Sharon's blood destroyed the bacteria. The diagrams show how they can do this.

3 Look at the diagrams of the white blood cells. Write down the ways they can destroy bacteria and other microorganisms.

Some white cells make **antibodies**. These destroy **microorganisms**. Each kind of antibody works against only one kind of microorganism.

When a new kind of bacterium or virus gets into your body, white cells have to start making a new kind of antibody. It takes time for the cells to make enough of the right kind of antibody. That is why it takes time to get better.

Bacteria make poisons called **toxins**. White blood cells make **antitoxins** which destroy toxins. Each kind of antitoxin works against only one kind of toxin.

4 Where are antitoxins made?

5 Toxins have time to make you ill before they are all destroyed. Why do you think this is?

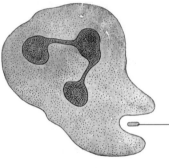

Some white cells surround and then digest bacteria. We say they **ingest** them.

bacterium

Other white cells make antibodies or antitoxins.

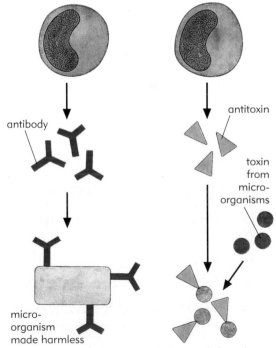

antibody

micro-organism made harmless

antitoxin

toxin from micro-organisms

toxins made harmless

■ Why didn't Daneya get whooping cough?

Daneya is Sharon's best friend. They spend most of their time together. But Daneya didn't get whooping cough. Two years ago she had an injection of a weak form of the bacteria which cause whooping cough. We say that she was **vaccinated** against the disease. Her white blood cells made antibodies against the bacteria.
So Daneya is **immune**.

6 Look at the diagrams. Explain what happens when bacteria from Sharon get into Daneya's blood.

7 Daneya's brother Adil had whooping cough last year. Will he catch it again? Explain your answer.

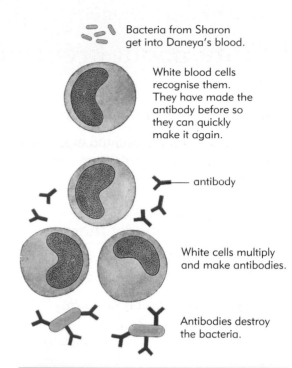

Bacteria from Sharon get into Daneya's blood.

White blood cells recognise them. They have made the antibody before so they can quickly make it again.

— antibody

White cells multiply and make antibodies.

Antibodies destroy the bacteria.

■ What if your defence system doesn't work?

Some medical treatments damage the white cells which destroy bacteria. HIV (human immunodeficiency virus) also destroys some kinds of white cells.

The HIV infects white blood cells. These cells then cannot do their job. They cannot make antibodies.

8 Illnesses which are normally quite mild can kill people with HIV who develop AIDS.
Why do you think this is?

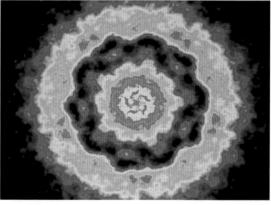

Human immunodeficiency virus (HIV).

What you need to remember [Copy and complete using the **key words**]

Humans against microorganisms

White blood cells help to defend the body against the _____ which cause disease.

Some white cells take the microorganisms into their cells and digest them. We say they _____ them.

Some white cells destroy bacteria or viruses by making _____.

Poisons or _____ made by microorganisms also have to be made harmless.

Some white cells make _____ to do this.

Once they have made antibodies against a particular microorganism, white cells can quickly do this again. That is why a person who has had a disease or who has been _____ against it does not become ill. We say that the person is _____ to the disease.

More about breathing

■ How do you get air into your lungs?

Movements of your ribs and **diaphragm** help to get air into your lungs. They do it by altering the volume of your thorax.

■ Looking at a model thorax

In this model, you can get air into the balloons by pulling the rubber sheet downwards.

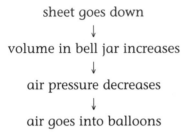

sheet goes down
↓
volume in bell jar increases
↓
air pressure decreases
↓
air goes into balloons

1 An important movement is not shown in the model thorax. Describe the missing movement.

> **REMEMBER**
>
> Your **lungs** are in your thorax or chest.
>
> Breathing is taking air in and out of your lungs.

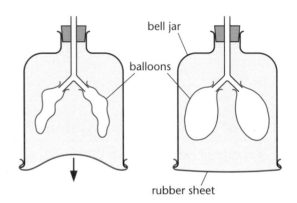

bell jar

balloons

rubber sheet

■ Your thorax

Your diaphragm is a bit like a rubber sheet. It flattens when the muscles contract. At the same time, the muscles between your ribs contract and pull your ribcage upwards and outwards. These movements of your diaphragm and ribcage increase the volume inside your thorax. As the volume <u>increases</u>, the pressure <u>decreases</u>. To keep the pressures inside and outside your thorax the same, air goes into your lungs.

2 Your thorax is air-tight. Describe the only route for air to go into your lungs.

3 Draw flow charts, like the one for the model thorax, to show why

   (a) air goes into your lungs

   (b) air goes out of your lungs.

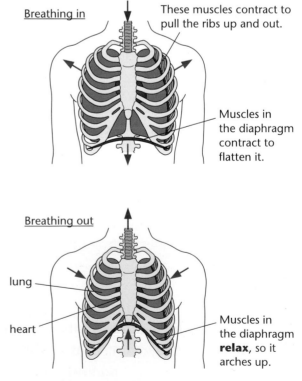

Breathing in

These muscles contract to pull the ribs up and out.

Muscles in the diaphragm contract to flatten it.

Breathing out

lung

heart

Muscles in the diaphragm **relax**, so it arches up.

We call the movement of air into and out of your lungs ventilation.

■ Inside your lungs

You absorb oxygen through your lungs. These have lots of 'folds' to increase their surface area. These 'folds' are called alveoli. Air reaches your **alveoli** through tiny tubes called **bronchioles**. The alveoli have a rich supply of capillaries. The walls of the alveoli and the capillaries are thin, so oxygen doesn't have far to diffuse. But it can only diffuse through cells in solution. So, the lining of the alveoli has to be moist.

Blood coming to your lungs contains only a little oxygen because the rest has been used in your body. The air in the alveoli has a higher concentration of oxygen than the blood, so oxygen **diffuses** easily from the alveoli into the blood. The blood then carries the oxygen away to the rest of your body.

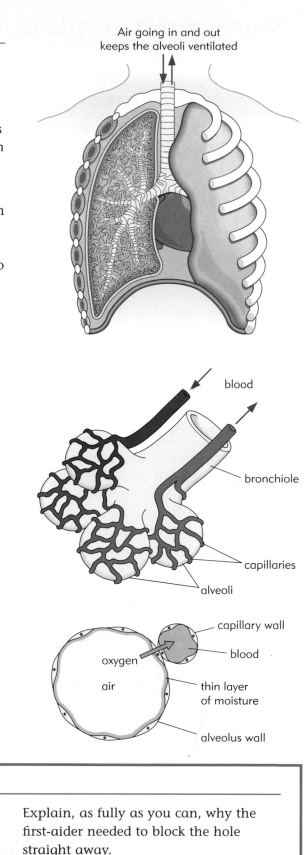

Air going in and out keeps the alveoli ventilated

blood

bronchiole

capillaries

alveoli

capillary wall

blood

thin layer of moisture

alveolus wall

oxygen

air

4 Copy and complete:

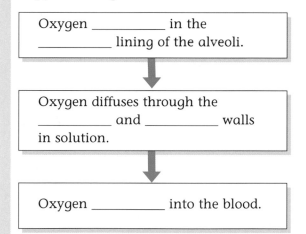

> Oxygen _____ in the _____ lining of the alveoli.

> Oxygen diffuses through the _____ and _____ walls in solution.

> Oxygen _____ into the blood.

5 Explain why each of the following features of an alveolus is important:

(a) the wall is thin;

(b) it has a rich capillary supply;

(c) the stale air inside is constantly being replaced with fresh air;

(d) the lining is moist.

Using your knowledge

1 Jo was stabbed. The knife went into her left lung. A first-aider could hear air being sucked in and out through the wound. She quickly blocked the hole so that air could go into Jo's lung again.

Explain, as fully as you can, why the first-aider needed to block the hole straight away.

More about respiration

Respiration happens in all living cells. Like other chemical reactions in cells, it is controlled by enzymes. Most energy is released in structures called **mitochondria**.

1 Look at the diagrams.
In what part of a cell are the mitochondria?

2 What are the raw materials for aerobic respiration?

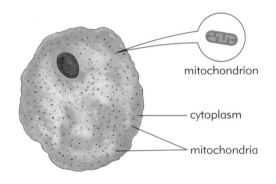

mitochondrion

cytoplasm

mitochondria

■ Another use of the energy from respiration

Substances often **diffuse** into or out of cells. This can only happen down a concentration gradient. Sometimes cells need to take in substances faster than they can diffuse in, or even <u>against</u> a concentration gradient. They use energy released in respiration to do this. So we call it active transport.

3 (a) Describe <u>two</u> differences between diffusion and active transport.

(b) Write down <u>four</u> uses for energy released in respiration.

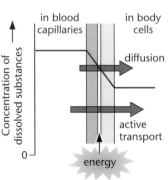

in blood capillaries   in body cells

Concentration of dissolved substances

diffusion

active transport

energy

Active transport can speed up the movement of dissolved substances into and out of cells or move substances against the concentration gradient.

■ Sometimes you can't take in enough oxygen

When you run, you pant and your heart beats faster. Both these things help to get more oxygen to your cells.

If they don't get enough oxygen your cells can release energy in another way. They do this by breaking down glucose into lactic acid. Lactic acid is a mild poison.

We call this process **anaerobic respiration**. Anaerobic means without air. The glucose isn't broken down completely so less energy is released in anaerobic than aerobic respiration.

Muscles produce lactic acid when they work hard for a long time.

4 Your cells can only release energy by anaerobic respiration for a short time. Why is this?

5 (a) Copy and complete the table.

	Aerobic respiration	Anaerobic respiration
Raw materials	_____ and _____	_____
Waste products	carbon dioxide and _____	_____ _____
Energy released	all	_____ _____

(b) Why is less energy released in anaerobic respiration than in aerobic respiration?

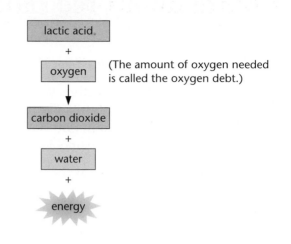

(The amount of oxygen needed is called the oxygen debt.)

■ You have to get rid of the lactic acid

Lactic acid is one cause of **muscle fatigue**. Your muscles get tired, ache and don't work as well as usual. You must get rid of this poison when the exercise is over. So, you have to breathe in more oxygen than usual so that you can break down the lactic acid. The extra oxygen that you need is called the **oxygen debt**.

6 What is:

(a) muscle fatigue?

(b) oxygen debt?

7 Look at the graph then write down:

(a) the lactic acid concentration before exercise;

(b) the highest lactic acid concentration reached;

(c) how long it then takes for the lactic acid concentration to go back to what it was before exercise.

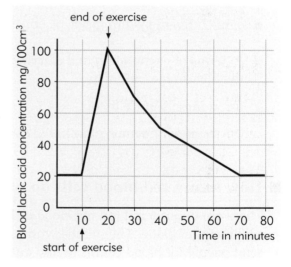

Lactic acid concentration in the blood of an athlete before, during and after exercise.

Using your knowledge

1 A high concentration of carbon dioxide or lactic acid in the blood reaching your brain makes you breathe faster and more deeply.

Why do you breathe faster and more deeply when you exercise?

2 In the first few minutes of exercise, is it carbon dioxide or lactic acid that makes you pant? Explain your answer.

H3   This extends *Humans as organisms* 13 for Higher Tier students

More about red blood cells

■ What is the job of red blood cells?

The job of the **red blood cells** is to carry oxygen around the body. They can do this because they are packed with a chemical called **haemoglobin**. Haemoglobin joins with oxygen to form oxyhaemoglobin.

haemoglobin + oxygen $\rightleftharpoons$ oxyhaemoglobin

1 The reversible reaction sign ($\rightleftharpoons$) shows that oxyhaemoglobin splits easily.
What is formed when it splits?

Red blood cells are unusual in another way. They have no nuclei. They lose their nuclei before they go into the bloodstream. Without a nucleus the cell has:

■ a larger surface area

■ as much haemoglobin inside as possible.

2 In terms of exchanging and carrying oxygen, explain the advantages of having

   (a) a large surface area;

   (b) as much haemoglobin in the cell as possible.

REMEMBER

Blood contains:

■ red cells, white cells and platelets

■ a liquid called plasma which has things dissolved in it.

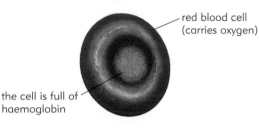

red blood cell (carries oxygen)

the cell is full of haemoglobin

■ How many red blood cells do we have?

There are about 5 million red blood cells in every cubic millimetre of blood. The number varies. Doctors can send people for blood counts to find out if they have enough. Technicians use a grid like the one on the right to help them to count the cells in a very tiny amount of blood.

3 (a) Count the red cells in one small square of the picture.

   (b) About how many red cells are there altogether?

   (c) About how many times more red blood cells are there than white blood cells?

4 What is there in blood that you cannot see in the picture?

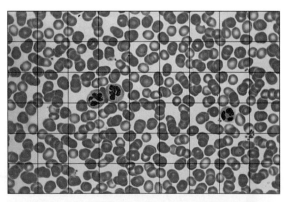

Blood seen through a microscope. White blood cells are stained purple so you can see them. Most of the cells are red blood cells. Blood also contains broken bits of cells called **platelets**.

■ Where is oxygen exchanged?

Look at the diagram which shows what happens to red blood cells as they move round the body.

5 The sentences below are in the wrong order. Put them into the correct order to show what's happening in the diagram. Start with:

- Blood carries the red cells to the lungs.

- The red cells are now bright red.

- In the lungs haemoglobin joins up with oxygen.

- Oxygen goes to the cells.

- Blood carries the red cells to the organs.

- Oxyhaemoglobin is formed.

- The red cells are now dark red.

- In the organs oxyhaemoglobin splits up into haemoglobin and oxygen.

What happens to red cells in the lungs.

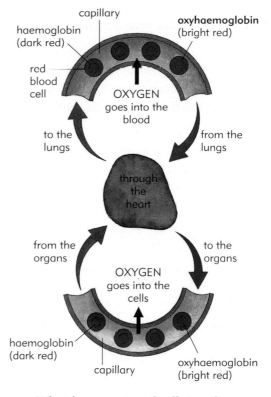

What happens to red cells in other parts of the body.

Using your knowledge

1 You use the iron in your diet to make haemoglobin. If you don't get enough iron, you become anaemic. You have:

- fewer red blood cells;

- less haemoglobin in each red cell.

Explain why people who are anaemic

(a) look pale;

(b) often feel tired and cold.

2 Look at the graph.

(a) What is the relationship between the number of red cells and the height above sea level?

(b) Suggest a reason for this relationship.

(c) Athletes often train at altitude before an important event. Explain why this could help them do better.

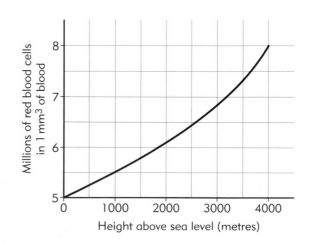

More about exchanges

■ Using what you know about exchanges

Plants and animals exchange substances with their surroundings. These exchanges happen in solution. Substances exchanged include gases such as oxygen and carbon dioxide, as well as nutrients such as sugars and mineral ions.

Exchanges also happen between cells and body fluids. To get in and out of cells, substances have to cross cell membranes.

1 (a) Write down <u>two</u> processes by which exchanges happen.

(b) What is the difference between the two processes?

■ Adaptations of efficient exchange surfaces

Remember, to work well an exchange surface has:

- ■ a large surface area
- ■ thin walls
- ■ a moist lining
- ■ a rich capillary supply.

2 Write down <u>one</u> reason for <u>each</u> of the features of a good exchange surface. If you need help, look back at spread 9.

In your examination, you may be asked to explain how other exchange surfaces work in humans and other organisms. Try applying the information on this page to the problems on page 55.

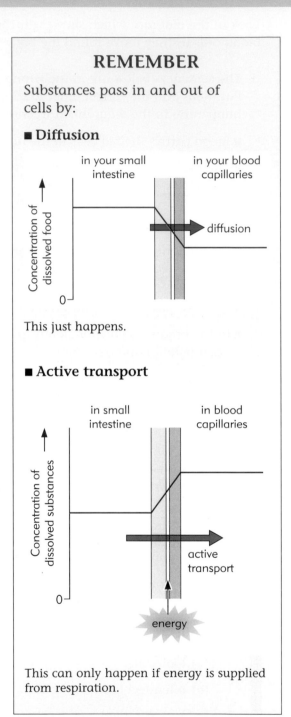

REMEMBER

Substances pass in and out of cells by:

■ Diffusion

This just happens.

■ Active transport

This can only happen if energy is supplied from respiration.

Using your knowledge

1   Some students cut some cubes of agar jelly and put them in red dye for 5 minutes. The diagrams show what happened.

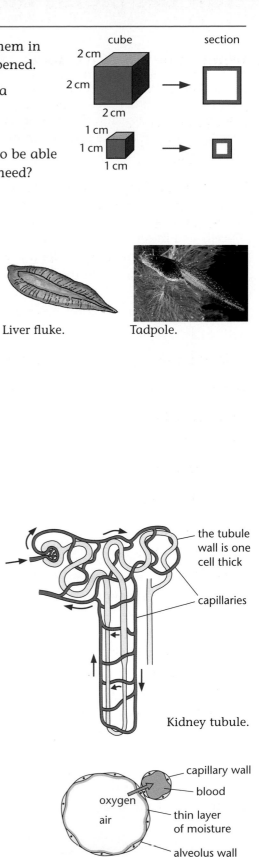

cube   section

2 cm

2 cm

2 cm

1 cm
1 cm
1 cm

(a) Which absorbs more of the red dye in 5 minutes, a large cube or a set of 8 smaller cubes?
Give a reason for your answer.

(b) Why are small cells more likely than larger cells to be able to obtain all the dissolved food and oxygen they need?

2   The liver fluke takes in oxygen and gets rid of carbon dioxide through its skin. The tadpole uses gills as well as its skin for this.

(a) Explain why the liver fluke can get enough oxygen through its skin but the tadpole can't.

(b) Design a tadpole gill. You can draw it or describe it. Explain your design.

Liver fluke.   Tadpole.

3   Alf smoked for 40 years. He had a bad 'smoker's cough' and easily got out of breath. His health got worse so he went to see his doctor. The doctor said that he had emphysema. She explained that coughing had damaged a lot of the alveoli in his lungs and reduced their surface area.

(a) Explain, as fully as you can, why Alf got out of breath easily.

(b) Alf's illness got worse. He couldn't walk very far and he had to breathe oxygen from a cylinder. Explain why.

4   The villi in the small intestine of people with coeliac disease don't work properly. These people don't grow as quickly as people with normal villi. Why is this?

the tubule wall is one cell thick

capillaries

5   Your kidneys are exchange surfaces. They are made of millions of tubules like the one in the diagram.

Using this information only, describe three features which make kidneys good exchange surfaces.

Kidney tubule.

6   (a) The diagram shows a section through an alveolus. Explain how oxygen passes from the air in the alveolus into the blood.

(b) Explain how oxygen passes from the blood to a body cell.

capillary wall

blood

oxygen

air

thin layer of moisture

alveolus wall

How are plants built?

All plants are made from tiny parts called **cells**.
Cells are so small that you can only see them using
a microscope.

The cells in the drawing on the right are the first ones
ever seen. Robert Hooke drew them more than
300 years ago.

1 Why do you think he called them cells?

2 Draw a line 1 centimetre (cm) long. About 400 plant
cells will fit along this line. Now use a sharp pencil to
mark off each millimetre along your line.
How many cells will fit into a space of 1 mm?

We know now that all plants are made up of cells.

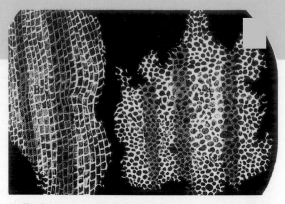

Cells from a cork oak plant.

These little spaces in a beehive are all the
same size and shape. They are called cells.

■ Do all cells look the same?

Some things are the same in all cells, but other things
are different. Look at the plant cells and the animal cell.

3 Write down <u>three</u> parts you can see in both
types of cell.

The **nucleus** controls what the cell does. The **cell
membrane** controls what passes in and out of a cell.
The **cytoplasm** is where most of the chemical
reactions take place.

4 Which part can you see in all three of the plant cells,
but not in the animal cell?

5 Write down the two parts you can see in some, but
not all, of the plant cells.

All plant cells have cell walls made of cellulose.
This makes the cells **stronger** and more rigid.
The spaces in plant cells called vacuoles are filled with
a watery fluid called **sap**.

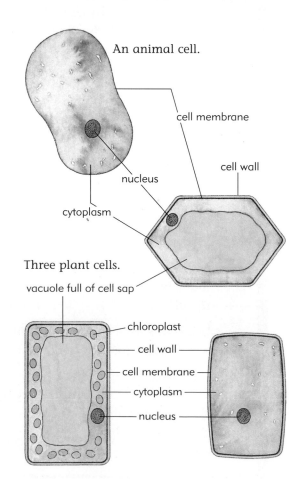

■ Why don't all plant cells have chloroplasts?

Chloroplasts contain **chlorophyll**. This is what gives plants their green colour. Chlorophyll absorbs light energy so that plants can make food. Chlorophyll is made only in the light. After a few weeks in the dark it disappears from the cells.

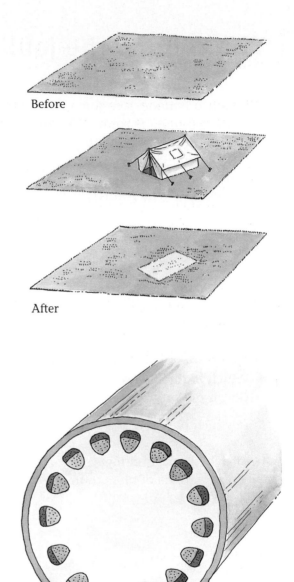

Before

After

6 Look at the pictures of the lawn.

   (a) What happens to the grass under the tent?

   (b) Why does this happen?

7 Root cells do not have chloroplasts. Why not?

8 The picture below shows a section cut through a stem of a plant. Only the outer layer is green. Why is it not green in the middle?

Potatoes are the underground stems of potato plants. They grow under the ground so they are not green, but they go green in the light.

■ The bad news: the green parts of potatoes are poisonous.

■ The good news: you would have to eat a lot to make you ill.

9 How should you store potatoes so they don't go green?

A slice across a stem.

What you need to remember [Copy and complete using the **key words**]

How are plants built?

All plants and animals are made up of small parts called _____.

Most plant cells and animal cells have a _____ _____,

_____ and a _____.

Plant cells also have cell walls to make them _____.

Plant cells often have other parts such as chloroplasts. The _____ in chloroplasts gives leaves their green colour.

Plant cells often have spaces called vacuoles. These are filled with a liquid called _____.

The cell for the job!

All plants are made from tiny parts called cells. But not all plant cells are the same. You can see this if you cut a slice through part of a plant.

1 You would need to look at the slice under a microscope. Why is this?

Different jobs in a plant are done by different kinds of cells. A group of cells with the same shape and job is called a **tissue**.

2 Write down <u>three</u> kinds of tissue shown in the leaf section.

3 What job does a leaf do?

4 Which of the tissues can make food? Give a reason for your answer.

5 In which part of a leaf is most of the food made?

The leaves, stems and roots of plants are called **organs**. Organs are made of more than one kind of tissue.

> ## REMEMBER
> Only plant cells which have chloroplasts can use light energy to make food.

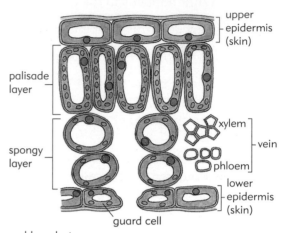

⬮ chloroplasts

A slice across a leaf.

■ Why do leaves have veins?

Plants use veins to transport substances. Veins are made of two main kinds of tissue. The first is called **xylem** tissue. (You say this word zy-lem).

In xylem tissue there are rows of dead cells with the ends missing. They form a long tube like a drinking straw. Water travels up xylem tissue from the **roots**.

Look at the drawing of xylem tissue.

6 What else besides water travels from the roots to the stems and leaves through the xylem tissue?

7 Xylem tissue also does another job. What do you think this job is?

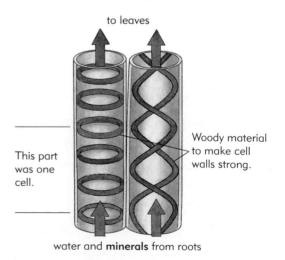

water and **minerals** from roots

Xylem vessels are made of dead cells.

The second kind of tissue is called phloem. (You say this word flo-em).

Look at the drawing of phloem tissue.

8 Write down <u>two</u> differences between xylem and phloem tissue.

Phloem carries **sugar** from where it is made to other parts of the plant.

9 (a) Which part of a plant does phloem transport sugar from?

(b) Where does phloem carry sugar to?

■ Where are the transport tissues?

10 Copy the drawings of the slice of a root and a stem. Then colour the tissue which transports water in one colour. Use a different colour for the tissue which carries sugar.
Add a key to show what your colours mean.

■ What other kinds of plant cells are there?

Other plant cells do other jobs. We say that they are **specialised** to do particular jobs.

11 What do you think each of the cells on the right is specialised to do? Choose from:

- support
- making new cells
- storage
- photosynthesis (making food)

Give a reason for each answer.

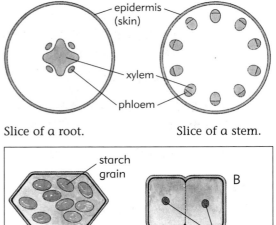

sugar from leaves

cytoplasm
end wall like a sieve
nucleus

sugar to **storage organs** and growing regions

Phloem tissue is made of living cells.

epidermis (skin)

xylem

phloem

Slice of a root.   Slice of a stem.

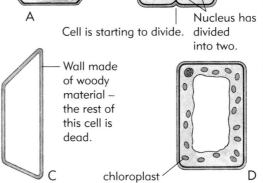

starch grain

B

A

Nucleus has divided into two.

Cell is starting to divide.

Wall made of woody material – the rest of this cell is dead.

C   chloroplast   D

What you need to remember [Copy and complete using the **key words**]

The cell for the job!

A group of cells with the same shape and job is called a _____.
Leaves, stems and roots are called _____; they are made of more than one kind of tissue.
Tissue called _____ transports water and _____ from _____ to stems and leaves. Tissue called phloem carries _____ from leaves to growing points, _____ _____ and other parts of plants.
Different plant cells do different jobs. We say they are _____.

[You should be able to look at a cell and work out its job like you did in question 11.]

How do plants get their food?

All living things need food to survive.
Green **plants** can make their own food.

Animals cannot do this.
They have to eat other animals or plants for food.

> **REMEMBER**
>
> The green parts of plants make food.
>
> They use light energy to do this.

1 Why do animals have to eat plants or other animals?

Animals have to eat plants or other animals to stay alive. They cannot make their own food.

Plants make their own food from water and
carbon dioxide.

2 If all the plants died, what would happen to animals
like sheep?

3 What would happen to us? Explain why.

■ What kind of food do plants make?

Plants use light energy to make glucose. **Glucose** is a
kind of sugar.

Plants can use glucose to make other foods. One of these
other foods is another sugar called sucrose. This is the
kind of sugar you use at home.

4 Where do plants get the energy from to make their
own food?

5 What type of food do plants make first using
light energy?

6 What plants do we grow for sugar

  (a) in hot countries?

  (b) in Britain?

Sugar cane grows in
hot countries.

Sugar beet grows in
cooler countries.

Where your sugar comes from.

■ What happens to the glucose plants make?

Plants make glucose. Then they use it in different ways. The diagram shows the ways plants use glucose.

7   Plants use glucose for respiration. What does this mean?

8   In what form do plants store the food they make?

9   Write down <u>three</u> other ways plants use glucose.

Some is reacted with oxygen. This releases energy for cells to live and grow. This release of energy is called **respiration**.

Some is made into sucrose.

Glucose

Some is made into **starch**. This is a food store.

Some is made into other substances.

potatoes

■ How do plants make starch?

Plants join together lots of the small glucose molecules they have made. This makes long starch molecules.

Starch is stored in the plant as a 'food store'. Starch is a good way of storing sugar because it is **insoluble** (it will not dissolve).

10   Copy and complete the diagram to show how plants change glucose into starch.

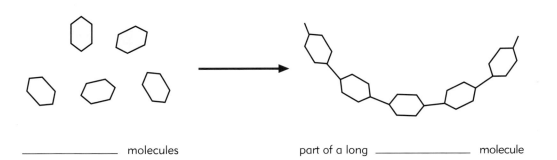

_____ molecules   part of a long _____ molecule

What you need to remember [Copy and complete using the **key words**]

How do plants get food?

Green _____ make their own food.

They produce a sugar called _____.

Plants use some of the sugar for _____ to release energy.

Some of the sugar is changed into _____.

The starch is stored.

Starch is a good storage substance because it is _____.

These ideas are extended, for Higher Tier students, in Maintenance of life H1 on page 100.

These ideas are extended, for Higher Tier students, in Maintenance of life H1 on page 100.

4

Food factories – the leaves

Plants use **light** energy to make food.
This is called **photosynthesis**.

You cannot see this happening, but you can prove that leaves make food. The diagrams show you how you can do this.

REMEMBER

Plants make glucose.
They then change some of this glucose into starch.

---

1 Copy and complete the following sentences.

You can remove the _____ colour from a leaf by putting it into hot _____.
You can then test the leaf with _____ solution.
A black colour shows where there is _____.

2 Plants use light energy to make food.
What do we call this process?

Take a leaf which has been in the light.

ethanol —— / —— hot water

Remove the green colour by putting the leaf in hot ethanol.

iodine solution

Test with iodine solution.
Any starch in the leaf goes black.

■ **Do all plant cells make food?**

Carol tested a leaf for starch. These are her results.

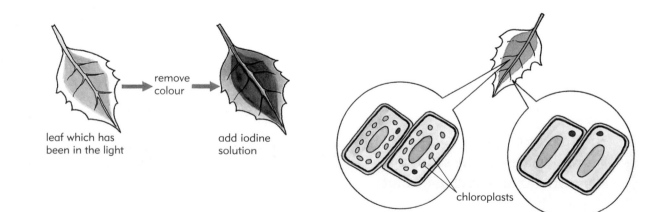

leaf which has been in the light

remove colour

add iodine solution

chloroplasts

---

3 Which parts of the leaf had starch in them?

4 What is the difference between the cells in the two parts of the leaf ?

■ Where do plants make their food?

The cells in the green parts of a plant contain
chloroplasts. These are filled with a green substance
called **chlorophyll**. Chlorophyll takes in light energy.
The cells use this energy for photosynthesis.

5 Why are the leaves of the potato plant green?

6 Which parts of the potato plant could not
photosynthesise? Explain why you think this is.

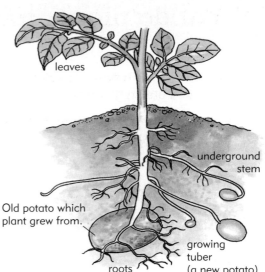

■ Why are leaves good at photosynthesis?

Most of a plant's chloroplasts are in its **leaves**.
Leaves are usually broad and flat.

7 How does the shape of a leaf help it to
photosynthesise? (Hint: imagine you are sunbathing.)

8 There are more chloroplasts in the palisade cells than
in the cells in the spongy layer. Why?

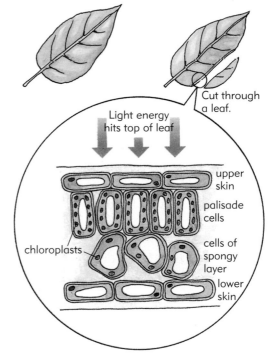

Slice of a leaf seen through a microscope.

What you need to remember [Copy and complete using the **key words**]

Food factories – the leaves

Green plants use _____ energy to make food.

This process is called _____.

A green substance called _____ absorbs the light energy.

Chlorophyll is found in the parts of cells called _____.

These are mainly in the _____ of plants.

5

What do plants make sugar from?

Some plant cells can make sugar using light energy. We call this **photosynthesis**.

The diagram shows what plants make the sugar from.

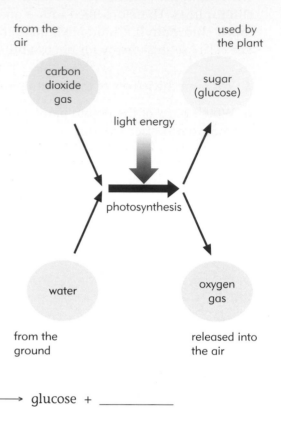

from the air

used by the plant

carbon dioxide gas

light energy

sugar (glucose)

photosynthesis

water

oxygen gas

from the ground

released into the air

1 What two substances do plants use to make sugar?

2 Where does each substance come from?

3 What else does the plant produce as it makes sugar?

4 Where does this other substance go?

We can write down what happens during photosynthesis as a word equation. Use the information in the diagram to complete the word equation.

_____ _____ + water + ⟨ _____ energy ⟩ ⟶ glucose + _____

■ Why do plants need light to make sugar?

You may have used a Bunsen burner to give you the energy needed to join chemicals together. Plants need energy to join carbon dioxide and water together.

Plants get the energy they need for photosynthesis from light.

5 Where do plants usually get this light energy from?

6 Copy the graph. Then copy these labels on to the right place on the graph:

| sunset | | sunrise |

7 No photosynthesis takes place at night. Explain why.

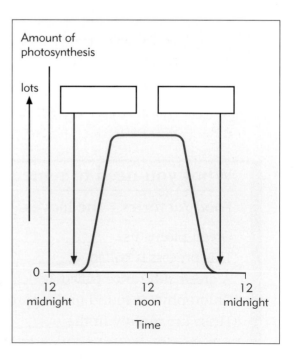

Amount of photosynthesis

lots

0

12 midnight

12 noon

12 midnight

Time

■ Investigating photosynthesis

A group of students learned that plants need light and carbon dioxide for photosynthesis. They decided to find out if this is true.

They set up four plants in different conditions. After 24 hours the students tested a leaf from each plant to see if it had starch in it.

8   Copy out the table.
    Fill in the results you think the students got.

Plant	How it was kept	Was starch found?
A	In the light with plenty of carbon dioxide.	
B	In the light with no carbon dioxide.	
C	In the dark with plenty of carbon dioxide.	
D	In the dark with no carbon dioxide.	

9   Tomato plants are usually grown in glasshouses.
    Extra carbon dioxide is sometimes added to the air.
    Why do you think this is?

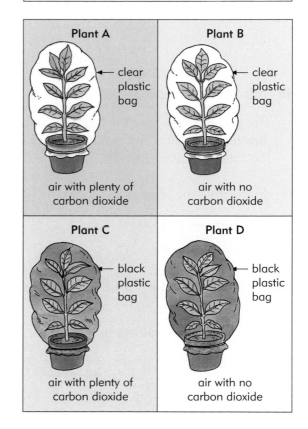

Plant A — clear plastic bag — air with plenty of carbon dioxide
Plant B — clear plastic bag — air with no carbon dioxide
Plant C — black plastic bag — air with plenty of carbon dioxide
Plant D — black plastic bag — air with no carbon dioxide

What you need to remember [Copy and complete using the **key words**]

What do plants make sugar from?

Plants make their own food by _____.

Copy the headings. Put these words in the right place in the table:
chlorophyll, light, water, oxygen, sugar, carbon dioxide

Things needed for photosynthesis	Things made by photosynthesis

6

Limits to plant growth

Even in Britain, wheat crops grow faster when farmers give them extra water.

1 To grow faster, a plant needs to make food faster. Write down <u>three</u> things that a plant needs to do this.

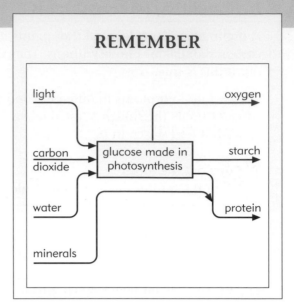

■ What affects plant growth?

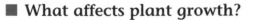

The graph shows how the amounts of **light** and **carbon dioxide** affect how fast a plant makes food. We call this the rate of **photosynthesis**.

2 Describe the change in the rate of photosynthesis:

  (a) between A and B.

  (b) between B and C.

3 Line A to D shows photosynthesis in the same plant. Write down:

  (a) <u>one</u> way it differs from line ABC;

  (b) <u>one</u> reason for the difference.

4 Look at the bottom graph. What limits the rate of photosynthesis:

  (a) in dim light?

  (b) in bright light?

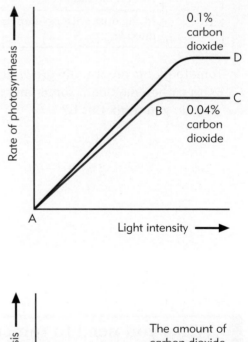

The table shows the results of a different experiment to compare rates of photosynthesis at different temperatures.

Temperature (°C)	Light intensity	Percentage of carbon dioxide	Rate of photosynthesis
20	3	0.04	15
25	3	0.04	18

5 Copy and complete the sentence: As you increase the _____, the rate of photosynthesis _____ .

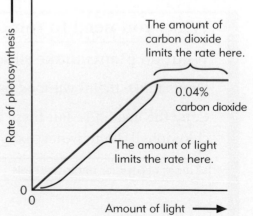

■ What else affects plant growth?

Tai grew the plants in the pictures from cuttings taken from one plant. He wanted to find out if the type of soil affected their growth.

6 Tai grew all the cuttings in exactly the same light and temperature. Why?

The soil that plant Q is growing in hasn't got enough nitrates in it. Plants need **nitrates** to make proteins and, like you, they need proteins for growing.

7 Write down <u>two</u> differences between plants P and Q.

8 Copy and complete the sentences.

Plant P had more _____ than plant Q, so plant P could make more _____ and grow _____ than plant Q.

Plants R and S are also short of minerals. These minerals are the ones they need to make chlorophyll.

9 Write down the names of the minerals which plants need to make chlorophyll.

10 Why do you think that the leaves of plants R and S are not as green as those of plant P?

11 When a plant cannot make much chlorophyll, it cannot grow well. Explain why.

Plant P in soil with plenty of minerals.

Plant Q in soil short of nitrates.

Plant R in soil short of magnesium.

Plant S in soil short of iron.

What you need to remember [Copy and complete using the **key words**]

Limits to plant growth

Plants need light, carbon dioxide, water and a suitable temperature so they can make food. We call this _____.

The rate of photosynthesis can be limited by:

■ low _____ intensity,

■ low _____ _____ concentration, or

■ low _____.

Plants also need minerals for healthy growth. For example they need _____ to make proteins.

These ideas are extended, for Higher Tier students, in Maintenance of life H1 on page 101.

Water that plant!

If plants don't get enough water, they **wilt**.

1 Describe what a plant looks like when it wilts.

A plant wilts when its cells lose water faster than it can take it in. Plants need water to hold them up. We say they need water for support.

2 What else does a plant need water for?

When cells are full of sap they are firm. They lose their firmness as they lose water.

It is the same with 'freeze pops' before you freeze them. Full freeze pops are firm. But freeze pops which aren't full flop over.

3 Is A or B the full freeze pop?

■ How do plants lose water?

There are lots of tiny pores in the bottom surface of leaves.

4 (a) What are these pores called?

   (b) Why do plants need them?

5 The pores can cause the plants to wilt. How?

Water evaporates from leaves, mainly through the stomata. Losing water in this way is called **transpiration**.

■ What can plants do to lose less water?

A plant wilts if it loses water faster than it takes it in. Some plants lose water faster than others. Most leaves have a **waxy** layer to slow down water loss.

6 Plants which grow in dry areas usually have the thickest waxy layers. Why do you think this is?

> ## REMEMBER
> Plants need carbon dioxide for photosynthesis. They take it in through tiny pores called **stomata**. Plants also need water for photosynthesis.

This plant has plenty of water.

This plant is short of water. It has wilted.

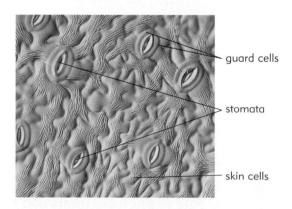

A   B

— guard cells

— stomata

— skin cells

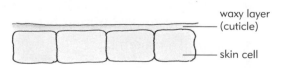

waxy layer (cuticle)

skin cell

Leaves have special cells to close their pores. We call them **guard** cells.

7 Look at the pictures of guard cells. Then copy and complete the following sentences.

When the guard cells lose water they change _____. This makes the leaf pores _____. The plant will then lose _____ water.

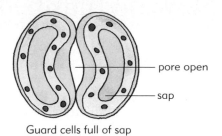

pore open

sap

Guard cells full of sap

■ When do plants lose most water?

Sue and Raj are trying to find out when plants lose most water. The diagram below shows what they do.

The plant takes in water to replace the water it loses. The faster the plant takes in water, the faster the bubble moves.

pore closed

Guard cells after losing water

How guard cells work.

8 Sue and Raj's results are shown in the table. They forgot to fill in two of the figures. What could the missing figures be? Give your reasons.

9 In which conditions did the plant take in (and lose) most water?

	Conditions	Average time (minutes) for bubble to move 100 mm
moist air around the plant	hot, windy	3
	hot, still	
	cool, windy	9
	cool, still	18
dry air around the plant	hot, windy	1
	hot, still	2
	cool, windy	3
	cool, still	

The leaves lose water.

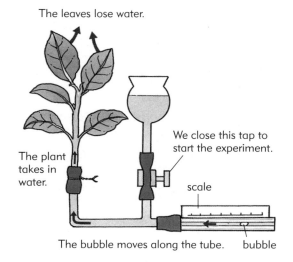

We close this tap to start the experiment.

The plant takes in water.

scale

The bubble moves along the tube.   bubble

What you need to remember [Copy and complete using the **key words**]

Water that plant!

The loss of water vapour from leaves is called _____.
Most leaves have a _____ layer to reduce this loss. Most of the water is lost through tiny pores called _____.
_____ cells can close the stomata when a plant loses water faster than it takes it in. This means the plant does not _____.
Transpiration is fastest when it is hot, dry and windy.

These ideas are extended, for Higher Tier students, in Maintenance of life H3 on page 104.

How do plants get the water they need?

■ Which parts of a root take in water?

Plants get water from the soil. The water is taken in by the roots. We say the roots absorb the water. Most of the water goes in through the **root hair** cells.
Root hairs increase the surface area of the root cells for **absorption**.

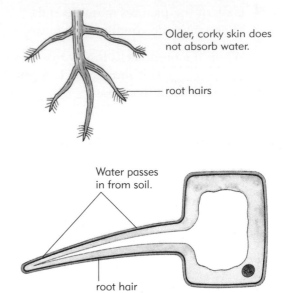

Older, corky skin does not absorb water.

root hairs

1 Where are the root hairs on a plant?
Describe this as clearly as you can.

Each root hair grows out from just one cell. Root hairs soon get worn away as the root grows through the soil.

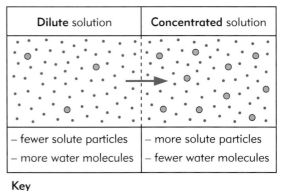

Water passes in from soil.

root hair

2 How big do you think root hairs are?
Give a reason for your answer.

3 Older parts of roots do not have root hairs.
Why do you think this is?

■ How do cells take in water?

Cell membranes are permeable to water. This means that water can diffuse through them from where it is in high concentration to where it is in low concentration.

Soil water is a very dilute solution of mineral ions.
So, water diffuses from the soil into root cells.

4 Look at the diagram.

Explain why the <u>water</u> concentration is higher in a dilute solution of mineral ions than in a concentrated solution of mineral ions.

Cell membranes control the passage of dissolved substances (solutes) such as mineral ions. So we say they are **partially permeable** membranes. The diffusion of water through a partially permeable membrane is called **osmosis**.

5 Copy and complete the sentence.

A dissolved substance is often called a _____.

Dilute solution	**Concentrated** solution

– fewer solute particles	– more solute particles
– more water molecules	– fewer water molecules

Key
⊙ solute particles (ions or molecules)

⟶ water diffuses in this direction

· water

6 Copy and complete the diagram.
Use the drawing of the cell to help you.

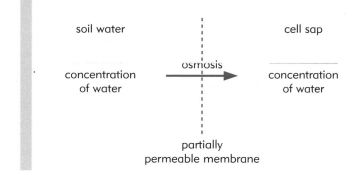

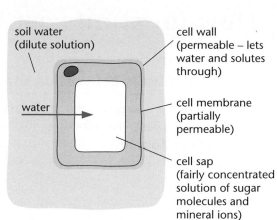

What happens in plant roots?

Plant roots take in water and minerals.

7 Put the following sentences in the right order to
describe where water goes in a plant.
The first one has been done for you.

Water passes through the cell membrane into a root
hair cell by osmosis.

- Water goes into the xylem.

- Water passes into the cell sap.

- Water passes to the stem and leaves.

- Water passes from cell to cell by osmosis.

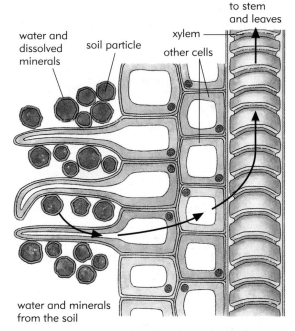

Soil water also covers the outside of the root.
The diagram doesn't show this.

What you need to remember [Copy and complete using the **key words**]

How do plants get the water they need?

Most of the water which goes into a plant is absorbed by the _____ _____ cells.
Root hairs increase the surface area for _____ .

Water diffuses from a _____ solution to a more _____
solution through a _____ _____ membrane.
We call this process _____ .

A partially permeable membrane is one that lets water molecules through but not
large solute molecules or ions.

These ideas are extended, for Higher Tier students, in Maintenance of life H2 on pages 102–103.

How do plants get the carbon dioxide they need?

■ Where do plants get carbon dioxide from?

Carbon dioxide is a gas in the air. Like other gases, it spreads out everywhere it can.
We call this **diffusion**.

> ### REMEMBER
>
> Plants need carbon dioxide and light for photosynthesis.
> Photosynthesis takes place in leaves.

1 Look at the diagrams. Then copy and complete the following sentences.

Carbon dioxide moves from places where there is a _____ concentration to places where there is a _____ concentration.

This is called _____.

2 Why do green leaves take in carbon dioxide?

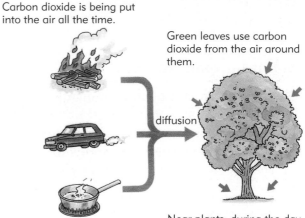

Carbon dioxide is being put into the air all the time.

Green leaves use carbon dioxide from the air around them.

diffusion

Near these things there is a lot of carbon dioxide.
The **concentration** of carbon dioxide is quite high.

Near plants, during the day, there is very little carbon dioxide.
The concentration of carbon dioxide is low.

■ How does carbon dioxide get inside leaves?

Carbon dioxide gas **diffuses** through tiny holes or pores in the skin of a leaf. We call these holes stomata.
The diagram shows where the carbon dioxide goes.

3 Copy the drawing. Then write down the following sentences in the right order:

- ■ Carbon dioxide diffuses through the spaces between the cells.

- ■ Carbon dioxide reaches the leaf by diffusion through the air.

- ■ Carbon dioxide diffuses into the cells.

- ■ Carbon dioxide diffuses into the leaf through tiny pores called stomata.

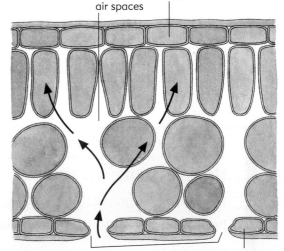

air spaces

upper epidermis (skin)

stomata (tiny pores)

lower epidermis (skin)

Carbon dioxide diffusing into a leaf.

■ How does carbon dioxide get into cells?

Carbon dioxide <u>gas</u> diffuses through the air spaces inside a leaf. But only <u>dissolved</u> carbon dioxide diffuses into cells.

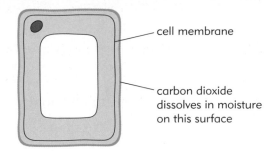

cell membrane

carbon dioxide dissolves in moisture on this surface

4 Look at the diagram.
All the cells inside a leaf have a moist surface like this. Explain way.

Substances can only pass through cell membranes if they dissolve first.

So, inside a leaf the exchange surface

■ is very thin;

■ is moist;

■ has a large area.

These are all features of an efficient exchange surface. The thin flat shape of a leaf also helps. Gases haven't far to diffuse and light can reach all the cells.

5 Why do leaf cells need light?

6 Look at the diagram of a squashed ball of plasticine.
Think of it as a model of a leaf.
In which form of the model will

(a) carbon dioxide reach cells more quickly?

(b) light reach more cells?

7 Look at the diagram of part of a leaf.
Which <u>two</u> tissues are in the veins of a leaf?

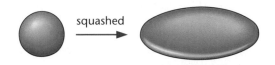

squashed

ball of plasticine

This thin, flat shape has the same volume but a larger surface area.

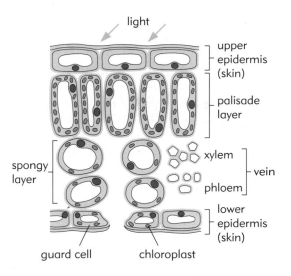

light

upper epidermis (skin)

palisade layer

xylem

vein

phloem

spongy layer

lower epidermis (skin)

guard cell   chloroplast

REMEMBER

In Maintenance of life 2 you found out that **xylem** carries water and minerals from the roots. **Phloem** carries sugar to growing points, storage organs and other parts.

What you need to remember [Copy and complete using the **key words**]

How do plants get the carbon dioxide they need?

Carbon dioxide goes in and out of leaves by _____. It spreads from where there is a higher _____ outside the leaves to where there is a lower concentration inside the leaves. We say that it _____.

Supplies of water and mineral ions reach leaves in _____ tissue. The tissue which carries nutrients such as sugars out of a leaf is called _____.

These ideas are extended, for Higher Tier students, in Maintenance of life H2 on pages 102–103.

10

How do plants know which way to grow?

Plants take in water through their roots and take in light energy through their leaves. So the roots of plants have to grow to where they can find water. The top parts of plants, the shoots, have to find **light**.

■ Shooting for the light

You may have noticed how a plant on a window sill grows towards the brightest light. This is because the shoot of the plant is **sensitive** to **light**.

Plants naturally grow straight up.

1 Look at the photo. Why do you think this plant is not growing straight up?

■ Do plant shoots know which way is up?

The Earth pulls everything down towards it. We call this the force of gravity. Jack thinks that plant <u>shoots</u> grow away from the force of **gravity**.

He decides to do an experiment to test this idea. He sets up his experiment in a dark box.

2 Why did he do this experiment in the dark?

3 What did he find out from his experiment?

At the start.   A few days later.

The force of gravity pulls this way.

Plant grown upside down.

■ Do plant roots know which way is down?

Leena has four bean seedlings with tiny roots and shoots. She wants to find out if gravity also affects plant <u>roots</u>.

The diagrams show what she does.
She then leaves the seedlings for a week to grow.

4 Where do you think Leena should put the seedlings to grow?

Give a reason for your answer.

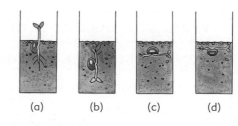

(a)   (b)   (c)   (d)

Seedlings grown in moist soil.

The diagrams show what happens.

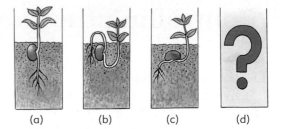

(a)   (b)   (c)   (d)

One week later.

5 What does this tell us

   (a) about the plant roots?

   (b) about the plant shoots?

6 Draw what you would expect to see in jar (d).

■ Can we confuse a seedling?

7 The diagrams show how you can make roots and shoots grow sideways.

   (a) What can you do to make roots and shoots grow sideways?

   (b) Why does this work?

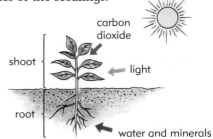

shoots have been cut off   roots have been cut off

The discs turn slowly, so that gravity pulls on all sides of the seedlings.

■ Why do shoots grow up and roots grow down?

The diagram shows how plants normally grow.

8 Why is it important that plants grow with their leaves above the ground?

9 Why should their roots grow below the ground?

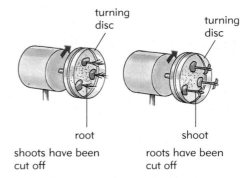

A plant growing normally.

■ Can plants find water?

Plant **roots** can usually find **water** by growing down. But sometimes there is more water to the side of a plant.

10 Sarah and Raj set up the experiment shown in the diagram.
What do you think they were trying to find out?
How would they know whether they were right?

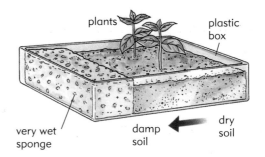

What you need to remember [Copy and complete using the **key words**]

How do plants know which way to grow?

Plants are _____ to gravity and water. They can also sense _____.
Shoots grow towards the _____ and away from the direction of the
force of _____.
_____ grow in the direction of the force of gravity and also
towards _____ .

11

Controlling the way plants grow

Plants can detect the direction light is coming from.
Their shoots then grow in this direction.

■ What part of a plant detects light?

Charles Darwin thought that plant shoots can detect light.
Over 100 years ago, he did an experiment to find out.

The diagrams show his results.

1 Which part of a shoot detects light?

Give reasons for your answer.

■ What makes the shoot bend towards the light?

Special chemicals affect the speed at which plants **grow**.
We call these chemicals **hormones**.

2 Look at the diagrams.
Then copy and complete the sentences.

When light shines on one side of a shoot there is
more growth _____ on the other side. So the
other side grows _____ and the shoot bends
towards the _____ .

■ Hormones to ripen fruit

Scientists can now make the hormones that plants
naturally make. We can use these hormones to make
plants do what we want them to do.

For example, we can use hormones to **ripen** fruit.

3 Look at the photograph.
Which tomatoes have been sprayed with hormone?

Sometimes farmers pick fruit before it is ripe.
This is because it is hard and doesn't get damaged.
Later it is sprayed with hormone to make it ripen.

4 Why do farmers pick their fruits before they are ripe?

5 Why are the fruits treated with hormones?

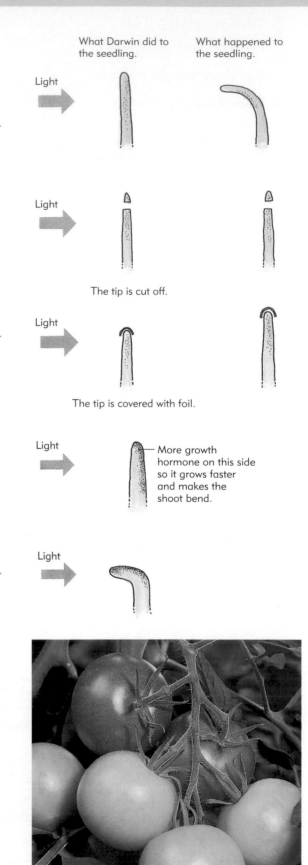

What Darwin did to the seedling.　What happened to the seedling.

Light

Light

The tip is cut off.

Light

The tip is covered with foil.

Light — More growth hormone on this side so it grows faster and makes the shoot bend.

Light

Hormones as killers

2,4-D is a hormone that kills weeds (unwanted plants). It makes plants grow so fast that they die.

2,4-D does not kill plants with narrow leaves.

The diagram shows some of the weeds growing on a lawn of grass.

6 Why is 2,4-D a good weed killer to use on the lawn?

7 Which plants will 2,4-D get rid of?

Give a reason for your answer.

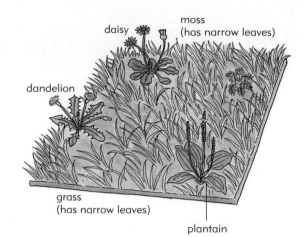

Plants on a lawn.

Getting bits of plants to grow roots

We can make new plants from small parts of older plants. We call these **cuttings**.

Cuttings produce better roots if we dip them in rooting hormone.

8 A friend wants to know how to make new plants from cuttings.
Write down the following steps in the right order.

■ Dip the cut end of the shoots into rooting hormone.

■ Cover the shoots with plastic bags to prevent them drying out.

■ Cut small young shoots from a larger plant.

■ Plant the shoots in compost and water them.

9 Why is it important to stop the cutting losing too much water?

Dip in rooting hormone.

Place in compost, water and cover with plastic bag.

Remove plastic bag when new roots have grown.

What you need to remember [Copy and complete using the **key words**]

Controlling the way plants grow

Hormones control the way plants _____.
Treating fruits with hormones helps us to _____ them.
We can also use _____ to kill weeds.
We can make new plants from small parts of older plants by taking _____.

Making sense – the nervous system

Animals must be able to detect things that are going on around them. For example, a rabbit needs to know when it is in danger from a fox.

1 Write down three parts of a rabbit's body that it can use to detect a fox.

Anything the rabbit detects with its senses is called a stimulus. For example, the scent of a fox is a stimulus. (When there is more than one stimulus we call them stimuli.)

2 Write down two other stimuli a rabbit can use to detect a fox.

■ How do we detect stimuli?

We detect **stimuli** with our eyes, ears, tongue, nose and skin. We call these our sense organs. Sense organs contain special cells called **receptors**. The receptors detect the stimuli. For example, receptors in your eyes detect **light**.

3 Make a table with the following headings.

Stimulus	Sense organ which detects it
salt	tongue

Then fill in your table as you read the story below. The first example has been done for you.

> **All at sea**
>
> You are on board a ship. You can taste the salt in the air and smell the fumes given off by the ship's engine.
>
> As the ship moves with the waves you can feel the soles of your feet pressing against the deck. A cold wind makes you shiver.
>
> You see a wave coming and hear it crash against the ship.

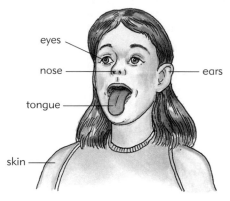

Your sense organs.

■ From sense organ to brain

The receptors in your sense organs are connected to your nervous system.

4 Look at the diagram.
Write down the parts of the nervous system.

Nerves carry information from receptors to the brain and spinal cord. The brain and spinal cord make sense of the information.

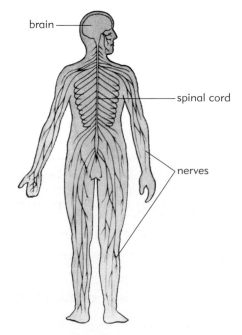

Your nervous system.

■ Taste and smell

There are thousands of receptors on your **tongue**. These are your taste receptors and they detect chemicals dissolved in water. The taste receptors are in groups called taste buds. There are four different kinds of taste buds. The diagram shows where they are.

5 List the <u>four</u> different tastes that your tongue can detect.

Receptors inside your **nose** detect chemicals in the air (smell). You need to taste and smell to get the full flavour of food.

6 Food seems tasteless when you have a cold. Why do you think this is?

■ Skin deep

Your skin also contains receptors. The diagram shows three different kinds of receptors in your skin.

7 What stimuli is your skin sensitive to?

■ Ears aren't only for hearing with

Your ears contain <u>two</u> kinds of receptors.

8 (a) Write down the two places in your ear where there are receptors.

(b) In each case say what the receptors are for.

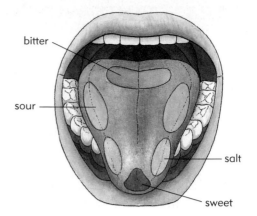

Your skin.

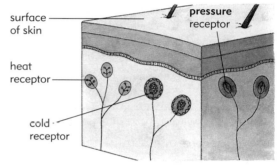

Your ear.

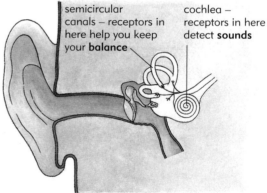

What you need to remember [Copy and complete using the **key words**]

Making sense – the nervous system

We use sense organs to detect _____ from the world around us. Sense organs contain special cells called _____. We can taste things because there are receptors on our _____. Receptors in our _____ help us to smell things. Our skin contains receptors sensitive to changes in temperature and _____ . Our eyes contain receptors which detect _____.

Our ears contain receptors sensitive to movement of our heads that help us keep our _____. Our ears also contain receptors sensitive to _____.

Eyes – your windows on the world

Your eyes are sense organs. They contain light receptors. Information from these receptors pass along nerve fibres to your brain.

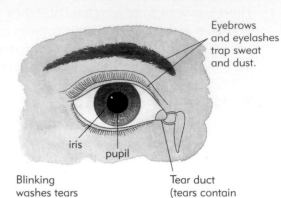

Eyebrows and eyelashes trap sweat and dust.

iris

pupil

Blinking washes tears over the surface of your eye.

Tear duct (tears contain chemicals which destroy microbes).

■ Your eye from the outside

Your eyes are in hollows, or sockets, in your skull. The bone protects your eyes from bumps and bangs.

1 Your eyes are protected in other ways. Describe <u>three</u> of these ways.

■ A look into your eye

The diagram shows all the different parts inside your eye. Use the diagram to answer the questions below.

2 (a) What is the white of your eye called?

  (b) Why do you think it has to be tough?

3 The cornea and lens are transparent.

  (a) What does this mean?

  (b) Why do they need to be transparent?

4 Suspensory ligaments hold the lens in place. What are they joined to?

5 Your pupil is a hole in a coloured ring. What is this coloured ring called?

6 (a) Which layer of your eye contains receptors?

  (b) What are the receptors sensitive to?

7 What carries information from light receptors to your brain?

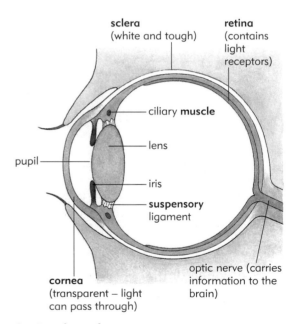

sclera (white and tough)

retina (contains light receptors)

ciliary **muscle**

lens

pupil

iris

suspensory ligament

cornea (transparent – light can pass through)

optic nerve (carries information to the brain)

Section through your eye.

■ Getting the right amount of light

Light gets into your eye through your **pupil**. You may have noticed that your pupil isn't always the same size. The muscles in the iris cause these changes in the size of the pupil.

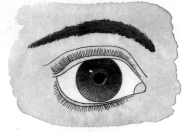

8 Copy the table. Use the information on the diagrams to fill in the spaces.

	What happens to pupil	What happens to iris	Why this happens
bright light			
dim light			

In bright light your pupil gets smaller. This stops too much light getting into your eye.

■ How can we see things?

The diagram shows what happens when you see a tree.

In dim light your pupil gets larger. This lets enough light into your eye.

9 Look at the diagram.
Then put these sentences in the right order.

■ The cornea and lens bend the rays of light.

■ Information is sent along the **optic** nerve to the brain.

■ Receptor cells detect the image.

■ Light from the tree reaches your eye.

■ An image of the tree forms on the retina.

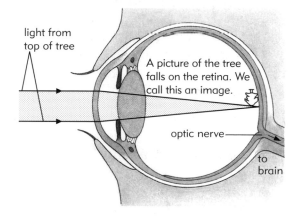

light from top of tree

A picture of the tree falls on the retina. We call this an image.

optic nerve

to brain

What you need to remember [Copy and complete using the **key words**]

Eyes – your windows on the world

A tough layer called the _____ surrounds the eye. The transparent part at the front is called the _____. The lens is held in place by _____ ligaments and ciliary _____. The muscular iris controls the size of the _____. This affects the amount of light reaching the retina. The _____ contains receptor cells which are sensitive to light.

Light from an object enters the eye through the pupil. The cornea and lens produce an image on the retina. Impulses are sent to the brain along sensory neurones in the _____ nerve.

[You need to able to label the following on a diagram of the eye:
optic nerve, lens, cornea, ciliary muscles, iris, suspensory ligaments, sclera, retina, pupil.]

These ideas are extended, for Higher Tier students, in Maintenance of life H5 on page 106.

Making decisions – coordination

Suppose you see a £10 note lying on the floor. You bend down and pick it up. You can do this because of your **nervous** system.

Your sense organs send information to your brain all the time. Your brain sorts out this information. It also controls what you decide to do. We say that your brain **coordinates** your actions.

■ How does your brain know about the money?

1 Look at the diagram. What type of stimulus travels from the money to your eye?

The receptors in your eyes send information to your brain. These are called nerve impulses.
They travel very quickly along a nerve to your brain.

■ What does your brain do next?

Your brain lets you react or respond. You decide what to do. Then your brain sends impulses to the muscles in your body to carry out your decision.

2 What is your response to seeing the £10 note?

3 Which parts of your body produce this response?

Your brain coordinates the actions of all the muscles you use to pick up the money. Your brain also makes sure that you do not fall as you bend over.

■ How information is carried to and from your brain

Nerve fibres need to be very long because they carry information to and from your brain. These fibres are parts of cells called neurones.

Sensory neurones carry impulses from your receptors to your brain. **Motor** neurones carry impulses from your brain to your muscles.

4 Describe the difference between the job of a sensory and a motor neurone.

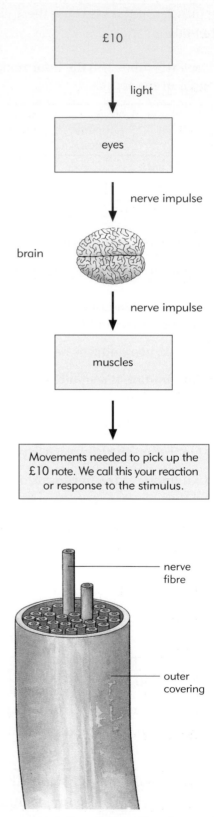

Nerves are made up of bundles of nerve fibres.

■ Ouch! That's hot

If you touch a hot plate, you move your hand away quickly without even thinking. The diagram shows what happens. We call a rapid, automatic response like this a **reflex** action.

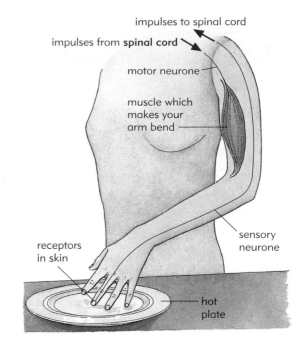

impulses to spinal cord

impulses from **spinal cord**

motor neurone

muscle which makes your arm bend

receptors in skin

sensory neurone

hot plate

5 Put the following sentences in the right order to explain what happens.

■ A muscle makes the arm bend away from the hot plate.

■ Receptors in the skin detect that the plate is hot.

■ The spinal cord sorts out the information.

■ Impulses travel along sensory neurones to the spinal cord.

■ Impulses from the spinal cord travel along motor neurones to the arm muscle.

Your body responds to some stimuli automatically. You do not 'think' of how you should respond, your body just does it for you.

6 Copy and complete the table to show how your body responds.

Stimulus	Automatic response
1 dust in eye	
2 bright light shone at eye	
3 food enters windpipe	

■ On your marks, get set …

Some athletes are ready to start a race. They must set off as fast as they can when they hear the starting pistol.

7 Describe, step by step, what happens inside an athlete's body when the starting pistol is fired.

What you need to remember [Copy and complete using the **key words**]

Making decisions – coordination

Your _____ system allows you to react to your surroundings.
Information from receptors passes along _____ neurones to your spinal cord and brain.
Your brain sends impulses along _____ neurones to your muscles.
We say that your brain _____ your responses to stimuli.

In _____ actions your response is fast and automatic. Impulses pass along sensory neurones to your _____ _____ then along motor neurones to muscles or glands. The muscles or glands bring about the response.

These ideas are extended, for Higher Tier students, in Maintenance of life H6 on page 107.

Keeping things the same inside your body

To work properly your body must be at just the right temperature. Your blood must also contain just the right amount of water, sugar and other substances.

Everything inside your body has to be kept at a **constant** level. You don't have to think about this. Your body controls these things **automatically**.

1 Look at the diagram.
   Then copy and complete the table.

Part of body	How it helps your body stay the same
skin	controls your body temperature
kidneys	
pancreas	
lungs	

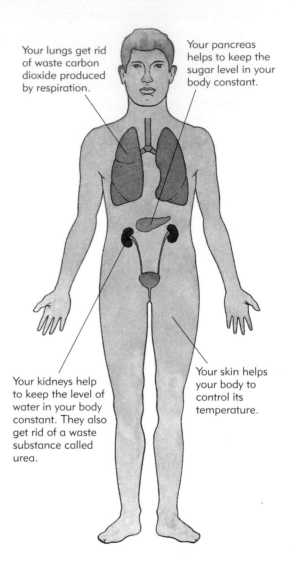

Your lungs get rid of waste carbon dioxide produced by respiration.

Your pancreas helps to keep the sugar level in your body constant.

Your kidneys help to keep the level of water in your body constant. They also get rid of a waste substance called urea.

Your skin helps your body to control its temperature.

■ How your skin can help you cool

Try licking the back of your hand and blowing on it. The wet part of your hand feels colder than the dry part. Heat from your body makes the water evaporate. This helps to **cool** you down.

The diagram shows how it does this.

2 What happens in your skin when you are hot?

3 Why does this cool you down?

4 Do you think you sweat much when you are cold? Give a reason for your answer.

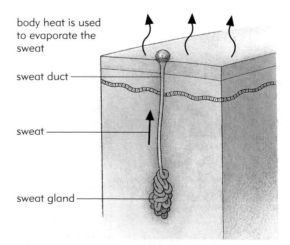

body heat is used to evaporate the sweat

sweat duct

sweat

sweat gland

When you are hot, your **skin** produces sweat.

How does your skin know when to sweat?

Your body constantly checks what temperature it is at. The diagram shows how it does this.

5 Which part of your body checks your temperature?

6 What should the temperature of your body be?

7 What happens if your body temperature is higher than this?

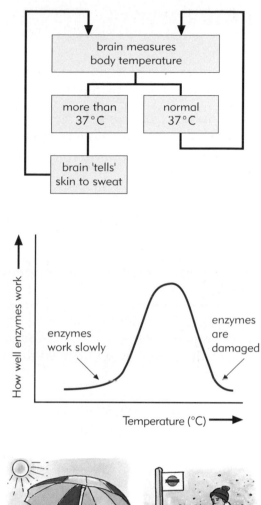

Why must your body be at 37 °C?

Chemical reactions happen all the time in your body. **Enzymes** are substances that make these chemical reactions happen. Your enzymes work best at 37 °C.

8 Copy the graph. Mark where you think the temperature 37 °C should be.

9 Why don't enzymes work as well

(a) above 37 °C?

(b) below 37 °C?

Helping your body stay at 37 °C

In very hot or very cold weather you can make it easier for your body to stay at 37 °C.

10 Explain how you can do this.

11 You need to drink more when the weather is hot. Why is this?

What you need to remember [Copy and complete using the **key words**]

Keeping things the same inside your body

For your body to work properly everything inside your body must be kept at a
_____ level. Your body controls these things _____.
You do not have to 'think' about it.
Your _____ helps control your body temperature.
Sweating helps to _____ your body. You need to replace the water that you lose when you sweat.
Your body must be at 37 °C so that _____ can work properly.

These ideas are extended, for Higher Tier students, in Maintenance of life H7 on pages 108–109.

16 Keeping your blood glucose concentration constant

It is important that the amount of sugar (glucose) in your blood is kept **constant**.

Read the newspaper article. It tells you what happened to Barbara when the amount of sugar in her blood was too low.

1 What effect did low blood sugar have on Barbara?

2 What did Ben do to solve this problem?

■ Does your blood glucose concentration change?

The amount of sugar in your blood goes up after a meal. It falls when you exercise. Usually your body detects these changes and returns the amount of sugar to normal.

3 Look at the graph. What do you think is normal blood glucose concentration?

4 At what time of day did this person have a meal? How do you know?

5 How long did it take for the blood glucose concentration to return to normal?

6 At what time of day did this person take exercise? How do you know?

■ How do you keep your blood glucose concentration constant?

If your blood glucose concentration changes, your pancreas releases special chemicals called hormones. These hormones make your blood glucose concentration go back to normal.

7 Copy and complete the table.
Use the diagram to help you.

Blood glucose concentration	Hormone released by pancreas	What then happens
higher than normal		
lower than normal		

Ben, 4, saves life of coma mother

Barbara, 25, told how four-year-old Ben kept her alive.

He knew exactly what to do when he found her unconscious.

He poured a bottle of his strawberry drink with extra sugar down her mouth then some glucose jelly, kept in the fridge for emergencies and finally some sugar-rich cough mixture.

Making the first telephone call of his life he dialled 999.

When the police arrived, Ben told them his mother was diabetic.

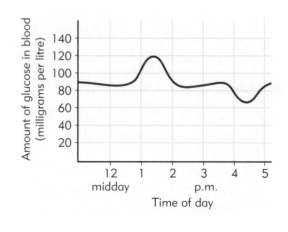

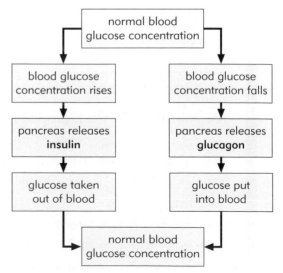

How do the hormones work?

Hormones are chemical messengers. Each hormone is produced by one organ in your body but travels through your blood and affects a different organ. The diagram shows some organs affected by hormones.

8 Which organ do the hormones insulin and glucagon affect?

9 How do the hormones reach this organ?

We say that the liver is the target organ for insulin and glucagon.

What happens if your pancreas is not working properly?

Barbara's pancreas does not work properly.
It does not produce enough **insulin**.

10 Without insulin, what happens to Barbara's blood glucose concentration?

Barbara's disease is called diabetes. She must take regular injections of insulin. This lowers the amount of sugar in her blood. She must also be careful about how much carbohydrate (sugar and starch) she eats.

Barbara's blood glucose concentration fell too low. She could have died.

11 How can you help someone in a diabetic coma? (Remember what Ben did.)

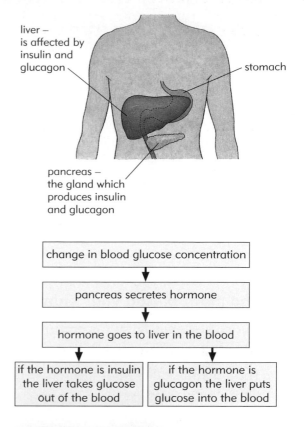

liver –
is affected by insulin and glucagon

stomach

pancreas –
the gland which produces insulin and glucagon

| change in blood glucose concentration |
| pancreas secretes hormone |
| hormone goes to liver in the blood |

| if the hormone is insulin the liver takes glucose out of the blood | if the hormone is glucagon the liver puts glucose into the blood |

Many diabetics have to inject themselves with insulin.

What you need to remember [Copy and complete using the **key words**]

Keeping your blood glucose concentration constant

Your blood glucose concentration must be kept _____.
If there is too much glucose, your pancreas releases the hormone _____.
If there is too little glucose your pancreas releases the hormone _____.
Diabetics cannot make enough _____ so the concentration of glucose in their blood rises too high. They need injections of insulin and have to be careful how much carbohydrate (sugar and starch) they eat.

These ideas are extended, for Higher Tier students, in Maintenance of life H7 on pages 108–109.

17 Cleaning blood and balancing water – your kidneys

The blood in your body is constantly passing through your kidneys. Your kidneys remove the poisonous substances which your cells produce. If your blood is not cleaned in this way you will soon die.

1 Write down <u>two</u> ways we can save the life of a person whose kidneys have stopped working.

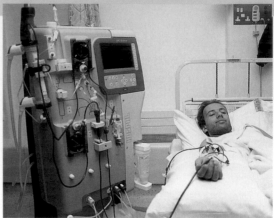

This man's kidneys have stopped working. His blood is cleaned by a kidney machine. He may be lucky enough to get a kidney transplant. Then he won't need the kidney machine.

■ The main poison your kidneys remove

Our bodies break down the protein in our food into **amino acids**.

The diagram shows what then happens to these amino acids.

2 What does your body use amino acids for?

3 What happens to any amino acids your body doesn't use?

Urea is made in the liver from amino acids. **Urea** is a poisonous substance. Your **kidneys** remove it from your blood. They also remove excess salts (ions) from your blood. The urea and salts are dissolved in water to make a liquid called urine.

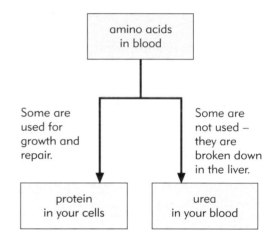

■ What happens to urine?

The diagram shows what happens to the urine your kidneys produce.

4 Copy and complete the sentences below. Use the diagram to help you.

Urine runs down tubes called _____ into your _____.

You then empty your **bladder** a few times each day.

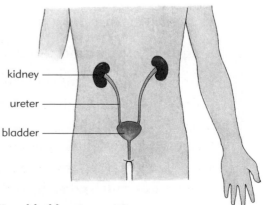

Your bladder stores urine.

■ A balancing act

Your body is about two-thirds water.

5 If you weigh 45 kg, how much of this is water?

The amount of water you lose must balance the amount you take in each day. The diagram shows the different ways you gain and lose water.

6 Copy and complete the table.

	Water lost by body (cm³)	Water gained by body (cm³)
drink		
food		
respiration		400
sweat		
faeces	300	
urine		
breathed out		
total		

7 Marathon runners must drink plenty of water. Explain why.

■ The kidneys and water control

Your kidneys control the amount of **water** in your body.

8 Look at the diagrams, then copy the table. Choose the correct answer from each box and put a ring round it.

	A lot of water in body	A little water in body
water in urine	a lot/a little	a lot/a little
urine colour	yellow/colourless	yellow/colourless

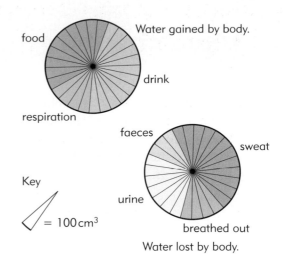

Key

= 100 cm³

Daily water balance.

Marathon runners breathe hard and sweat a lot for a few hours.

How much urine you make in one day ...

if your body has a lot of water. if your body has a little water.

What you need to remember [Copy and complete using the **key words**]

Cleaning blood and balancing water – your kidneys

A poisonous waste substance called _____ is made in the liver from broken down _____ _____.

The _____ remove urea from the blood.

The kidneys also control the amount of _____ and salts (ions) in the body. Urine is stored temporarily in the _____.

These ideas are extended, for Higher Tier students, in Maintenance of life H8 on pages 110–111.

18

People and drugs

A **drug** is a substance that can change the way your body works. Some drugs, such as painkillers and antibiotics, are useful. We use antibiotics to kill bacteria in our bodies. But other drugs such as **solvents**, **alcohol** and chemicals in **tobacco** may harm the body.

Drugs aren't a new problem. People have been using drugs for thousands of years.

■ Alcohol – an old drug

We know that people made beer in Babylon 8000 years ago. The Egyptian picture writing from nearly 4000 years ago warns people not to drink too much.

1 What dangers of drinking alcohol are mentioned in this writing?

2 (a) Make a copy of this picture.

(b) What do you think it means?

■ Smoking milestones

Native Americans smoked tobacco 1000 years ago.

Look at the information about smoking in England.

3 When did tobacco houses become common in England?

4 When did it become illegal to sell cigarettes to those under 16 years old?

The number of people who smoke has gone down a lot since 1950.

5 What do you think are the three most important reasons for this?

6 (a) Why is smoking banned on the London Underground?

(b) What other useful effect does this ban have?

Don't make yourself helpless by getting drunk in the pub. Because the things you say slip out from your mouth without you knowing what you said. Falling down arms and legs breaking and no one will give a hand to help you up friends drunk on beer, will get up and say, "Outside with this drunk."

Egyptian picture writing (hieroglyphics).

1492	European sailors see cigars being smoked in Cuba
1625	Many tobacco houses open in England
1908	Illegal to sell cigarettes to children under 16 years of age
1947	43 per cent rise in cigarette tax
1951	Medical report shows smoking causes lung cancer
1965	Ban on cigarette advertising on TV
1971	Message on cigarette packs: 'Warning by HM Government: Smoking can damage your health'
1974	Tobacco tax increased by 20 per cent
1985	London transport bans smoking on Underground after a fire which killed many people

■ Another ancient habit that is growing

People have sniffed substances for thousands of years. Over 3000 years ago Greeks sniffed oils, herbs and spices as part of their religion. Some Greeks still burn olive leaves in their homes as part of their religion.

In the 1700s some people sniffed a gas called nitrous oxide. Nitrous oxide puts people to sleep. Smaller amounts make people feel relaxed and happy. They tend to laugh a lot.

7 (a) Why do you think people sniffed nitrous oxide?

   (b) Why is nitrous oxide sometimes called 'laughing gas'?

During the last 100 years some people have started sniffing solvents, such as those used in glues and paints.

Using solvents in this way can harm people and even kill them. Sniffing solvents is called solvent abuse. The graph shows how the number of deaths from solvent abuse changed from 1971 to 1990.

8 What was the number of deaths from solvent abuse.

   (a) in 1972?

   (b) in 1987?

9 How did deaths from solvent abuse change from the early 1970s to the late 1980s?

People can become dependent or **addicted** to a drug. They get **withdrawal** symptoms when they cannot get the drug.

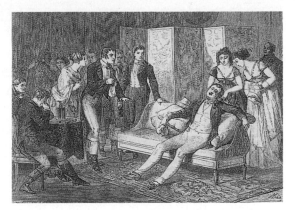

The person on the left of the picture is sniffing nitrous oxide.

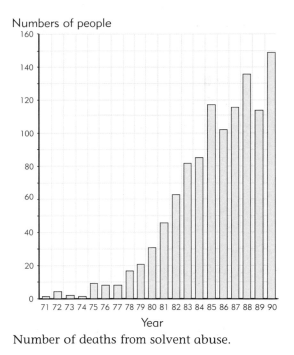

Number of deaths from solvent abuse.

What you need to remember [Copy and complete using the **key words**]

People and drugs

A substance that can change the way your body works is called a _____.
There are many different types of drugs. These include _____,
_____ and the chemicals in _____ smoke.
Some people become dependent on a drug. They have _____ symptoms
when they cannot get it. We say they are _____.

The dangers of sniffing solvents

Solvents are found in many products. They are in aerosol sprays, glues, correcting fluids and petrol.

■ Solvents and the body

When you breathe a solvent in, the fumes go into your lungs. The solvent passes into your blood and travels to other parts of your body. Some of the effects are shown in the diagram.

1 What are the main organs which solvents damage?

2 How does a solvent get to the brain, the lungs and the liver?

3 What other effects do solvents have?

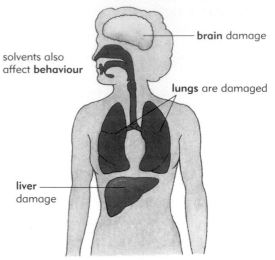

solvents also affect **behaviour**

brain damage

lungs are damaged

liver damage

Organs that are damaged by solvents.

■ How can you tell if someone is sniffiing solvents?

Some of the warning signs are shown on the right.

4 You need to look for a few of these signs and not just one. Why do you think this is?

5 Which three signs of solvent abuse could you spot just by looking at someone?

Warning signs of solvent abuse
(a) the person smells of solvent
(b) red, glassy or watery eyes
(c) wide pupils
(d) slurred speech
(e) loss of appetite
(f) lack of concentration
(g) does poorer work at school
(h) bad coordination

■ Darren died of solvent abuse

Many people **die** after the <u>first time</u> they sniff a solvent.

Darren was 16 years old when his mother found him dead. He died of solvent abuse.

"I will never stop grieving over the death of my son. I will never stop crying when I remember he will never have another birthday, never have another girlfriend, never ever be able to dash out and meet his friends"

Darren's mother

6 Why do you think this mother wants to tell others how she feels?

7 How do you think the families of those who use solvents feel?

■ Who are the main solvent abusers?

The graph gives total figures for a 20-year period.
It shows the number of people who died after sniffing
solvents at different ages.

8 Which age group had the largest number of deaths
from solvent abuse?

9 (a) How many 18-year-olds died of solvent abuse in
the 20 years from 1971 to 1991?

   (b) How many is this, on average, each year?

10 (a) 12 per cent of all those who died of solvent
abuse in 1991 were females.
What was the percentage of males?

   (b) How many times more males than females died
of solvent abuse?

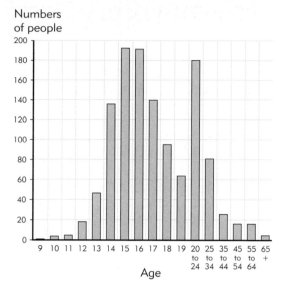

Numbers of people

Age

Deaths in the UK from solvent abuse (1971–91).

■ Are all parts of the UK affected?

Some parts of the UK have more of a problem
than others.

11 What part of the UK has the greatest problem?

12 Copy the following headings.

Region	Number of deaths from solvent abuse

Then use the information from the map to complete
your table.

Put the region with the highest number of deaths at
the top of your table and the region with the lowest
number of deaths at the bottom.

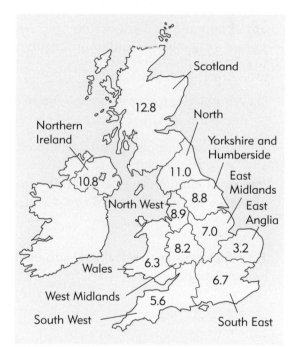

Number of 10- to 24-year-olds dying of solvent
abuse every year for every million people.

What you need to remember [Copy and complete using the **key words**]

The dangers of sniffing solvents

Products like glue, aerosol sprays and petrol contain _____.

Solvents cause damage to your _____, _____ and

_____ and also affect your _____.

There is a high chance that people will _____ if they sniff solvents.

93

What's your poison – alcohol?

Beers, wines and spirits like whisky contain alcohol.
Alcohol is a drug. Its effects on the body have been
known for a long time.

1 Look at Morton's description of how alcohol
affects behaviour.
Copy the following headings.
Then complete the table.

Numbers of drinks	How Morton says that people behave	What do you think he means?

*'One drink and you act like a monkey; two drinks, and
you strut like a peacock; three drinks, and you roar like
a lion; and four drinks – you behave like a pig.'*
Henry Vollam Morton (1936)

■ Effects of alcohol on the body

Small amounts of alcohol slow your reactions.
Larger amounts can make you unconscious or even go
into a **coma**.

2 What does alcohol do to your body that makes it
dangerous to drink and drive?

3 What can happen if you drink too much alcohol?

Your liver changes the alcohol into harmless substances.
However, too much alcohol can damage organs in your
body.

4 Which organs in your body can be damaged
by alcohol?

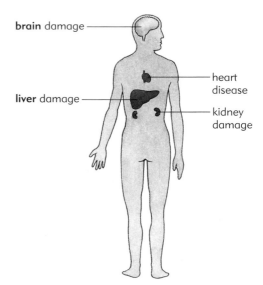

If you keep drinking too much alcohol.

■ How much alcohol is there in different drinks?

The drinks shown in the diagram all contain the same
amount of alcohol.

This is called one unit.

5 Tony drinks two pints of ordinary beer.
Alex drinks one pint of strong beer and
one single whisky.
Nassia drinks two glasses of wine.

How many units of alcohol does each person drink?

How much drink gives one unit of alcohol.

■ What is reasonable drinking?

Alcohol is a poison. It slows your **reactions** and it affects your behaviour.

You can become dependent on alcohol or **addicted** to it. This means that you can't do without it. But small amounts of alcohol can help some people to relax.

The diagram shows how many units of alcohol many health workers think it is safe to drink each week.

6 (a) What is the maximum number of units a man should drink each week?

(b) How much strong beer is this each day?

7 A woman drinks three glasses of wine and a single whisky each day.

(a) How many units of alcohol is this in a week?

(b) What advice would you give the woman?

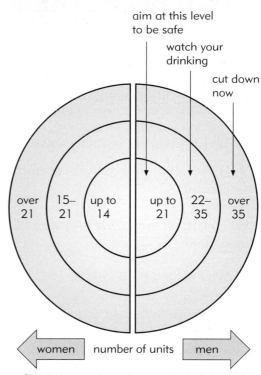

aim at this level to be safe

watch your drinking

cut down now

| over 21 | 15– 21 | up to 14 | up to 21 | 22– 35 | over 35 |

← women   number of units   men →

Children are affected more than adults and women more than men.

Safe drinking – units per week.

What you need to remember [Copy and complete using the **key words**]

What's your poison – alcohol?

Alcohol can damage the _____ and _____ , as well as many other parts of the body. It also slows down your _____.

If people drink too much they can lose self-control. They can become unconscious and even go into a _____.

People can become dependent on alcohol.

We say that they are _____ to it.

95

Legal but harmful – tobacco

■ What is in cigarette smoke?

Cigarette smoke contains many harmful chemicals. Some of these are shown in the table.

1 Which chemical is an addictive drug?

2 Which substance contains chemicals that cause lung cancer?

When carbon monoxide is in your blood your heart has to work harder.

3 Why do you think this is?

It is the carbon monoxide in car exhaust fumes that can kill people. If gas fires aren't working properly they can also release carbon monoxide.

Some insecticides contain nicotine.

Nicotine is a natural poison found in many plants. The plants produce it to stop insects eating them.

4 What effect does nicotine have on your body?

5 Why is nicotine useful to gardeners?

■ The dangers of smoking

6 Draw a table with the following headings.

Organ affected	Name of disease	What the disease does

Complete the table using the information in the diagram.

REMEMBER

You can become addicted to some drugs. This means you feel that you can't do without them.

Chemical	Addictive drug	Poison	Effect on body
tar (1000 different chemicals)		✓	causes cancer
nicotine	✓	✓	increases blood pressure, raises pulse rate
carbon monoxide		✓	blood can carry less oxygen

If you smoke you have …

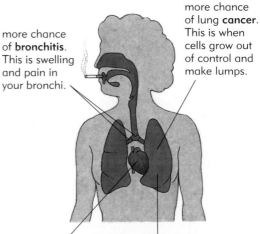

more chance of **bronchitis**. This is swelling and pain in your bronchi.

more chance of lung **cancer**. This is when cells grow out of control and make lumps.

more chance of a **heart attack**. This is when your heart stops working.

more chance of **emphysema**. This is when alveoli break down because of coughing. You have less lung surface to take in oxygen.

■ Does it matter whether you smoke?

The table shows how smoking affects your chance of getting lung cancer.

Number of cigarettes smoked per day	Increased chance of cancer compared with non-smokers
5	4 ×
10	8 ×
15	12 ×
20	16 ×

7 Write down, as carefully as you can, what the table tells you.

> **Facts and figures**
>
> **A** Out of every 1000 teenagers who smoke, about 250 will eventually die of smoking related diseases.
>
> **B** On average, smokers die 10 to 15 years earlier than non-smokers.
>
> **C** Over 90 per cent of people who die from lung cancer are smokers.
>
> **D** The babies of pregnant women who smoke weigh, on average, 200 g less than the babies whose mothers do not smoke. We say that the babies have a low **birth mass**.
>
> **E** Pregnant women who smoke are more likely to have a miscarriage or still birth.

8 Look at the photograph. What message is the photograph trying to get across to people?

9 The fetus (developing child) inside a pregnant woman who smokes is likely to get less **oxygen** than it should. Why is this?
(Hint: Look at the table on page 96.)

10 Write down <u>one</u> effect of lack of oxygen on the baby.

Would you like a cigarette?

No!

> ## What you need to remember [Copy and complete using the **key words**]
>
> ### Legal but harmful – tobacco
>
> Smoking can cause diseases of the lungs like _____ , _____ and _____ .
>
> Smoking also affects your heart and can increase your chance of having a _____ _____ .
>
> In a pregnant woman the fetus can be deprived of _____ so the baby has a low _____ _____ .

These ideas are extended, for Higher Tier students, in Maintenance of life H4 on page 105.

Smoking and lung cancer

Sir Walter Raleigh brought tobacco to Britain in the sixteenth century. It was smoked mainly in pipes. Cigarettes became popular during and after the 1914–1918 War. Few women smoked before 1920.

■ Deaths from lung cancer increase

In the years after World War I, the number of men dying from lung cancer increased. At first many people suggested that the figures weren't really true. It was just that doctors were getting better at recognising lung cancer. This could have explained some of the increase. But people began to look for other reasons.

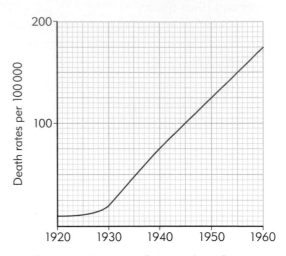

Death rates of men aged 45–64 from lung cancer in England and Wales.

1 Look at the graph.
  What was the death rate from lung cancer in

  (a) 1920?

  (b) 1940?

■ Why were deaths from lung cancer increasing?

About 50 years ago in Britain, Professor Richard Doll and Dr Bradford Hill thought that there might be a link between cigarette smoking and lung cancer.
Other scientists were thinking about and working on similar ideas in the United States. This idea is not strange to us now.

2 Why did Doll and Hill think that smoking and lung cancer were linked?

Doll and Hill decided to test their idea by doing a survey. They asked a group of men with lung cancer about their smoking habits. They selected a group of men of similar ages and backgrounds who didn't have lung cancer. They asked the men the same questions. These men were the control group.

3 What was the idea or hypothesis that Doll and Hill were testing?

4 Why did they need a control group?

5 Look at the table.
  Do the results support the hypothesis that there is a link between smoking and lung cancer?

	Lung cancer patients	Control group
smokers	99.7%	95.8%
non-smokers	0.3%	4.2%

■ Looking for more evidence

In 1951 Doll and Hall decided to do some longer-term studies. They recorded the smoking habits, the health and the death rates of a group of doctors over 5 years.

	Deaths of doctors from lung cancer (per 100 000)
non-smokers	7
light smokers	47
moderate smokers	86
heavy smokers	166

6 Look at the table.

  (a) Which group of doctors was at most risk from lung cancer?

  (b) How many times greater was the risk of lung cancer for heavy smokers than for non-smokers?

At the same time as Doll and Hall were researching the health of doctors, scientists at New York University began testing the chemicals in cigarette smoke to find out if any of them caused cancers in animals. They found that many did.

In 1962 a report summarising the research was published in Britain. It concluded that there was a relationship between lung cancer and smoking. Not everyone agreed. Many people looked for other explanations.

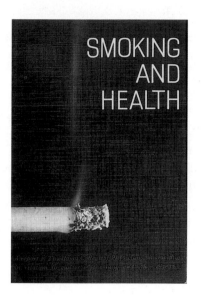

7 Who produced the report and what was it called?

Following the report, there was only a 4% fall in the number of cigarettes smoked. One group that did take notice of the report was the doctors. Large numbers of doctors gave up smoking. The death rates of doctors from lung cancer fell.

"My factory makes millions of cigarettes every year."

"Not all smokers get lung cancer."

8 What action did large numbers of doctors take that provided further evidence of a link between smoking and lung cancer? Explain your answer.

9 Some groups of people did not want to accept that there was a link between smoking and lung cancer. Think of <u>two</u> reasons for this.

"Non-smokers can get lung cancer too."

By the end of the twentieth century, even the tobacco companies had to agree that tobacco smoking increases the chances of developing lung cancer.

What you need to remember

Smoking and lung cancer

You do not need to <u>remember</u> any information from this topic. You must be able to <u>interpret</u> information you are given in the same sort of way.

Plant nutrition

REMEMBER

Plants make food in a chemical reaction called **photosynthesis**.
We can describe this using a word equation:

$$\text{carbon dioxide} + \text{water} \xrightarrow{\text{light energy}} \text{glucose} + \text{oxygen}$$

Plants need minerals to make amino acids and chlorophyll.

Lack of light or lack of only one nutrient can limit the growth of a crop (and its yield).

■ What do plants use glucose for?

Plants release energy from glucose when they respire. They use the energy released to build other sugar molecules into larger molecules such as starch, cellulose, **lipids** (fats or oils) and amino acids. They need nitrates and other minerals, as well as glucose, to make amino acids.

glucose + nitrates + other minerals + energy

↓

amino acids

↓

proteins for **growth**

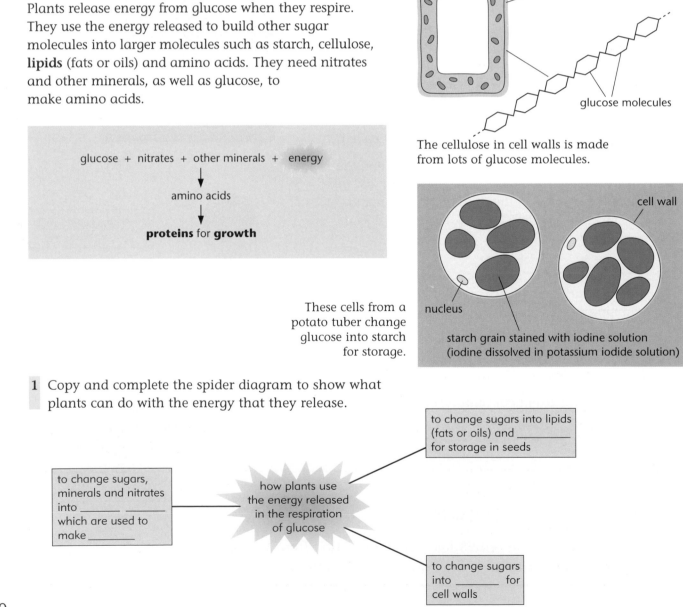

cell wall

glucose molecules

The cellulose in cell walls is made from lots of glucose molecules.

cell wall

nucleus

starch grain stained with iodine solution
(iodine dissolved in potassium iodide solution)

These cells from a potato tuber change glucose into starch for storage.

1 Copy and complete the spider diagram to show what plants can do with the energy that they release.

to change sugars into lipids (fats or oils) and _____ for storage in seeds

to change sugars, minerals and nitrates into _____ _____ which are used to make _____

how plants use the energy released in the respiration of glucose

to change sugars into _____ for cell walls

■ What do plants use minerals for?

If a plant can't get enough minerals, its growth may be stunted. Lack of a particular mineral will have a particular effect. This is because different minerals do different jobs. The big <u>three</u> minerals are:

- ■ <u>nitrate</u>
- ■ <u>phosphate</u>
- ■ <u>potassium</u>.

Nitrate is used to make the amino acids and proteins needed for growth.

Phosphate is needed for energy transfers in photosynthesis and respiration. Plants which don't get enough phosphate have tiny leaves and their younger leaves are purple.

Potassium helps photosynthesis and respiration by making sure the enzymes can do their jobs well. Plants which lack potassium have yellow leaves with dead spots.

Healthy tomato leaf.

Effect of shortage of nitrate on older leaves.

Healthy vine leaf.

Effect of shortage of a mineral.

2 Look at the photographs.

   (a) Write down <u>one</u> effect of lack of nitrate on older leaves.

   (b) Is the unhealthy vine leaf from a plant short of phosphate or potassium?

Using your knowledge

1(a) The yield of wheat in a farmer's best field was less than usual. He thought that the soil <u>might</u> be short of nitrate so he decided to add some next year. His son suggested that he should have analysed the soil first. Why was this good advice?

  (b) The farmer could add a natural fertiliser such as manure instead of an artificial nitrate fertiliser. Why is natural fertiliser more likely to solve any problem?

2 Plants need magnesium and iron to make chlorophyll. Explain exactly which parts of a plant are affected by a lack of these minerals.

3 Some crops take large amounts of one particular mineral out of the soil. If a farmer grows the same crop on a field year after year, the soil then lacks that mineral. The crop yield gets smaller.

Explain why shortage of just one mineral affects the yield of a crop.

How dissolved substances get into plants

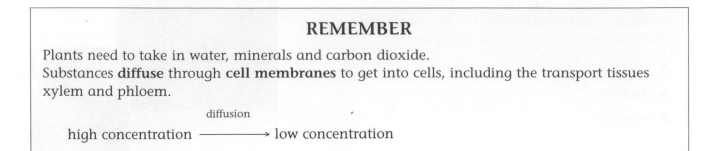

REMEMBER

Plants need to take in water, minerals and carbon dioxide.
Substances **diffuse** through **cell membranes** to get into cells, including the transport tissues xylem and phloem.

diffusion

high concentration ⟶ low concentration

■ Diffusion and concentration gradients

Molecules in liquids and gases move in all directions. So, they spread out.

Look at the diagrams. There are more molecules of dye at A than B. So, more of them move towards B than A. We say that they diffuse along a **concentration gradient**.

Substances such as potassium ions diffuse from one cell to another. There are more potassium ions in cell A than in cell B. So, more of them move from A to B than from B to A.

1　Copy and complete the diagram of cells A, B and C. Don't forget to draw some potassium ions in cell C.

Suppose a cell needs to take in potassium ions from a very dilute solution such as soil water. The ions cannot diffuse in against the concentration gradient.
The diagram shows how the cell absorbs them.

2　Copy and complete the sentences.

The cell has to use its own energy to absorb a substance against a _____ gradient. Because it uses energy, we call this process _____ _____.
The energy comes from the _____ of glucose.

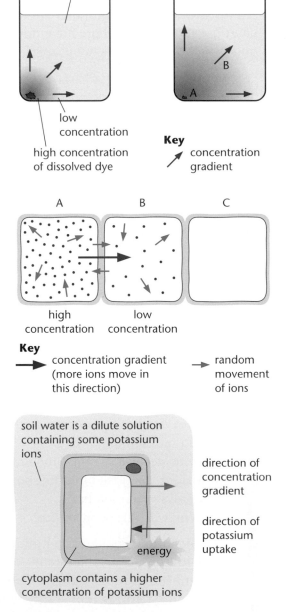

The cell uses energy from respiration to absorb potassium ions by **active uptake (active transport)**.

■ Diffusion of gases in and out of leaves

Leaves are adapted to exchange gases with the air.
In the dark, they take in oxygen for respiration and give
out carbon dioxide. In daylight, they make more oxygen
than they need for respiration so they give out the rest.

3 Look at the diagram, then copy and complete
the sentences.

The thin, flat shape of a leaf gives it a large surface
area compared with its volume. A leaf has lots of
spaces inside it. Gases go in and out of these spaces
through _____. Each leaf cell exchanges
with this air. So, leaves have a large, moist exchange
surface inside them. Gases _____ in the
moisture, then _____ into the cell in solution.

Good exchange surfaces:

■ are thin

■ are moist

■ have a large surface area.

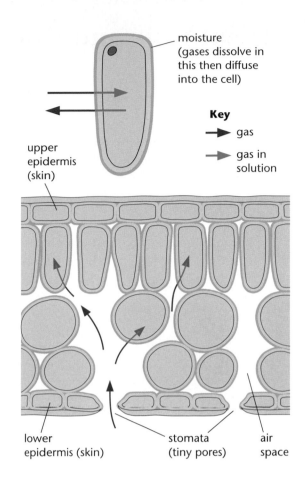

Using your knowledge

1 The drawings show simplified 'leaves'.

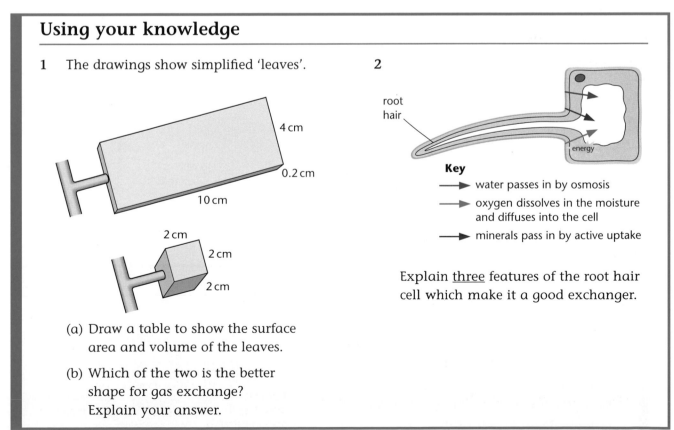

4 cm

0.2 cm

10 cm

2 cm

2 cm

2 cm

(a) Draw a table to show the surface
area and volume of the leaves.

(b) Which of the two is the better
shape for gas exchange?
Explain your answer.

2

root
hair

energy

Key

→ water passes in by osmosis

→ oxygen dissolves in the moisture
and diffuses into the cell

→ minerals pass in by active uptake

Explain <u>three</u> features of the root hair
cell which make it a good exchanger.

Plant cells and water

■ What happens when a plant doesn't take in enough water?

For your body to work properly, the water, sugar and ion content are important. These things are also important for plants.

The plant on the right in the picture has wilted. Its leaves and leaf stalks are soft and bendy. This is because its cells have lost more water than they have taken in. If plant cells take in enough water, they remain firm or rigid. We say that they have **turgor**.

Woody tissue helps to support the stem.

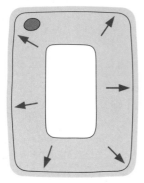

This cell has taken in enough water. Its contents are pressing against the cell wall. So the wall is firm and rigid. Rigid cells provide a plant with support.

This cell is short of water. Its contents aren't pressing against the wall. So the wall is not firm. When its cells are like this, a plant is **wilting**.

1 (a) The plant in the picture relies on the rigidity of its cells for support. What makes its cells rigid?

(b) Explain why the main stem of this plant has stayed upright.

2 Look at the diagram then copy and complete the sentences.

When water moves into a cell by _____, the pressure inside the cell _____. The cell wall stretches, but it is _____ enough not to burst as a result of the pressure. This pressure keeps the cell _____. We say that it maintains the cell's _____.

Water goes into the cell by osmosis.

Strong cell wall withstands pressure.

So the pressure on the wall increases.

How a cell's turgor is maintained.

Using your knowledge

1 Look at the picture.

(a) The guard cells take in minerals by active uptake from the cells next to them. Explain why water then passes into the guard cells.

(b) As water passes into the guard cells, the pore opens. Explain why.

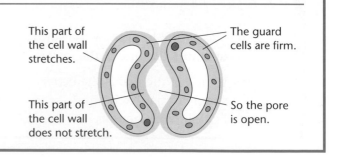

This part of the cell wall stretches.

The guard cells are firm.

This part of the cell wall does not stretch.

So the pore is open.

Carbon monoxide and your body

When fuels such as petrol and natural gas burn completely, they produce carbon dioxide and water. If there isn't enough oxygen to burn them completely, some **carbon monoxide** is produced too.

■ Why is carbon monoxide a problem?

Carbon monoxide is a poisonous gas. We can neither see it nor smell it. That is why many people now have detectors for it in their homes.

1   Look at the pictures. Describe the symptoms of carbon monoxide poisoning.

■ How does carbon monoxide poison you?

The **haemoglobin** in your red cells absorbs carbon monoxide more easily than it absorbs oxygen. So it soon picks up any carbon monoxide that you breathe in.

Carbon monoxide combines with haemoglobin to form cherry-red carboxy-haemoglobin. This reaction is <u>irreversible</u>. So this haemoglobin can no longer carry oxygen. The brain is the first organ to suffer from lack of oxygen.

2   Write a word equation for the reaction between haemoglobin and carbon monoxide.

3   Explain how this reaction is different from the reaction between haemoglobin and oxygen.

4   Explain the symptoms of carbon monoxide poisoning.

"My head aches and I feel confused."

"I'm finding it hard to breathe."

"He's in a coma."

The flue from Carl's gas heater is blocked. The pictures show what happened to him.

haemoglobin + oxygen ⇌ oxyhaemoglobin
   (dull red)   (bright red)

In your tissues, oxyhaemoglobin gives up its oxygen. The reaction is reversible.

Using your knowledge

1   A chemical was added to some blood to stop it clotting. Then it was divided between three beakers. A different gas was bubbled into each beaker. The gases were carbon monoxide, carbon dioxide and oxygen. The pictures show the results.

(a) Which gas was bubbled into which beaker?

(b) Oxygen was then bubbled into all three beakers. The colour changed in only one of them. Which one was it and why?

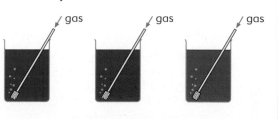

gas   gas   gas

Clear images

> ### REMEMBER
>
> The **cornea** and **lens** focus images on the retina.
>
> The **retina** is made of light sensitive cells.
>
> These cells convert light energy into nerve impulses.

■ Producing a clear image

You have to focus a lens to get a clear image. With a glass lens you do this by changing the distance between the lens and the screen.

Your eyes need to focus but you cannot change the distance between the lens and the retina. However, the lens can change shape. Lenses of different shapes focus at different distances. So, you can use the same lens to focus on near and distant objects.

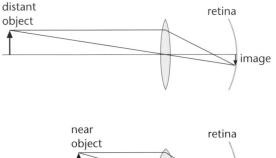

1 Look at the diagrams below.
Copy and complete the table.

Part of the eye	How your eye focusses on	
	near objects	distant objects
ciliary muscle		
suspensory ligament		
lens		

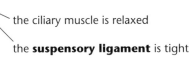

the ciliary muscle is relaxed

the **suspensory ligament** is tight

the lens is thin

The eye is focussed on a distant object.

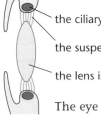

the ciliary muscle contracts

the suspensory ligament goes slack

the lens is fat

The eye is focussed on a near object.

Using your knowledge

1 Some people say that cats can see in the dark.

(a) Explain why this is not true.

(b) What do they really mean?

2 Good advice to readers is to look into the distance from time to time to relax your eyes.

Explain why looking at a book can strain your eyes but looking into the distance relaxes them.

More about coordination

REMEMBER

Receptor cells in your sense organs detect changes in your surroundings.
Your brain and spinal cord (**central nervous system**) coordinate your reactions.
Nerve impulses are tiny electrical impulses along neurones that carry the information.

■ Pathways in your nervous system

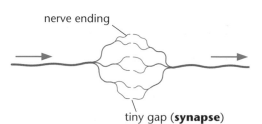

nerve ending

tiny gap (**synapse**)

Some reactions, such as picking up a £10 note, are **voluntary** – you decide whether or not to do them. Other reactions don't involve thinking – if you touch a hot pan you don't want to waste time thinking about it before you move your hand. This quick, automatic reaction is called a **reflex action**.

In both voluntary and reflex actions, the pathway of the impulse is similar.

There is a tiny gap between one neurone and the next. A chemical released at the end of one neurone causes an impulse to start in the next one.

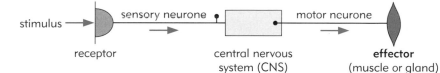

stimulus → receptor — sensory neurone → central nervous system (CNS) — motor neurone → **effector** (muscle or gland)

As well as sensory and motor neurones a reflex action usually involves a **relay neurone** in the CNS (brain or spinal cord).

1 (a) What is a synapse?

   (b) How does a nerve impulse cross it?

2 Look at the diagram. Then, write down the following sentences in the correct order.

   ■ The effector (a muscle or a gland) responds.
   ■ Impulses from a receptor pass along a sensory neurone.
   ■ A muscle responds by contracting, a gland by releasing (secreting) chemical substances.
   ■ In the central nervous system, impulses pass from a sensory to a relay neurone, then to a motor neurone.

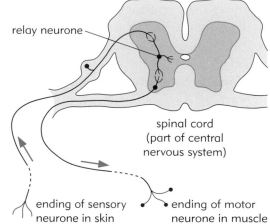

relay neurone

spinal cord (part of central nervous system)

ending of sensory neurone in skin   ending of motor neurone in muscle

---

Using your knowledge

1   When Liam saw his dinner, his mouth started to 'water' (his brain caused his salivary glands to secrete saliva).

   (a) Why is this reflex action useful?

(b) For this reflex action, what is:

   ■ the stimulus?   ■ the effector?
   ■ the receptor?   ■ the response?
   ■ the coordinator?

H7   This extends *Maintenance of life* 15 and 16 for Higher Tier students

Homeostasis

REMEMBER

For your body to work properly, the internal environment must stay the same.
The conditions which are controlled include the water, **glucose** and ion content
of your blood and your core temperature.

■ Controlling temperature

Your inner body temperature or **core temperature** should be about 37 °C.
It is safe for your skin and some other parts to get hotter or colder than this. Part of your brain acts like a <u>thermo</u>stat. We call it the **thermoregulatory centre**. It checks the temperature of the blood passing through your brain. It also receives impulses from temperature receptors in your skin.

If your core temperature is too high or too low, your thermoregulatory centre sends impulses to your skin and muscles. These affect muscles, sweat glands and the blood vessels to your skin. Evaporation of sweat cools your body. Shivering muscles are contracting muscles. To contract, they use the energy from respiration. Some of this energy is released as heat.

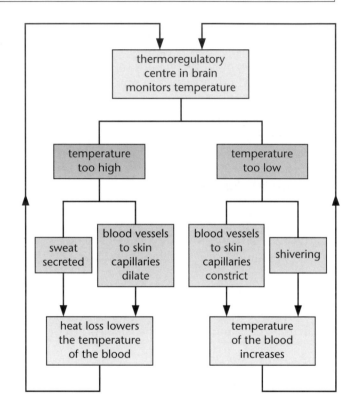

1 (a) Where is your thermoregulatory centre?

   (b) Explain how it helps to control your body temperature.

2 (a) Look at the top diagram, then copy and complete the table:

When your core temperature is:	
too high	**too low**
no shivering	
	no sweat
blood vessels supplying your skin capillaries dilate (widen)	

   (b) What is shivering and why does it warm you?

   (c) Look at the diagram that shows why you lose less heat when the blood vessels in your skin constrict. Draw a similar diagram to show what happens when these blood vessels dilate.

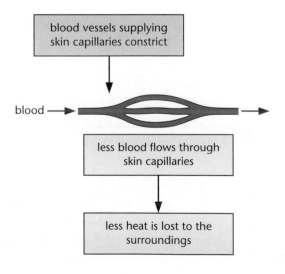

Controlling the concentration of glucose in your blood

Having too little or too much glucose in your blood is dangerous. Either of these can cause coma and death. Your pancreas monitors your blood glucose concentration. If this concentration is too high (or too low) the pancreas releases **insulin** (or **glucagon**) into your blood. We say that the **pancreas** <u>secretes</u> these hormones.

Both hormones affect your **liver** cells. Without them, your liver cells can't control the concentration of glucose in your blood. Insulin enables liver cells to take glucose out of your blood and store it as insoluble **glycogen**. Glucagon causes the reverse to happen. It enables liver cells to change glycogen into soluble glucose which is released into your blood.

3 Your pancreas and your liver control your blood glucose concentration. Explain, as fully as you can, the part played in lowering the concentration of glucose in your blood by:

(a) your pancreas;

(b) your liver.

4 Copy and complete the diagram.

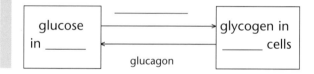

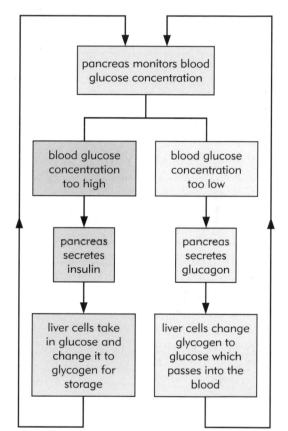

We call the maintenance of a constant internal environment **homeostasis**.

You will see how your kidneys act as organs of homeostasis as well as excretory organs on pages 110 and 111.

Using your knowledge

1 These are some discoveries about the pancreas.

1889 – Mering and Minkowski removed a dog's pancreas. The dog's blood glucose concentration went up.

1922 – Banting and Best tied the tube from a dog's pancreas to its small intestine. The parts of the pancreas which make digestive juices stopped working but other parts carried on working. Injection of an extract made from these parts lowered the blood glucose concentration of a diabetic dog.

What could each group of scientists conclude from <u>its own evidence alone</u>?

2 Why does your skin look flushed when you are hot?

H8   This extends *Maintenance of life* 17 for Higher Tier students

More about your kidneys

REMEMBER

Your **liver** breaks down excess amino acids producing waste **urea**.

Urea is a poison and your body must get rid of it.
This is one of the jobs your **kidneys** have to do.

They also regulate the amount of water and salt in your body.

■ Filtration of blood

Your kidneys get rid of urea and the excess water and salts from your blood. Over one litre of blood passes through your kidneys every minute. **Urine** trickles out of them continuously and travels down tubes called **ureters** into your **bladder**.

Each kidney is made of millions of tiny tubules with walls only one cell thick. Water, ions, glucose and urea are <u>filtered</u> from the blood into the tubules at high pressure. Your body needs to keep <u>all</u> the glucose and <u>some of</u> the water and ions. So, these are <u>re-absorbed</u> into your blood.

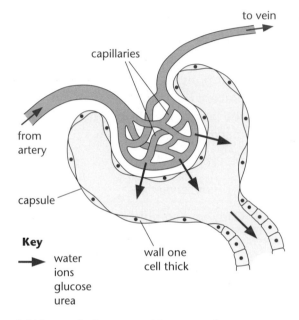

Key

→ water
    ions
    glucose
    urea

wall one
cell thick

A kidney tubule starts with a capsule that is like a cup.

1 Copy and complete the sentences.

Kidney tubules _____ blood at high _____. Water, glucose, ions and urea pass into them. All the _____ and the ions and _____ that the body needs are _____ into the blood.

■ Re-absorption of the things you need

The concentration of ions and glucose in your kidney tubules is as high or higher than their concentration in your blood. This means that your kidneys re-absorb them against a **concentration gradient**. They need energy to do this, so re-absorption is by **active uptake**.

As glucose and ions pass into your blood, the fluid in the tubules becomes more dilute. So, water then passes into your blood by **osmosis**.

2 Explain how glucose, water and dissolved ions are re-absorbed into your blood.

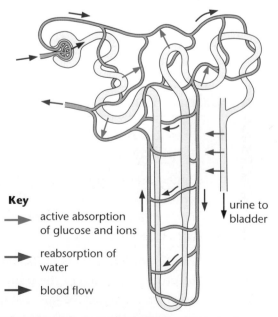

Key

→ active absorption
    of glucose and ions

→ reabsorption of
    water

→ blood flow

urine to
bladder

One kidney tubule and its blood supply.

■ Why does the amount of water re-absorbed vary?

If the concentration of ions in your blood is too high, your kidneys get rid of the extra ions and re-absorb as much water as possible. So, you produce less urine, but it is more concentrated.

If the water content of your blood is too high, less water is re-absorbed and your urine is more dilute.

3 Look at the pictures.

 (a) Which <u>three</u> of these people probably have too little water in their blood?

 (b) Will their urine be dilute or concentrated?

■ What controls the re-absorption of water?

The **pituitary gland** in your brain monitors the amount of water in your blood. It releases a **hormone** called **ADH**. Its effect is to make your kidney tubules re-absorb water into your blood.

4 Look at the diagram, then copy and complete the table:

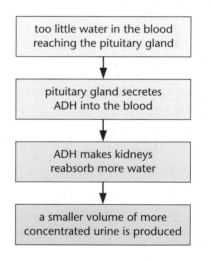

too little water in the blood reaching the pituitary gland

↓

pituitary gland secretes ADH into the blood

↓

ADH makes kidneys reabsorb more water

↓

a smaller volume of more concentrated urine is produced

	Too much water in the blood	Too little water in the blood
Pituitary secretes	_____ ADH	more ADH
Kidney tubules	re-absorb _____ water	re-absorb _____ _____
Urine volume	large	_____
Urine concentration	low (dilute)	_____

Using your knowledge

1 Look at the diagram. Three tubes, A, B and C are connected to the kidney.

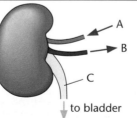

to bladder

 (a) Which one carries unfiltered blood?

 (b) Which one carries filtered blood?

 (c) Which one carries urine?

 (d) Which one should contain least urea?

 (e) Which one should not contain glucose?

2 What would be the effect of the following things on your urine volume and concentration:

 (a) drinking four mugs of unsweetened tea?

 (b) eating lots of salted crisps?

 (c) playing a football match on a hot day?

3 Organs suitable for exchanges have thin, moist surfaces, a large surface area and a good capillary supply. Describe how the kidneys satisfy all these conditions.

Staying alive

It is hard to survive in some places on Earth. In some places it is sometimes too <u>hot</u> or too <u>cold</u>. Or there might not be enough <u>light</u>. Sometimes there might not be enough <u>water</u> or <u>oxygen</u> or carbon dioxide.

We call all of these things <u>physical</u> factors. These factors vary according to the time of day and time of year.

1 Write down a list of physical factors which affect plants and animals.

2 Between which temperatures do most plants and animals live?

3 Why do you think not many organisms live below 0 °C?

4 Not many organisms live above 40 °C. Why?

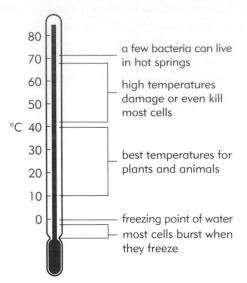

■ Day and night

During the day, the Earth gets heat and light from the Sun.

5 Copy and complete the following sentences.

During the day the Sun _____ the Earth so temperatures _____. At night temperatures _____ because heat _____ into space.

These daily changes in temperature and light affect animals and plants.

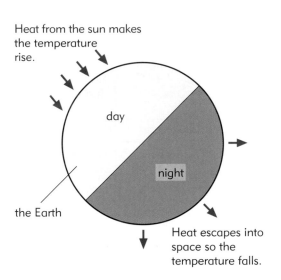

■ Seasons of the year

In tropical rainforests there are many different kinds of plants and animals which <u>live</u>, <u>grow</u> and <u>breed</u> there all year round. In countries like Britain, some plants and animals can be seen all the year round. But others can be seen only at some times of the year. This is because they live, grow and reproduce only when conditions are right for them.

6 The diagram shows how the temperature in Britain changes with the seasons. Write down <u>two</u> other physical factors that change with the seasons.

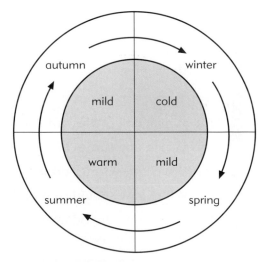

How plants survive the winter

Frost can damage plants, and plants cannot get enough water when it is frozen in the soil. Different plants have different ways of surviving in cold weather.

Some plants like the poppy complete their life cycle in one growing season. They are called <u>annuals</u>.

7 Which part of an annual plant survives the winter?

Winter	Spring	Summer	Autumn
seeds	seeds germinate	flowers	seeds are spread, plants die

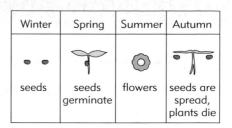

Annual plants

Two kinds of trees

Some plants, including trees, live for many growing seasons. They are called <u>perennials</u>. Different trees and other woody plants have different ways of surviving frost and water shortage.

8 Why do broad-leaved trees lose their leaves in winter?

9 Evergreen trees do not need to lose their leaves in winter. Write down <u>two</u> reasons why.

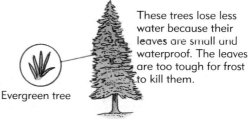

Broad-leaved tree
winter   summer

These trees lose their leaves in autumn. This stops the tree losing water from the leaves.

These trees lose less water because their leaves are small and waterproof. The leaves are too tough for frost to kill them.

Evergreen tree

winter and summer

How animals survive the winter

Animals also have problems in **winter**. It is cold and food is in short supply.

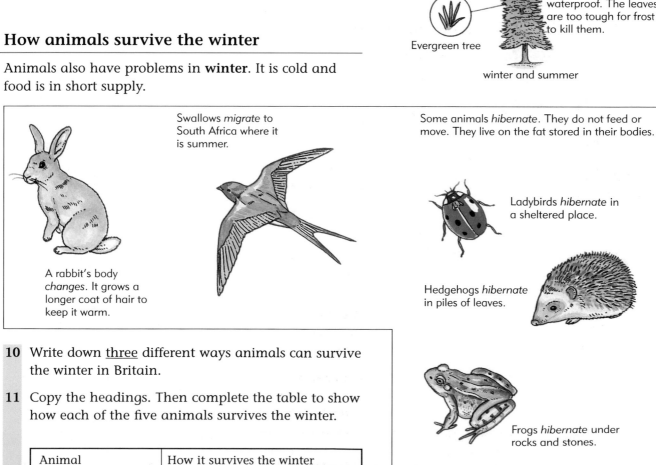

Swallows *migrate* to South Africa where it is summer.

A rabbit's body *changes*. It grows a longer coat of hair to keep it warm.

Some animals *hibernate*. They do not feed or move. They live on the fat stored in their bodies.

Ladybirds *hibernate* in a sheltered place.

Hedgehogs *hibernate* in piles of leaves.

Frogs *hibernate* under rocks and stones.

10 Write down <u>three</u> different ways animals can survive the winter in Britain.

11 Copy the headings. Then complete the table to show how each of the five animals survives the winter.

Animal	How it survives the winter

Surviving in different places

■ Some places are hard to live in

Humans live in most parts of the world. In many places they can survive only by making clothes, houses and many other things.

1 How is the Inuit in the picture able to live in the extreme cold?

People in other parts of the world survive in different ways.

2 Write down some of the ways that Bedouins use to survive in the desert.

Different kinds of animals and plants live in different places. They live, grow and reproduce in places where **conditions** are suitable for them. We say that they are **adapted** to the conditions in which they live.

Inuit.

Bedouin.

■ How animals are adapted to cold places

The Arctic fox is adapted to live in the cold, but the Fennec fox is adapted to live in the heat of the Sahara.

3 Look at the pictures. Write down <u>two</u> differences between the Arctic and Fennec foxes.

Fennec foxes have long bodies and ears. This means that they have a large **surface area**. They have hardly any fat and very short fur. All these things mean that lots of heat can escape from their bodies. They stay cool!

Arctic foxes have a shorter body, small ears, lots of fat and thick fur. The small surface area, and thick **fur** and **fat** cut down on heat loss. They stay warm!

Fat and fur are good for stopping heat escaping. We say that they are good insulators.

4 How do you think these features help Arctic foxes to live in cold climates?

Some animals have colours which match their surroundings. We say that they are camouflaged.

5 Arctic foxes have white coats in winter and dark coats in summer.
Explain how this helps them to survive.

Arctic fox.

Fennec fox.

How animals and plants are adapted to desert life

In the desert there is very little water.
Gerbils survive by living in burrows in the desert.
The burrows stay cool during the day. Droplets of water (condensation) collect on the walls. Each day a gerbil produces only one or two drops of very concentrated urine.

6 Write down <u>two</u> ways that a gerbil can survive the shortage of water in the desert.

The cactus is a desert plant.

7 Look at the picture. Write down <u>two</u> ways the cactus is adapted to live in dry places.

8 The camel is well adapted to life in the desert. Copy and complete the table to show how.

Adaptation	How it helps
Can drink large amounts of water.	Does not have to drink very often.

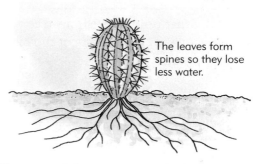

The leaves form spines so they lose less water.

The roots of the cactus spread a long way so they can take in a lot of **water** when it rains.

A camel's hump is a fat store. It can break down fat to release water.

Coarse wool on top of its body protects the camel from the sun

A camel can drink large amonts of water.

Its mouth is tough so it can eat thorny plants like cacti.

Short hair underneath the camel lets heat escape.

Its big flat feet stop it sinking into the sand.

What you need to remember [Copy and complete using the **key words**]

Surviving in different places

Organisms live, grow and reproduce in places where _____ are suitable for them.
We say that they are _____ to their conditions.

You need to be able to explain how adaptations of plants to dry conditions are related to how well they take in _____ and keep it in.

You also need to be able to explain how adaptations of animals to desert and Arctic conditions are related to
- body size and _____ _____;
- amount of insulating _____ and _____;
- camouflage.

115

Surviving in water and on land

Animals have features which help them to survive in the conditions in which they live. They are **adapted** to their habitats. Some animals are adapted to live in water. Other animals are adapted to live on land.

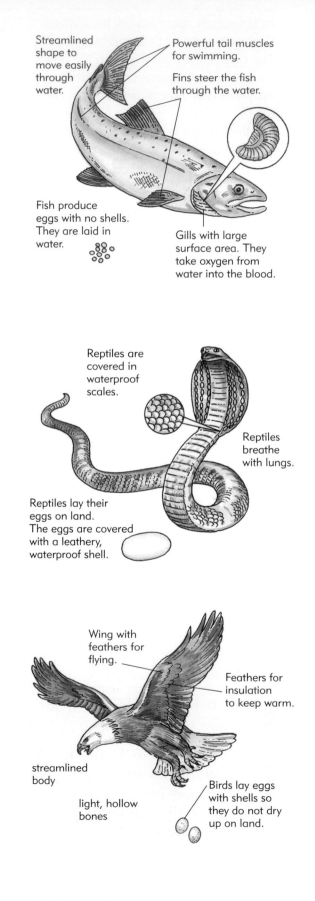

Streamlined shape to move easily through water.

Powerful tail muscles for swimming.

Fins steer the fish through the water.

■ Life in water

Like all other animals, fish need oxygen to survive. Fish live in water, so they must get the oxygen they need from the water.

Fish produce eggs with no shells. They are laid in water.

Gills with large surface area. They take oxygen from water into the blood.

1   How do fish get oxygen from water?

2   Write down <u>three</u> ways that fish are adapted to move easily through the water.

■ Life on land

Some snakes and other reptiles live on land. All animals which live on land must stop too much water escaping from their bodies. Reptiles and birds lay their eggs on land.

Reptiles are covered in waterproof scales.

Reptiles breathe with lungs.

3   How do reptiles stop water escaping from their bodies?

4   How do reptiles take in oxygen from the air?

5   Why do you think that reptiles and birds lay eggs with waterproof shells?

Reptiles lay their eggs on land. The eggs are covered with a leathery, waterproof shell.

Nearly all birds are adapted for flying.

6   Write down <u>three</u> ways in which birds are adapted for flying.

7   What else do feathers help birds do?

Wing with feathers for flying.

Feathers for insulation to keep warm.

streamlined body

light, hollow bones

Birds lay eggs with shells so they do not dry up on land.

Many mammals are adapted to life on land. The diagram shows some of the features of a land mammal.

8 Copy and complete the table to show how this mammal is adapted to life on land.

Feature	Purpose
covered in hair/fur	to keep warm

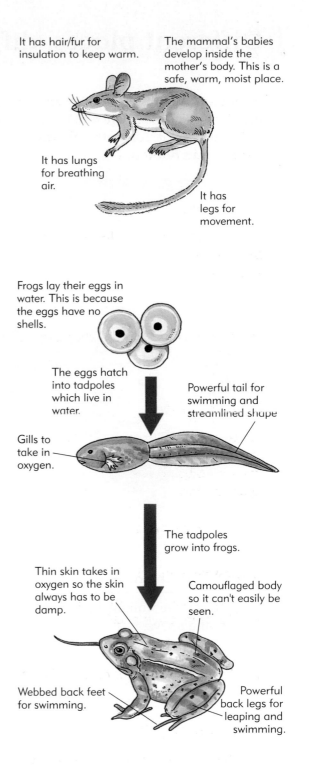

It has hair/fur for insulation to keep warm.

The mammal's babies develop inside the mother's body. This is a safe, warm, moist place.

It has lungs for breathing air.

It has legs for movement.

■ Life on land and in water

Some animals, like the frog, start their lives in water but then spend a lot of time on land.

9 What would happen to a frog's eggs if it laid them on land?

10 Write down <u>two</u> ways that a tadpole is adapted to living in water.

11 We usually find frogs in damp places. Why is this?

Frogs spend most of their time on land but come back to water to mate and lay their eggs.

12 Copy the headings below. Then complete the table to show how a frog is adapted to life on land and life in the water.

How an adult frog is adapted	
to life on land	to life in water

Frogs lay their eggs in water. This is because the eggs have no shells.

The eggs hatch into tadpoles which live in water.

Powerful tail for swimming and streamlined shape

Gills to take in oxygen.

The tadpoles grow into frogs.

Thin skin takes in oxygen so the skin always has to be damp.

Camouflaged body so it can't easily be seen.

Webbed back feet for swimming.

Powerful back legs for leaping and swimming.

What you need to remember [Copy and complete using the key words]

Surviving in water and on land

To survive, animals must be _____ to the conditions in which they live.

[You should be able to look at a picture of an animal and say how it is adapted to its surroundings.]

Different places, different plants

Plants and animals live in places where **conditions** are suitable. The place where a plant or animal lives is called its habitat. A plant or an animal is **adapted** to survive in its **habitat**.

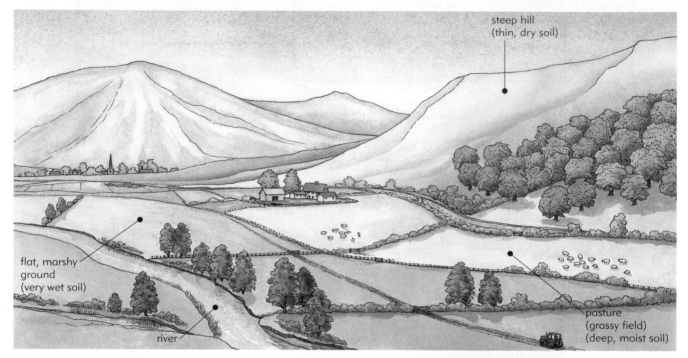

steep hill
(thin, dry soil)

flat, marshy
ground
(very wet soil)

river

pasture
(grassy field)
(deep, moist soil)

■ A walk in the country

Imagine you are walking up the hill from the river in the drawing above.

1 Copy the table. Then complete it to describe the three types of land you walk through.

	What the soil is like	What grows there
flat, marshy ground		
pasture		
steep hill		

2 Explain, as fully as you can, why:

(a) oak trees grow on the hill but not by the river;

(b) alder trees grow by the river but not on the hill.

Alder trees can survive in wet soil. They cannot compete with other trees in dry soil.

Oak trees survive in well-drained soil.

Why don't trees spread to the pasture?

Sheep are eating the grass in the field. They are grazing. Seeds from the trees fall on the pasture and some of them start to grow. Sheep eat the tops of the tiny trees. Look at the drawings of the tree seedling and grass.

3 Sheep usually kill young trees. Explain why.

4 Grass can survive grazing by sheep. Explain why.

5 What would happen to the pasture if there were no sheep on it for several years? Explain your answer.

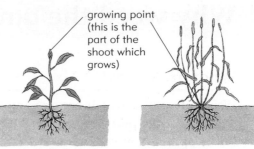

growing point
(this is the part of the shoot which grows)

Tree seedling   Grass plant

Into the woods

It gets darker as you go into the wood. The plants are different from those in the field. They are adapted to different conditions.

6 Write down <u>two</u> differences between conditions in the wood and in the field.

14 °C

25 °C

To the mountains

As you go over the top of the hill you can see mountains in front of you. The trees above you are all conifers.

As you walk up the mountain it gets colder and more windy.

Water evaporates more quickly in windy places. Trees living in windy places can easily lose too much water. To survive they have to lose as little water as possible.

7 Write down <u>two</u> ways conifers are adapted to stop them losing water from their leaves.

8 Higher up the mountain there are no trees at all. Why do you think this is?

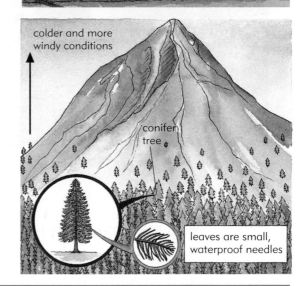

colder and more windy conditions

conifer tree

leaves are small, waterproof needles

What you need to remember [Copy and complete using the **key words**]

Different places, different plants

Plants and animals live in places where _____ are suitable.
A plant is _____ to survive in its _____.
That is why different plants live in different places.

[You need to be able to explain why particular plants or animals live where they do, just like you have done on these pages.]

4

Why weed the garden?

■ What are weeds?

Weeds are plants which are growing where they are not wanted. People plant poppies in their flower gardens, but poppies are weeds in a farmer's crop.

1 Write down the names of <u>three</u> weeds in the picture on the right.

■ What is wrong with weeds?

Gardeners don't like weeds because they take the things flowers, fruit and vegetables need to grow. They **compete** with the gardeners' plants. So, gardeners try to get rid of weeds so that their plants can grow better.

2 Write down <u>four</u> things the crops and weeds compete for. (Use the remember box to help you.)

Pull them up.

Cut them down.

Use weedkiller.

3 Write down <u>three</u> ways of getting rid of weeds.

■ Weeding is a constant battle

A garden is overgrown.
The weeds are all crowded together.

A family clears the weeds and plants some vegetables. The last picture shows the same garden a few months later.

4 Describe <u>two</u> differences between the weeds in the first and last pictures.

5 Why are there weeds in the garden a few months later?

> ### REMEMBER
>
> Plants need the right conditions to grow well. They need **water** and **nutrients** from the soil, **carbon dioxide** from the air and **light**.

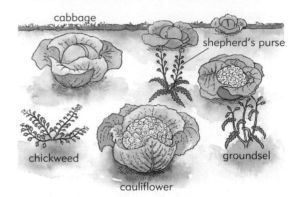

cabbage

shepherd's purse

chickweed

groundsel

cauliflower

This weed grew from a seed blown into the garden.

This weed grew from a bit of root that was left in the soil.

How weeds can start to grow again.

■ Competition between weeds

The groundsel plants on the right were taken from the garden shown on the last page. Both of these plants took three months to grow.

6 Describe <u>one</u> way in which they are similar.

7 Describe <u>one</u> difference between them.

The first plant has grown tall because the garden was overcrowded. The plant was competing with many other plants.

8 What are the plants competing for when they grow tall?

9 Which parts of the plant would you expect to grow bigger in the competition for water and nutrients?

Plants compete for light as well as for water and nutrients from the soil. Plants can get what they need more easily if they have plenty of **space**.

■ What happens if we never weed a garden?

The picture shows the same garden but it has not been weeded for many years.

10 What plants have taken the place of many of the smaller weeds?

11 Why do you think the smaller weeds died out?

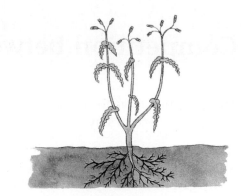
Groundsel from a very weedy garden.

Groundsel from a less weedy garden.

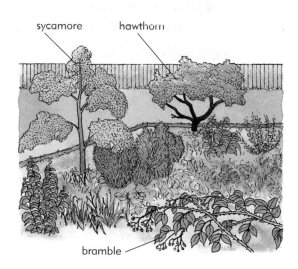
sycamore   hawthorn
bramble

What you need to remember [Copy and complete using the **key words**]

Why weed the garden?

Plants need the right conditions to grow well.

They need: _____ and _____ from the soil;

_____ _____ from the air;

and plenty of _____.

When plants grow close together they _____ with each other for these things.

If plants have plenty of _____ they get all the things they need more easily.

[You should be able to suggest what plants are competing for if you are given information about a particular habitat.]

Competition between animals

Animals often have to **compete** with each other for the things they need to stay alive.

If you keep gerbils as pets, you have to supply them with food, water, nesting material and shelter. If you keep too many gerbils in one cage they will be overcrowded and uncomfortable. This is cruel.

1 What would the gerbils be competing for in an overcrowded cage?

Animals most often compete with each other for **food**, **water** and **space**.

■ Competition between fish

Animals which don't compete very well for food and other things they need may die.

The graph shows how the number of fish in a tank affects the number of young fish which die. If you are a fish farmer, the more fish you rear the more profit you make.

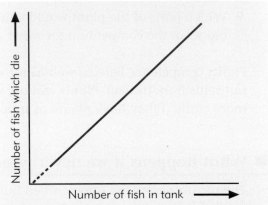

2 Why is it a bad idea to keep too many fish in one tank?

3 Why do you think more young fish die in an overcrowded tank?

■ Competition between flies

Animals which don't compete very well for food and other things they need may not be able to breed.

A fruit fly

Scientists often keep fruit flies for breeding experiments. The graph shows what happens if they keep too many flies in the same space.

4 What happens to the number of eggs that are laid as the number of fruit flies goes up?

5 Why do you think this happens?

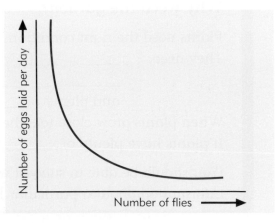

Competition between squirrels

So far we have talked about animals of the same kind, or **species**, competing with each other. But as well as competing with members of their own species animals compete with those of other species.

If two different species compete for exactly the same things they cannot live together. One of the two species will win the competition and so survive.

The graph shows what happens when grey squirrels arrive in an area where red squirrels live.

6 Describe what happens to the numbers of the two types of squirrels.

This probably happens because the two types of squirrel are in competition.

7 What do you think that these two species of squirrel could be competing for?

Competition between birds

Blackbirds and song thrushes live in parks and gardens. Although they eat similar food they can still live together in the same place.

8 What two differences in their diet means that blackbirds and song thrushes can live in the same place?

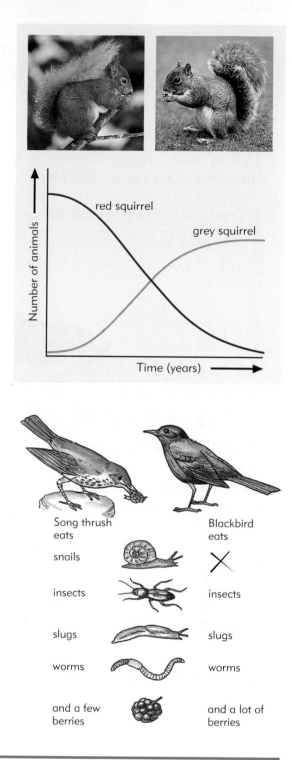

Song thrush eats

snails

insects

slugs

worms

and a few berries

Blackbird eats

X insects

slugs

worms

and a lot of berries

What you need to remember [Copy and complete using the **key words**]

Competition between animals

Animals of one species often _____ with each other. They also compete with members of other _____.

They may compete for _____, _____ or _____.

[You need to be able to suggest what animals are competing for when you are given information about a particular habitat.]

6

Predators and their prey

Spiders use webs to trap insects for food.

Animals which eat other animals are called **predators**. The animals they eat are their **prey**.

1 Copy and complete the following sentences.

The spider is a _____.

The fly is its _____.

Lioness and wildebeest.

Blackbird and earthworm.

2 Copy the table and complete it using the predators and prey in the three pictures above.

Predator	Prey
spider	fly

Usually **predators** feed on more than one kind of animal. For example, a lion doesn't just eat wildebeest.

3 Write down the name of another animal it can eat.

Lion on savannah with wildebeest and zebra.

An animal can be preyed upon by several predators. For example, mice are not just eaten by owls.

4 Write down the names of <u>two</u> other animals which eat mice.

■ Stoats and rabbits

Stoats are predators. They eat rabbits and other animals. We call all the rabbits which live in one place a **population**. The size of the population is limited by the amount of food available.

Mouse being watched by a cat, a kestrel and an owl.

5 Look at the graph. What happened to the size of the rabbit population between 1930 and 1950?

If the population of rabbits increases, there is more **food** for the stoats.

6 (a) What do you think happened to the number of stoats as the population of rabbits went up?

  (b) Give a reason for your answer.

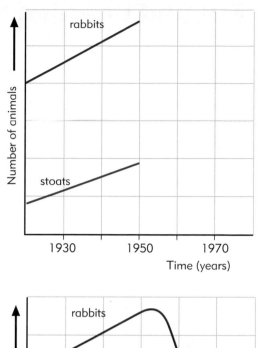

■ A disaster for rabbits (and for stoats)

In the 1950s rabbits were infected with a **disease**. Most of them died. The stoats did not catch this disease, but 95 per cent of them still died.

7 Copy and complete the following sentences.

The rabbit population went down because of _____. The stoat population went down because they had less _____.

8 The graph shows what happened to the rabbit population after 1953. Copy the graph and continue your line for the stoats as far as 1960.

In the 1960s the number of stoats began to go up again. This is because they started to eat different **food** such as a lot more small birds, mice and even earthworms instead of rabbits.

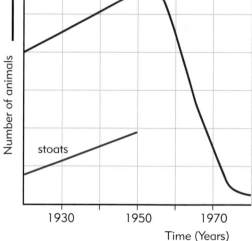

9 Draw a line on your graph to show this increase. Label the line with a reason for the increase.

What you need to remember [Copy and complete using the **key words**]

Predators and their prey

Animals which kill other animals for food are called _____.
The animals they eat are called their _____.

The number of animals of a species is called its _____. This is usually limited by the amount of _____ available.
If the population of prey increases, predators have more _____ so the number of _____ also increases.
The size of a population can also be affected by _____.

Kill and be killed

■ Predators of the Great Barrier Reef

The Great Barrier Reef is off the east coast of Australia. It is made of coral. Coral is an animal which feeds on microscopic sea-life called plankton.

The crown-of-thorns starfish feeds on coral.
So the starfish is a predator, and the coral is its prey.
Starfish themselves are prey for other predators.

1 Write down the names of <u>three</u> predators of the starfish. Use the diagram below to help you.

Many people visit the reef and collect shells. They also catch trigger fish, Napoleon fish and puffer fish.
So numbers of all these have gone down.

2 The number of starfish is going up. Why is this?

3 What effect does the increase in the number of starfish have on the coral population?

4 Copy and complete the following sentence.

When the population of a predator increases, the population of its prey _____.

In some parts of the reef, the starfish have eaten most of the coral animals. Only the skeletons are left. Scientists are worried because they think the coral will take 20 years to grow back.

Some scientists think that people should not be allowed to collect shells or to fish on the reef. A ban on fishing and collecting could help to save the coral.

5 There is an increase in the number of trigger fish. Draw a diagram, similar to the one on the right, that shows how this affects the starfish population.

The populations of different species which live in the same place are called a **community**.

> ### REMEMBER
> The population of a species is usually limited by the amount of food available.

The Great Barrier Reef.

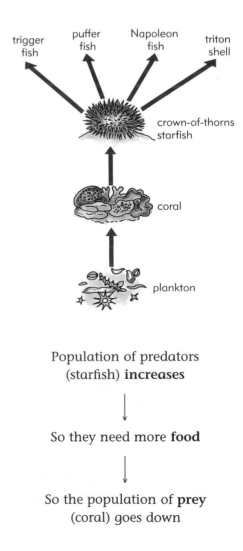

Population of predators
(starfish) **increases**

↓

So they need more **food**

↓

So the population of **prey**
(coral) goes down

The balance of nature

In nature, the numbers of predators and prey stay in overall balance. On the Great Barrier Reef, people have upset this balance.

6 What did they do to upset it?

The balance in nature doesn't always mean steady numbers. Sometimes the numbers of predators and prey go up and down every few years. This is what happens in Canada with the lynx and the snowshoe hare. The lynx prey on the hares.

The graph shows how the numbers of lynx and hares changed over 30 years.

7 Describe what happened to the population of the hare during the first 10 years.

During this time, the population of the lynx also changed.

8 Describe <u>one</u> similarity between the population change for the lynx and that for the hare.

9 Describe the differences between the two population changes.

10 The population changes for the lynx are always behind the hares by about two years. Why do you think this is?

Lynx (predator) and snowshoe hare (prey).

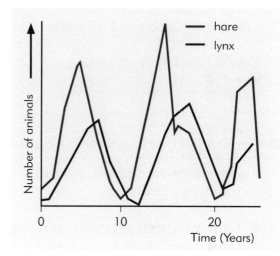

Population cycles of snowshoe hare and lynx.

What you need to remember [Copy and complete using the **key words**]

Kill and be killed

The populations of different species in the same place are called a _____.
In a community the number of animals of a particular species depends on the amount of _____ available.

If the number of predators goes up (_____), they need more food.
This means that the population of their _____ goes down (decreases).

Food chains, webs and pyramids

■ Food chains

Food **chains** are a way of showing what animals eat.
They always begin with green plants.

animal
↑
animal
↑
plant

Each arrow in a food chain means 'is **eaten** by'.
The food chain on the right tells you that the **grass** is
eaten by the rabbit and the **rabbit** is eaten by the fox.

1 What does this food chain tell you?

barley ——→ mouse ——→ owl

■ Drawing your own food chains

If you know what different animals eat, you can draw
your own food chains.

2 Look at the sets of pictures on the right.
Draw a food chain for each set.

Plants are called **producers** because they produce or make
food. This is why food chains begin with **green plants**.

Animals consume food made by plants or they eat
animals which have eaten plants.
So they are called **consumers**.

The diagram shows what the words mean in a food chain.

3 Go back to the food chains you drew for question 2.
Write 'producer', '1st consumer' or '2nd consumer'
next to each member of the chains.

The food produced by green plants is where all of the
minerals and energy in a food chain come from. So the
arrows in a food chain show the transfer of materials
and energy from one organism to another.

4 Copy the diagram. Complete the arrow to show the
direction of transfer of energy and materials.

fox
↑
rabbit
↑
grass

caterpillar

blackbird

caterpillar

cabbage

slug

lettuce

slug

frog

adder

frog

frog

fox	2nd consumer
↑	↑
rabbit	1st consumer
↑	↑
grass	producer

fox
↑
rabbit
↑
grass

direction of
transfer of
materials
and
energy

■ Food webs

Most animals don't eat just one thing.
So they belong to more than one food **chain**.

When different food chains contain the same animals we can join them together. We then get a food **web**.

5 Copy the food web. The missing animals are an earthworm and a fox. Write their names in the correct boxes.

6 Blackbirds eat earthworms. Falcons eat rabbits and blackbirds. Add falcons and blackbirds to your food web to show this.

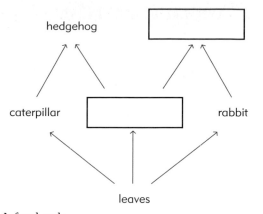

A food web.

■ Pyramids in food chains

7 Copy and complete the following sentences.

To stay alive the owl eats _____.
So there must be lots of mice for each _____. The mice stay alive by eating _____. So there must be lots of wheat plants for each _____.

The numbers of plants and animals in this food chain make a pyramid. We call this a **pyramid of numbers**. The diagram shows a simple way of drawing the pyramid:

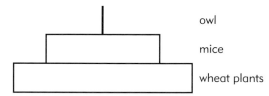

owl
mice
wheat plants

8 The diagram shows this food chain in a field:

daisy ⟶ caterpillar ⟶ blackbird

(a) Count the number of each of daisies, caterpillars and blackbirds. Set out your results in a table.

(b) Draw a pyramid of numbers for this food chain. Use a scale of 1 mm to represent one plant or animal.

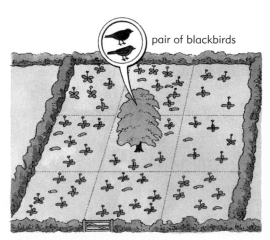

🌿 daisies ◠ caterpillars

Energy for life

To stay alive, plants and animals need a constant supply of energy. The diagram shows how they get the energy they need.

1 How do plants get the energy they need?

2 What do plants do with the energy once they have got it?

Plants only use a small amount of the energy which reaches them from the Sun. Some of the energy that they trap is then passed along the food chain.

3 How do animals get the energy they need?

4 What else do plants and animals use food for besides providing energy?

This is the food chain shown opposite:

lettuce ──→ snail ──→ thrush

Food, or stored energy, passes along the chain:

lettuce ──→ snail ──→ thrush

food (stored energy)

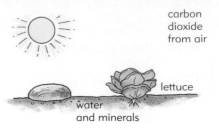

carbon dioxide from air

lettuce

water and minerals

Plants capture **light** energy from the sun. They use this to make **food**. Food is a store of chemical energy.

Animals eat plants. They use some of the energy from food to move. They use some of the food to grow. Energy is then stored in the animals' bodies.

thrush

Animals may be eaten by other animals. Part of the energy stored in the food is used to move or to keep warm. Some food is used to grow so the energy is stored in the animals' bodies.

■ Less and less energy

Animals use a lot of the energy from their food to **move** about. Some animals also use energy from food to keep **warm**. All of this energy ends up in the surroundings as **heat**.

Animals use some of their food to **grow**. This means that the energy in the food is stored in the animals' bodies.

The diagram shows what happens to the energy stored in the bodies of plants and animals as you move up a food chain. The higher you go, the less energy there is.

5 Draw, and label, a similar diagram for the food chain:

cereals ──→ chickens ──→ humans

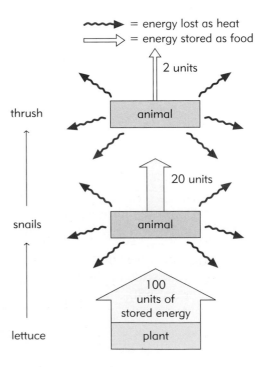

= energy lost as heat
= energy stored as food

thrush

animal

2 units

snails

animal

20 units

lettuce

plant

100 units of stored energy

■ Energy loss and food supplies

In some countries many people don't get enough to eat. If we **reduce** the number of stages in a food chain, we can feed more people. We call it 'eating lower in the food chain'. It means eating plants instead of meat.

6 Explain why more people could be fed if we all ate lower in the food chain.

The amount of land needed to feed one person on:

■ chicken

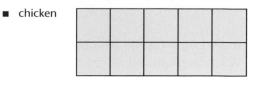

■ grain

■ Another kind of pyramid

The materials which animals and plants are made of store energy. We call these materials <u>biomass</u>.

At each stage in a food chain there is less and less energy. So there is also less biomass. We can show this by drawing a **pyramid** of biomass.

7 One thrush has a bigger mass than one snail. But the pyramid of biomass shows a bigger mass for the snails. Why is this?

The diagram shows the pyramid of numbers and the pyramid of biomass for another food chain.

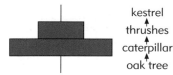

kestrel
↑
thrushes
↑
caterpillar
↑
oak tree

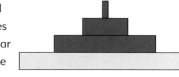

Pyramid of numbers.   Pyramid of biomass.

8 What difference is there between the pyramids? Explain the reason for the difference.

REMEMBER

A pyramid of numbers shows how many plants and animals there are at different stages in a food chain.

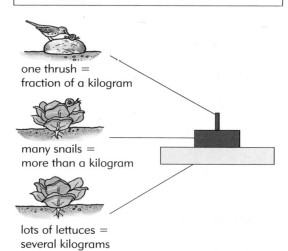

one thrush =
fraction of a kilogram

many snails =
more than a kilogram

lots of lettuces =
several kilograms

Pyramid of biomass.

What you need to remember [Copy and complete using the **key words**]

Energy for life

Plants capture _____ energy from the Sun and store the energy in _____.
When animals eat plants they only use a part of this food to _____ .
A lot of the energy in the food is used to _____ and to keep
_____. This energy is lost to the surroundings as _____ so less
energy is passed to the next stage of a food chain. This means there is less biomass to
pass along a food chain. We can show this by drawing a _____ of biomass.
We can improve the efficiency of food production for humans if we
_____ the number of stages in the food chain.

[You need to be able to draw and to interpret pyramids of biomass.]

These ideas are extended, for Higher Tier students, in Environment H1 and H2 on pages 152–154.

Recycling minerals

It isn't only people who produce waste.
Waste is produced all the time in nature.

Look at the picture of the wood. The woodland floor is
covered in dead leaves. This is called leaf litter.

1 What sort of things do we usually call litter?

2 As well as dead leaves, other things are found in
leaf litter. List <u>four</u> of these things.

animal   acorns   woodlice   twigs   leaves
droppings

■ What happens to fallen leaves?

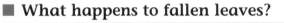

Leaves fall from trees and then **decay** or rot. If they
didn't, leaf litter would get deeper and deeper every year.
Animal droppings and the dead bodies of plants and
animals in the leaf litter also decay. All these things
break down into simple **chemicals** as they decay.

3 Write down the names of <u>three</u> substances which are
made when dead plants and animals decay.

4 Leaves disappear as they rot. But the chemicals they
break down into can't just disappear.
Where do they go to?

carbon dioxide goes
into the air

dead leaves

water and **minerals** go
into the soil

Dead leaves decay into simple substances.

■ What causes decay?

Tiny living things called <u>microorganisms</u> make plant
and animal waste decay. Microorganisms digest the
waste and take it into their cells. It is their food.
Like you, they need food for energy and growth.

Some of the microorganisms which digest waste are
bacteria. Others are fungi.

5 The microorganisms which break down waste are
often called decomposers.
Why do you think this is?

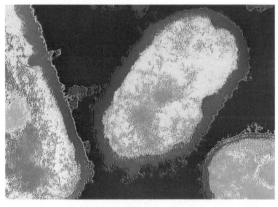

Bacteria (magnified 85 000 times)
which decompose waste.

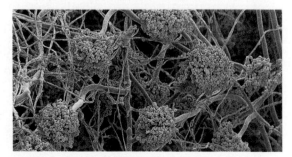

Fungi (magnified 300 times) which decompose
waste.

■ Does all waste decay?

Microorganisms break down waste from living things. We call this **biodegradable** waste.

Unfortunately, microorganisms cannot break down some of the litter we drop. This litter is non-biodegradable.

6 Make a copy of the table.
Complete it by adding things which people drop as litter. (Try to add at least <u>three</u> things to each column.)

These rot or decay (biodegradable)	These do not rot (non-biodegradable)
orange peel	cola can

6 months later

■ Why is decay important?

All living things depend on plants for food. So new plants must grow all the time. When plants grow they take minerals from the soil. But the soil doesn't run out of minerals, because the same minerals are used over and over again. We say that the minerals are **recycled**.

7 Copy and complete the following sentences.

To grow, plants need _____ from the soil. When plants die_____ break them down. Some plants are eaten by _____. Microorganisms also break down the animal _____, and their bodies when they _____. This releases minerals which go back into the _____. These minerals are then used again by _____.

In a stable community such as natural woodland, there is a balance between processes that:
■ remove materials from the environment;
■ replace materials into the environment.

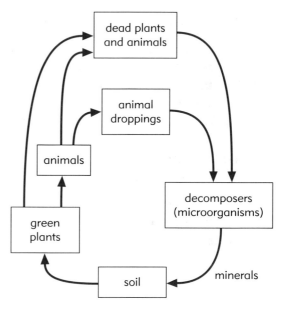

How minerals are recycled.

What you need to remember [Copy and complete using the **key words**]

Recycling minerals

Dead parts of plants and animals _____. They break down into simple _____ like carbon dioxide and water. Waste which can be broken down by microorganisms is called _____ waste. The decay also produces _____ which can then be used again by plants to grow. So the same minerals are used over and over again.
We say that the minerals are _____.

Microorganisms – little rotters!

Microorganisms do a very useful job in gardens. They recycle waste so that plants can use it again to grow.

■ Microorganisms in soil

Just one teaspoonful of soil may contain a billion bacteria and 100 metres (m) of fine threads of fungi.

Look at the diagrams.

1 How many rod-shaped bacteria will fit end to end in 1 centimetre (cm)?

2 How can you get so many bacteria in a teaspoonful of soil?

These bacteria and fungi feed on **waste** such as dead plants and animal droppings. We call this organic waste. The diagrams show what the microorganisms do to this waste.

3 Copy and complete the following sentences.

The organic waste is first broken down into _____. Then it is broken down into carbon dioxide, water and _____. Plants use these substances to grow.

■ Recycling waste in the garden

Many gardeners use compost heaps to recycle plant waste from kitchens and gardens.

4 Copy and complete the flow diagram below:

Gardeners put dead parts of plants on to a compost heap.

↓

Microorganisms break these down into _____.

↓

Gardeners put the compost into the _____.

↓

Plants use _____ from the soil to help them to _____.

5 List <u>ten</u> things you could put in a compost heap. (Remember they must be biodegradable.)

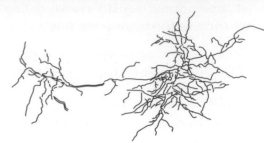

These threads of fungi are magnified 125 times.

This bacterium is magnified 2000 times.

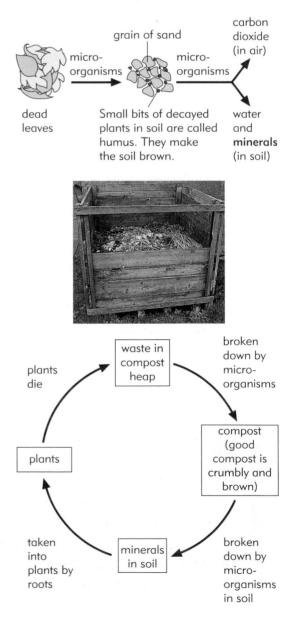

How to make a good compost heap

Microorganisms digest waste in a compost heap faster in **warm** conditions. They produce heat as they do this.

6 Look at the pictures. Which heap, A or B, is best for keeping this heat in? Explain why.

7 Mice sometimes make their nests in the middle of compost heaps. Why do you think this is?

Most microorganisms digest waste faster when they have plenty of **oxygen**. They also need moisture. But no air gets in if a heap gets too wet.

8 Look at the design of heap B. How does air get in?

9 What could the gardener do to stop the heap getting too wet in winter?

10 Compost is dark and crumbly when the microorganisms have done their work. You cannot see what it was made from. Why not?

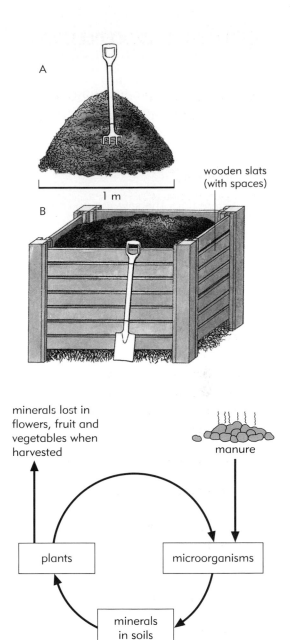

Why do gardeners need to add fertiliser to soil?

Gardeners often pick flowers, fruit and vegetables. So the minerals from these things do not naturally go back into the soil. Plants cannot grow without minerals, so gardeners have to replace them.

11 Write down <u>two</u> ways that gardeners can put minerals back into their soil.

12 Manure is animal droppings, often mixed with straw. What happens to manure in soil?

13 Chemical fertiliser can be used straight away by plants. Explain why.

What you need to remember [Copy and complete using the **key words**]

Microorganisms – little rotters!

Some microorganisms are useful in the garden.

They feed on organic _____ in compost heaps and in soil. They release _____ and carbon dioxide from this waste. Plants need these substances to grow. Microorganisms digest materials faster in _____ , moist conditions. Most work better when there is also plenty of _____ .

These ideas are extended, for Higher Tier students, in Environment H4 on page 156.

Down the drain

Towns and cities produce huge amounts of watery waste. We call this **sewage**.

1 Write down <u>three</u> ways that we produce sewage in our homes.

2 Where does the sewage go to when it leaves our homes?

To stop sewage polluting our rivers and seas we usually treat it in sewage works.

There, organic waste in sewage is broken down by microorganisms.

3 (a) What percentage of sewage in Britain is treated in sewage works?

 (b) What happens to the rest of the sewage?

4 Which part of the sewage from our homes contains most organic waste (contains the most carbon compounds)?

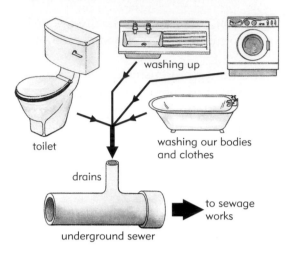

washing up

toilet

washing our bodies and clothes

drains

to sewage works

underground sewer

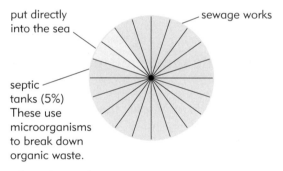

put directly into the sea

sewage works

septic tanks (5%) These use microorganisms to break down organic waste.

Where Britain's sewage goes.

■ Separating the sewage into parts

First, different parts of the sewage are separated from each other. The diagram shows how this is done.

5 Copy and complete the table to explain how the sewage is separated.

Part of sewage	Where it is separated	How it is separated
big bits of rubbish		
grit		
solid waste from toilets		
watery waste		

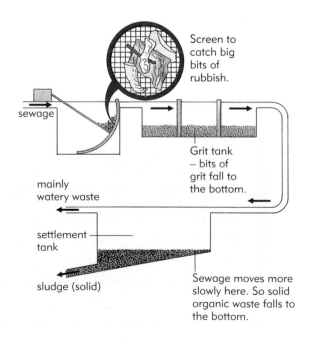

Screen to catch big bits of rubbish.

sewage

Grit tank – bits of grit fall to the bottom.

mainly watery waste

settlement tank

sludge (solid)

Sewage moves more slowly here. So solid organic waste falls to the bottom.

■ Cleaning the mainly watery waste

The watery waste in sewage still contains small bits of organic material. We use microorganisms to break this down.

The diagrams show two ways of doing this. Both ways give the microorganisms plenty of **oxygen**. This means that they can digest the waste more quickly.

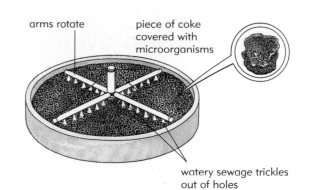

arms rotate piece of coke covered with microorganisms

watery sewage trickles out of holes

Trickle filter method.

6 Copy and complete the table.

	Microorganisms come from:	Microorganisms get oxygen from:
trickle filter		
activated sludge		

The watery waste is stirred up by the air bubbling through it.

This process uses microorganisms already in the sewage.

Activated sludge method.

After treatment some sludge settles out. The water is clean enough to put into the river.

■ What happens to the sludge?

Sludge can be dried and burnt, or dumped in the sea. In many sewage works different **microorganisms** break sludge down in a digester. These microorganisms do not need **oxygen**. They make the sludge safe to use as fertiliser. They also make methane gas which can be used as fuel. Some sewage works use it for heating, others bottle it and use it to run their vans.

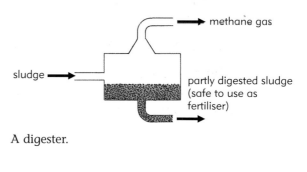

methane gas

sludge

partly digested sludge (safe to use as fertiliser)

A digester.

7 (a) Write down <u>two</u> things that can be made from sewage sludge.

(b) How much of the sludge is used in this way?

(c) What happens to the rest of the sludge?

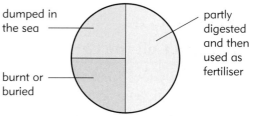

dumped in the sea

burnt or buried

partly digested and then used as fertiliser

What happens to the sludge.

What you need to remember [Copy and complete using the **key words**]

Down the drain

Watery waste from homes, factories and gutters is called _____.
Microorganisms are used at sewage works to break down the waste in sewage.
The microorganisms used to treat the watery waste are more active when there is plenty of _____.
Sludge can also be digested using different _____. These microorganisms do not need _____.

The carbon cycle

Carbon, like minerals, is constantly being recycled. All living things are made from substances called carbohydrates, fats and proteins. These substances all contain carbon. We call them **carbon** compounds.

■ Where do carbon compounds come from?

Plants take carbon dioxide from the **air**. They join carbon dioxide with water to make glucose. Plants use light energy to do this so we call it photosynthesis.

Next, plants use the glucose to make other **carbohydrates** as well as **fats** and **proteins**. Plants use these carbon compounds to grow.

1 Write down <u>three</u> carbohydrates plants make.

2 (a) What substances do plants use to make glucose?

(b) Which <u>one</u> of these substances contains carbon?

The diagram shows plants taking in carbon dioxide from the air. This is just one part of the <u>carbon cycle</u>.

3 You can make your own diagram of the carbon cycle. It is easier to do this one step at a time. Start by copying the diagram on the top half of a clean page.

■ Why isn't all the carbon dioxide used up?

There is only a very small amount of carbon dioxide in the air. Plants keep using carbon dioxide to grow. It doesn't all get used up because animals and microorganisms feed on plants. They use some of the carbon compounds in plants to supply energy. This process is called **respiration**. It puts **carbon dioxide** back into the air.

4 Add the extra boxes and arrows to your diagram.

Plants also respire. So when there isn't enough light for photosynthesis, they put carbon dioxide into the air.

Decomposers also use animal wastes and dead animals for food.

5 Add these two arrows to your diagram.

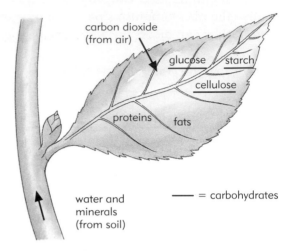

Foods made in a leaf.

What happens to carbon.

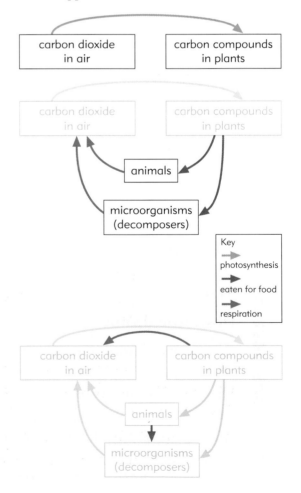

◼ Nature's balanced carbon cycle

In nature the amount of carbon dioxide in the air stays the same. The same carbon is used over and over again. This is why we call it the carbon **cycle**.

6 Look at the diagram.

   Why does the amount of carbon dioxide in nature stay the same?

◼ How humans upset the balance

Coal, gas and oil are the fossil remains of plants and animals from millions of years ago. These fossil fuels contain a huge amount of carbon. When we burn these fuels, we add a lot of extra carbon dioxide to the atmosphere.

7 Add the extra box and arrows to your carbon cycle diagram.

8 Look at the diagram.
   Then copy and complete the following sentences.

   Burning _____ makes more carbon dioxide than plants can use for photosynthesis.

   This means that the amount of carbon dioxide in the air keeps on _____.

The two sides **balance**. So the amount of carbon dioxide in the air stays the same.

Carbon dioxide in nature.

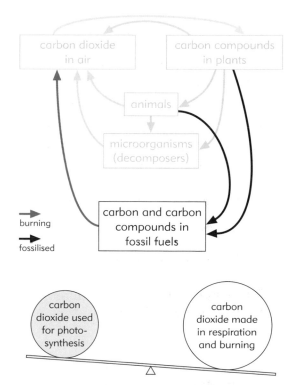

Human effect on carbon dioxide.

What you need to remember [Copy and complete using the **key words**]

The carbon cycle

Carbon dioxide is taken from the _____ by plants.
They use it to make _____, _____ and _____.
These _____ compounds are used by animals and microorganisms to provide energy. This is called _____ and releases _____
_____ into the air.

In nature the amount of carbon dioxide released into the atmosphere in respiration and the amount taken out for photosynthesis _____.
The constant recycling of carbon is called the carbon _____.

[You should be able to show all of these things on a diagram of the carbon cycle. Check that your diagram is correct.]

Sustainable development

In the rest of this section you will look more closely at some of the ways in which humans harm the environment. As the population increases and as we all try to improve our standard of living, the problem gets worse.

In 1983 an international commission on environment and development was set up. Gro Harlem Brundtland was in charge. The Commission produced a report called 'Our Common Future' in 1987. The report talked about the needs of human beings, the environment and the availability of resources. The findings pointed out that there was a difference between what humans <u>want</u> and what they actually <u>need</u> to live comfortably.

Gro Harlem Brundtland, former Prime Minister of Norway.

1 Look at the pictures. Which one should be labelled 'I need' and which 'I want'? Explain your answer.

In 1992, the Earth Summit in Rio de Janeiro agreed on a document called Agenda 21. This document sets out what we need to do to make sure that humans can survive in the twenty-first century. To meet the needs of the poor, there must be economic development. But this must be done in a way that won't damage the Earth and so that development can keep going. The people of the future will then have what <u>they</u> need.
We call this **sustainable development**.

2 What is sustainable development?

3 Brundtland said 'It is both futile and indeed an insult to the poor to tell them that they must live in poverty to protect the environment.'

(a) What do you think she meant?

(b) Do you agree with her?

Millions of people don't get enough food and water or the fuel they need to cook and to keep warm.

"I need some Nike trainers."

"I haven't eaten today. I need some food."

■ Getting the energy we need

We burn fuels for cooking, heating and to make electricity.

4　We can burn wood or fossil fuels or biogas which is made from organic waste. Which <u>one</u> of these is <u>not</u> sustainable? Explain your answer.

5　(a) Why is it more sustainable to make electricity from wind or solar energy than by burning fuel?

　　(b) Write down <u>one</u> use that is better than burning for each of fossil fuel, wood and organic waste.

■ Getting the food we need

Collecting and growing food has energy costs too. To survive, people must gain more energy from their food than they use getting it. Hunter-gatherers in Africa get 5 to 10 times more energy from their food than they use getting it. So they can easily collect enough food for a family.

A European farmer grows enough food for many families. The energy in the food is many times more than the energy the farmer uses. But we must not forget that the farmer will have used up lots of energy from fossil fuels.

6　Look at the pictures. Write down <u>three</u> ways in which modern farming uses the energy from fossil fuels.

7　Write down <u>one</u> way in which the way the hunter-gatherer gets food is more sustainable than that of the farmer.

8　Write down <u>two</u> advantages for local people of organic farming.

It takes lots of energy to make and use equipment and chemicals. Some chemicals harm the environment too.

Organic farmers don't use weedkillers. So we've got jobs weeding the carrots.

What you need to remember

Sustainable development

You do not need to remember any information from this spread.
You need to be able to <u>form judgements</u> about **environmental issues**, including the importance of **sustainable development**, like you have done on this spread.

Think about sustainable development as you study the environmental issues in the rest of this section.

More people, more problems

Nowadays, people have a much bigger effect on the environment than they used to. One reason for this is that there are a lot more people. We say that the human **population** is increasing.

■ How the human population has grown

The graph shows the change in world population since 1800.

1 Copy and complete the following sentences.

In 1850 there were _____ people in the world. By 2010 there will probably be _____ people.

2 What does the shape of the graph tell you about how fast the human population is rising?

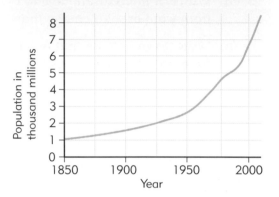

■ More people means less trees

More people need more land for growing food. The last great forests in the world are in danger. They are being cut down to provide land for farming and wood to make things with.

3 (a) What are these forests called?

(b) How long will they last if we keep chopping them down at the present rate?

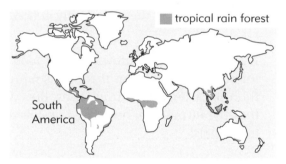

The biggest area of tropical rain forest is in South America. About 1 per cent is being cut down each year.

■ More farming means more pollution

Using more land for farming means that we pollute water more.

4 There is much less pollution of water when land is covered with trees. Explain why as fully as you can.

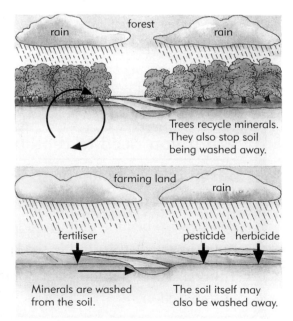

Trees recycle minerals. They also stop soil being washed away.

Minerals are washed from the soil.

The soil itself may also be washed away.

■ We all use more things

There are a lot more people in the world than there used to be. Many of these people have a lot more things like fridges, cars and TV sets. We say they have a high **standard** of living.

This also affects the world around us.

5 (a) Where do we get the raw materials to make all these things?

(b) What will eventually happen to the supply of these raw materials?

6 The things we use eventually wear out. What further problem does this cause?

■ More energy means more air pollution

We don't just need energy to make new things. We also need energy to use them. For example, people travel in cars, trains and planes and all these use fuel. The more fuel we burn, the more waste gases we produce and the more we **pollute** the air.

7 Copy the headings. Then complete the table.

Waste gases	Environmental problem

■ Polluting the whole Earth

Humans have always affected the local area where they live. But there are now many more people, and they are having a bigger effect.

8 (a) How does burning fuels in Britain affect nearby countries?

(b) How does it affect the whole Earth?

Raw materials from the ground. (These will eventually run out.)

ores to make metals   oil to make plastics   oil, coal, gas for energy

These are thrown away when finished with.

Old products are thrown away. They can pollute the land.

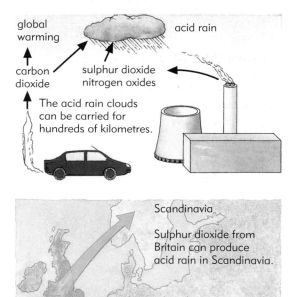

global warming   acid rain

carbon dioxide   sulphur dioxide nitrogen oxides

The acid rain clouds can be carried for hundreds of kilometres.

Scandinavia

Sulphur dioxide from Britain can produce acid rain in Scandinavia.

Carbon dioxide from Britain can affect the air all over the Earth.

What you need to remember [Copy and complete using the **key words**]

More people, more problems

The human _____ keeps on increasing. Many people have a high _____ of living. This means that the _____ materials we need to make things are being used up faster. It also means that we produce more waste and _____ the air and water a lot more.

How humans have changed the landscape

People don't just affect water and air.
They also change the land that they live on.

After the last Ice Age, 60 per cent of the British Isles was woodland. The maps show how this had changed by the year 1086.

1 Copy and complete the following sentences.

In 7000 BC, _____ per cent of Britain was covered with trees. By 1086 AD this had fallen to _____ per cent. This means that there were _____ times as many trees in 7000 BC as in 1086 AD.

2 Was more woodland lost from the north or the south of Britain?

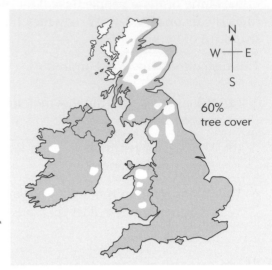

7000 BC – British Isles after the last Ice Age.

■ What happened to the trees?

From 7000 BC   The land was cleared of **trees** for animals to graze and then to grow crops.

From 500 BC   Wood was first used to make charcoal to get iron from iron ore.

The number of people increased. More land was cleared for **farming**. More wood was needed for building.

From 1086 AD   As the population continued to increase, more land was needed for farming and building. More trees were cut down.

3 Write down <u>three</u> reasons for cutting down trees.

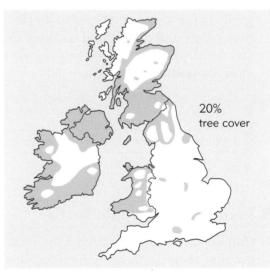

1086 AD – Domesday survey.

■ Twentieth-century forests

Millions of acres of trees were cut down during the First World War. Timber was needed for pit-props in coal mines, paper and building. The war ended in 1918. By this time trees covered only 4 per cent of the British Isles.

4 What was done, after 1918, to increase the numbers of trees in Britain?

About 10 per cent of Britain is now covered by trees.

The Forestry Commission was set up after the First World War. Large areas of new forests were planted.

Effects of losing the trees

Many woodland plants and animals can survive only in shady and damp conditions. When woods are cut down, there are fewer places for them to live.

5 Some woodland plants survive in hedges. Why do you think this is?

6 During the last 50 years many hedgerows have been pulled up to make bigger fields. Why do you think many people are worried about this?

Hedgerows.

What else do people use land for?

People use land for other things besides farming. We use land for **buildings** and **roads**. We also use land for **quarries** for stone, and for **landfill** sites where we dump rubbish.

When land is used in these ways, many plants and animals can no longer live there. We say we have destroyed their **habitats**.

The map shows land use in a small area.

7 What is most of the land in this area used for?

8 What is shown in square B4?

9 Land is also used for quarrying and for dumping waste. In which squares can you find evidence for these activities?

Open fields.

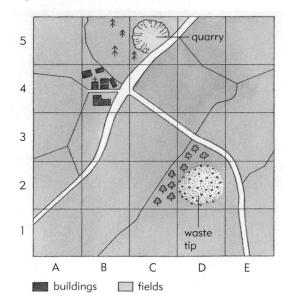

What you need to remember [Copy and complete using the **key words**]

How humans have changed the landscape

Humans often change the land around them. They do this by:

- cutting down _____ and using the land for _____ ;
- taking stone from _____ and using it to make _____ and _____ ;
- dumping waste in _____ sites.

All these things can destroy the _____ of many plants and animals.

[You need to be able to describe the effects of humans on landscapes when you are given information about them just like you have done on these pages.]

How humans affect water

We treat most of our sewage so that it doesn't pollute rivers and seas. The diagram shows what can happen when untreated **sewage** gets into a river.

1 What happens to fish in a river polluted with large amounts of sewage?

2 Why isn't there enough oxygen in the water?

We also pollute water with the chemicals we use on farms and in factories.

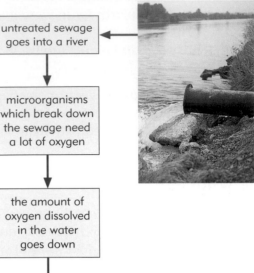

untreated sewage goes into a river

↓

microorganisms which break down the sewage need a lot of oxygen

↓

the amount of oxygen dissolved in the water goes down

↓

fish die because they can't get enough oxygen

■ Chemicals we use on farms

Farmers spray chemicals on to their crops. **Pesticides** and **herbicides** are two examples of these chemicals.

Farmers use pesticides to kill the insects and other animals that feed on their crops.
They use herbicides to kill weeds.

Pesticides and herbicides are toxic.
This means that they are poisonous.

3 Why do farmers want to get rid of weeds?

4 Organic farmers try not to use chemicals on their crops. Why is this?

These poppies are competing with the wheat crop. They take some of the water, minerals and light.

How pesticides and herbicides can pollute water

The diagrams show what can happen to the herbicides and pesticides that farmers spray on their crops.

5 How do pesticides and herbicides get into streams and rivers?

6 What other chemicals can also get into streams and rivers?

7 Where do the chemicals eventually end up?

Farmers spray chemicals on to their crops.

pesticides to kill insects that eat crops

herbicides to kill weeds

fertilisers to help crops to grow

the dissolved chemicals get into streams and rivers

when it rains, chemicals dissolve and seep into the soil

river flows into the sea

Industrial waste

Factories make waste that can cause pollution.

In the 1960s a chemical factory in Minamata Bay, Japan, let out poisonous waste containing mercury into the sea. By 1969 many people were ill and 68 people had died.

8 Look at the diagram.
How did the mercury poison get into people's bodies?

local people catch fish in the bay

waste from the factory

Acid rain

Many lakes in Europe now have no fish.

9 Why have the fish in these lakes died?

Acid rain makes lakes acidic. The rain is more acidic than it should be because people have polluted the air.

You can read about this on the next page.

There are now no fish in this lake.
The water has become too **acidic**.

What you need to remember [Copy and complete using the **key words**]

How humans affect water

Humans can pollute water in many ways:

- with untreated _____;

- with chemicals like _____ and _____ which farmers use to protect their crops, or _____ which they use to make crops grow better;

- by causing acid rain which can make the water in lakes _____.

These ideas are extended, for Higher Tier students, in Environment H5 on pages 158–159.

How humans affect the air

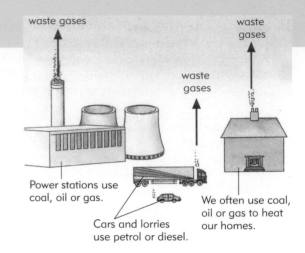

We are constantly putting waste gases into the air around us.

1 Write down <u>three</u> places where we produce waste gases.

2 How are these waste gases produced?

waste gases

Power stations use coal, oil or gas.

Cars and lorries use petrol or diesel.

We often use coal, oil or gas to heat our homes.

Burning fuels produces smoke and waste gases. These go into the air.

These waste gases pollute the **air**.

They can cause acid rain and many other problems.

■ What causes acid rain?

Fuels often contain sulphur. When fuels are burnt, this sulphur produces a gas called **sulphur dioxide**.

When we burn fuels, nitrogen and oxygen from the air also react to produce **nitrogen oxides**. The diagram shows how these gases make acid rain.

3 Copy and complete the following sentences.

Burning fuels produces smoke and waste gases called _____ _____ and _____ _____. These gases _____ in rain and make it _____. Acid rain can kill _____. It also makes lakes and rivers too _____ for plants and animals to survive.

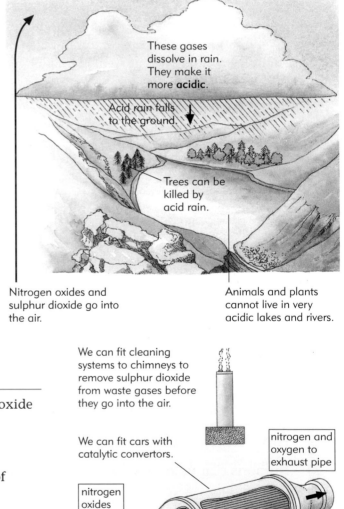

These gases dissolve in rain. They make it more **acidic**.

Acid rain falls to the ground.

Trees can be killed by acid rain.

Nitrogen oxides and sulphur dioxide go into the air.

Animals and plants cannot live in very acidic lakes and rivers.

■ What can we do about acid rain?

To make rain less acid we must put less sulphur dioxide and nitrogen oxides into the air.
The diagram shows some ways of doing this.

4 Write down <u>two</u> ways of reducing the amount of sulphur dioxide we put into the air.

5 (a) How can we remove nitrogen oxides from car exhaust fumes?

(b) What harmless gases are produced from this?

We can fit cleaning systems to chimneys to remove sulphur dioxide from waste gases before they go into the air.

We can fit cars with catalytic convertors.

nitrogen and oxygen to exhaust pipe

nitrogen oxides from engine

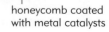

honeycomb coated with metal catalysts

Helping to reduce acid rain.

■ Asthma

Tom has asthma. When he has an asthma attack he cannot breathe in enough air. A serious attack could kill him.

Some scientists believe that pollution in the air could be one thing that can cause these attacks.

Children with asthma who live near a main road seem more likely to have serious attacks.

6 Why do you think this could be?

Tom uses his inhaler to get medicine inside his lungs when he has an asthma attack.

■ Global warming

Coal, gas and oil all contain a lot of carbon. When they burn a gas called **carbon dioxide** is produced.

7 Look at the graph. What has happened to the level of carbon dioxide in the air since 1750?

The rising level of carbon dioxide in the air may be making the Earth a warmer place.
This is called **global** warming.

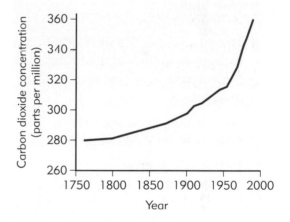

What you need to remember [Copy and complete using the **key words**]

How humans affect the air

Coal, oil, and gas are all _____.
Burning fuels produces waste gases which pollute the _____.
These gases include:

_____ _____

and

_____ _____

_____ _____

These gases dissolve in rain and make it _____.

This may cause _____ warming.

Are we changing the climate?

The amount of **carbon dioxide** in the atmosphere depends on:

■ the amount of **fuel** (including wood) burned:

■ the amount of decay of waste by microorganisms;

■ the amount of photosynthesis.

The carbon dioxide taken up by tree leaves for photosynthesis 'locks up' carbon in wood for many years.

Microorganisms growing without oxygen put **methane** into the atmosphere. These microorganisms live in rice fields, marshes and the guts of animals such as cattle.

The size of the human population affects all of these things.

1 The pictures tell the story of a family in Java. Explain how each of the things in the picture affects the amount of carbon dioxide or methane in the atmosphere.

2 Look at the pie charts.
   Write down the <u>two</u> main sources of:

   (a) carbon dioxide,

   (b) methane.

3 Many people blame deforestation in tropical countries for the increase in the amount of carbon dioxide in the atmosphere. Are they right to do so? Use evidence from this page to support your ideas.

We cut down some trees and sold them for timber.

We burnt the rest of the trees to get rid of them.

We grow rice on some of the land.

We also keep some cattle.

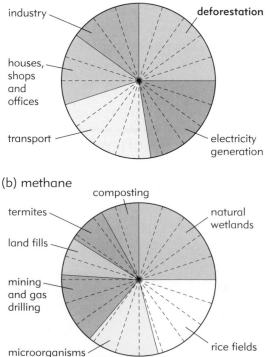

(a) carbon dioxide

industry

deforestation

houses, shops and offices

transport

electricity generation

(b) methane

composting

termites

natural wetlands

land fills

mining and gas drilling

rice fields

microorganisms in guts of animals e.g. cattle

The pie charts show the percentage of the increase in greenhouse gases in the atmosphere caused by various activities.

■ Is the amount of these gases a problem?

No-one is sure about the answer to this question. Some scientists think that the increasing amounts of these gases are causing an increase in the average temperature of the Earth.
They call this **global warming**.

The Earth's atmosphere controls the amount of heat energy that reaches and leaves the Earth. If more energy reaches the Earth than escapes, it will warm up.
We call this the **greenhouse effect**. Carbon dioxide and methane are two of the gases that are particularly good at keeping the heat in.
So we call them greenhouse gases.

4 Copy and complete the sentences.

Two of the gases that cause the greenhouse effect are _____ and _____ _____.

An increase in the amounts of these gases in the atmosphere may cause _____ _____.

■ Is the Earth getting warmer?

5 Write down <u>one</u> piece of evidence <u>from the charts</u> which supports the idea that

(a) global warming is happening;

(b) the rise in temperature is part of a natural cycle of temperature changes.

■ Some effects of global warming

The temperature will only have to increase by a few degrees Celsius to cause big changes on Earth. It may melt a lot of the ice so that the **sea level** rises. It may affect the amount of rain and where that rain falls. It may affect the winds and the lengths of the seasons. **Climate** change may also affect the types of plants that grow in different parts of the Earth.

6 (a) Write down <u>three</u> effects of global warming.

(b) Write a few sentences about how these changes may affect humans.

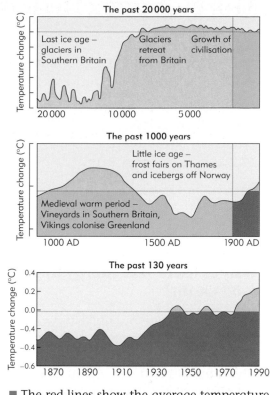

■ The red lines show the average temperature in the second half of the twentieth century.
■ Notice that the scales on the three graphs are different.

What you need to remember [Copy and complete using the **key words**]

Are we changing the climate?

The amounts of _____ _____ and _____ in the Earth's atmosphere are increasing. This may increase the _____ _____ and cause _____ _____ .

Global warming may cause _____ change and a rise in _____ _____ .

Some causes of the increase in the amounts of greenhouse gases are _____, burning _____, keeping cattle and growing rice.

[You need to be able to consider evidence about environmental issues such as global warming.]

These ideas are extended, for Higher Tier students, in Environment H3 on page 155.

H1   This extends *Environment* 8 for Higher Tier students

More about efficient food production

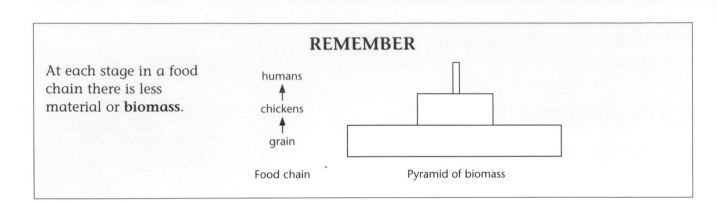

REMEMBER

At each stage in a food chain there is less material or **biomass**.

humans
↑
chickens
↑
grain

Food chain   Pyramid of biomass

■ Why is there less energy at each stage of a food chain?

If there is less material at each stage of a food chain, there is also less energy. So, a pyramid of biomass is also a **pyramid of energy**. Look at the diagram. It shows what happens to the food that a chicken eats. Some of the food is digested and absorbed into its body as sugars, fats and amino acids. All these contain energy. The undigested waste also contains energy.

The cells of the chicken release energy from food when they respire. Chickens, like other birds (and also like mammals), have constant body temperatures. In Britain, this body temperature is usually higher than the temperature of their surroundings. This means that chickens are constantly transferring thermal energy to their surroundings. So, much of the energy released from their food ends up as thermal energy in the surroundings. The chicken stores the rest of the food in its cells or uses it for growing. Only these parts of its food can be passed on to the next animal in the food chain.

1 (a) Draw a pyramid of energy for the food chain:

   grain → chicken → human

   (b) Describe what happens to the biomass and the amount of energy along this food chain.

2 (a) Copy the Sankey diagram and add figures to show what happens to each 100 J of energy stored in grain.

   (b) Draw the arrow that shows the energy for the next step in the food chain in one colour. Draw the arrows that show energy loss from the food chain in a different colour.

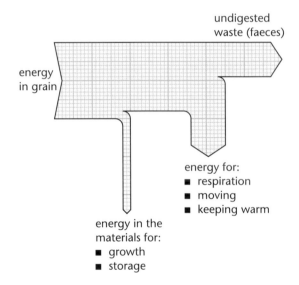

undigested waste (faeces)

energy in grain

energy for:
■ respiration
■ moving
■ keeping warm

energy in the materials for:
■ growth
■ storage

This Sankey diagram shows what happens to the energy in a chicken's food.

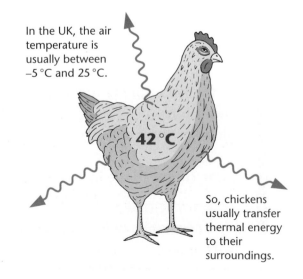

In the UK, the air temperature is usually between −5 °C and 25 °C.

42 °C

So, chickens usually transfer thermal energy to their surroundings.

■ Can we reduce this energy loss?

Most farm animals are mammals or birds. These animals use a lot of the energy in their food for moving and keeping warm. They use less energy if we keep them in warm conditions and we stop them moving about very much.

Then they use a bigger proportion of their food for growing.

3 (a) Explain how farmers benefit when they keep chickens crowded together in barns or in cages.

(b) Explain why some people object to keeping chickens like this.

If we can reduce this energy loss, we can increase food supplies. Another way of feeding more people is to eat more plants and less meat. We call this eating lower in the food chain.

4 Look at the pyramids.

(a) How many times more food do humans get if they eat grain instead of feeding it to chickens?

(b) So, how many more times more people can be fed?

The chickens haven't much room to move about. They keep each other warm.

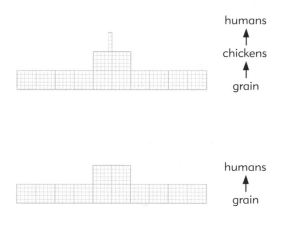

Using your knowledge

1 The diagram shows a pyramid of numbers.

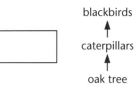

blackbirds
↑
caterpillars
↑
oak tree

(a) Draw a pyramid of energy for the same food chain.

(b) Explain why the two pyramids are different shapes.

2 A farmer insulated the floor, roof and walls of her chicken huts.

(a) Explain the advantages of keeping farm animals in warm conditions.

(b) Why is insulating huts better than heating them with electricity?

3 Fish do not keep their body temperature constant. Birds and mammals do.

The conversion rate (amount of growth) for each 100 g of food is:
   fish   25 g;
   chicken 10 g.

(a) What is the difference in the conversion rates of food for fish and chickens?

(b) Explain the reason for this difference.

H2   **This extends *Environment* 8 for Higher Tier students**

Getting more food to the consumer

A lot of fruit and vegetables are grown a long way from our homes. They have to be harvested, packed and transported to the shops. We want them to be in good condition when we buy them.

1 Look at the pictures.
Write down <u>three</u> reasons why a lot of fruit is spoiled.

Scientists and technologists have researched the best conditions for harvesting, storing and transporting fruit. They have also developed new varieties that stay in good condition for longer after they have been picked. They did this by selective breeding and genetic engineering. Some people object to this.

2 Look at the spider diagram.

(a) Write down <u>one</u> change to the tomato itself that makes it last longer.

(b) Explain why market gardeners usually harvest tomatoes before they are ripe.

Tomatoes are picked and stored when they show the first signs of a pink colour. Extra carbon dioxide in the air stops them ripening. When it is time to ripen them, the plant **hormone** ethene is used. The tomatoes become softer and sweeter as they ripen. But they are not as sweet as those left to ripen on the plant.

The new breeds of tomatoes with thick skins stay fresh for a long time, but they were not bred for flavour. Also some people don't like the thick skins.

3 Some people pay extra for tomatoes that were ripened on the plant. Explain why.

4 Write down <u>two</u> disadvantages of the new breeds of tomatoes.

Many fresh fruits and vegetables are easily bruised and damaged.

Microorganisms soon spoil soft fruits.

Some fruits soon become over-ripe.

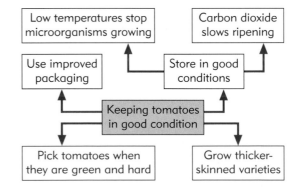

Keeping tomatoes in good condition
- Low temperatures stop microorganisms growing
- Carbon dioxide slows ripening
- Use improved packaging
- Store in good conditions
- Pick tomatoes when they are green and hard
- Grow thicker-skinned varieties

Using your knowledge

1   Explain the advantages and disadvantages of picking tomatoes when they are green

(a) for the growers and distributors;

(b) for consumers.

You need to be able to point out the advantages and disadvantages of managing food production and distribution, and to recognise the need to compromise.

More about climate change

Methane and carbon dioxide are **greenhouse gases**. They cause the greenhouse effect, which is what keeps the Earth warm. **Global warming** is the increase in the average temperature of the Earth.

Without its atmosphere, the average temperature of the Earth would be about 38 °C cooler than it is.

1 Look at the diagrams.

(a) What kind of rays does the Earth radiate?

(b) Write down <u>two</u> things that can happen to this radiation?

(c) How does this affect the average temperature of the Earth?

But, the amount of the greenhouse gases in the atmosphere is increasing. Some scientists think that this will make the Earth warmer than it otherwise would be.

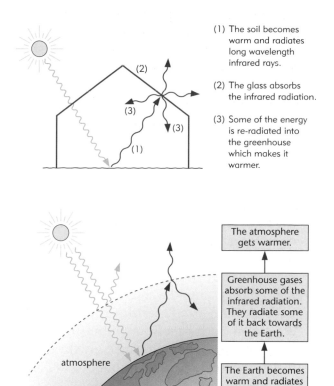

(1) The soil becomes warm and radiates long wavelength infrared rays.

(2) The glass absorbs the infrared radiation.

(3) Some of the energy is re-radiated into the greenhouse which makes it warmer.

The atmosphere gets warmer.

Greenhouse gases absorb some of the infrared radiation. They radiate some of it back towards the Earth.

The Earth becomes warm and radiates long wavelength infrared rays.

atmosphere

Earth

Using your knowledge

The table shows how different greenhouse gases can affect global warming. They are based on comparing the effect of 1 kg of a gas with 1 kg of carbon dioxide.

Gas	Carbon dioxide	Methane	Other gases
concentration before industry	280 ppm	0.8 ppm	0.28 ppm
concentration now	353 ppm	1.72 ppm	0.31 ppm
years it stays in the atmosphere	50–200	10	65–150
global warming potential 20 years	1	63	5800
100 years	1	21	5400
500 years	1	9	3000
Percentage contribution to global warming now	55%	15%	30%

1 Which gas causes most warming now?

2 If no more greenhouse gases are added to the atmosphere, which gas would lose its effect first?

3 Explain why 'other gases' have a higher warming potential than carbon dioxide, but cause much less warming.

4 Which gases will cause problems for the longest time?

H4   **This extends *Environment* 10 for Higher Tier students**

The nitrogen cycle

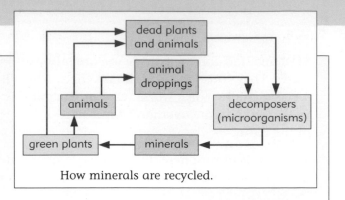

REMEMBER

Nitrogen is a gas in the air.

Ammonium compounds, nitrates and proteins all contain nitrogen.

Plants use nitrates to make proteins.
The proteins in plants pass along food chains.

How minerals are recycled.

■ Why don't plants run out of nitrates?

An **ecosystem** is made up of all the living and non-living things in an area. Farms and woods are both ecosystems. When farmers harvest crops, they take nitrogen away in the plants' proteins. If they don't put more nitrates into the soil, the next crop doesn't grow so well. So, farmers add **fertilisers** to the soil. In a natural ecosystem, such as a wood, nitrogen compounds are used over and over again. We say they are recycled. Animal waste, and dead animals and plants are the fertilisers.

Animals such as earthworms, dung beetles, woodlice and maggots eat this waste or detritus. So, we call them **detritus feeders**. The waste gives them materials and energy to grow.

Putrefying bacteria and fungi also get their energy and materials from this waste. They release ammonium compounds into the soil. These contain nitrogen, but plants cannot use them. Other bacteria change the ammonium compounds to nitrates.

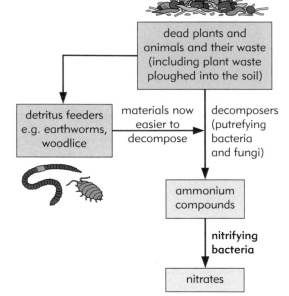

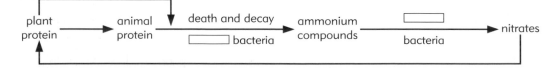

1   Copy the diagram above and complete the two blank boxes.

2   Detritus feeders and decomposers help to recycle dead plants and animals and their waste in soil.
    Describe how each of these two groups helps.

3   (a)   Which kind of microorganism changes ammonium compounds to nitrates?

    (b)   Why is this important for green plants?

■ What happens to the energy in the waste?

When **microorganisms** break down waste, they release energy as well as nitrogen compounds. So, by the time all the nutrients in waste have been recycled, <u>all</u> the energy in them will have been transferred. It is not recycled. It ends up as thermal energy in the surroundings. The diagram shows some of the energy transfers in an ecosystem.

4 (a) Where does the energy entering an ecosystem come from?

(b) Which living things capture this energy?

5 Name <u>two</u> kinds of living things to which the energy can be transferred.

6 Name the process in which living things release energy.

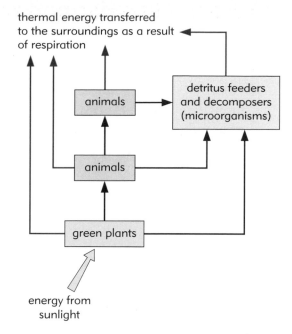

thermal energy transferred to the surroundings as a result of respiration

energy from sunlight

Using your knowledge

1 The diagram shows what happens to the nitrate used as fertiliser on a crop of wheat.

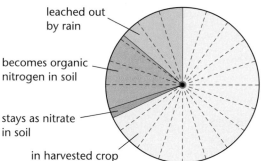

leached out by rain

becomes organic nitrogen in soil

stays as nitrate in soil

in harvested crop

Copy and complete the table.

What happens to the nitrate in fertiliser	%
stays as nitrate in the soil	2

2 Much of the nitrogen in soil is in the form of complex organic molecules which have come from the dead bits of plants. Explain, as fully as you can, how these will become useful to next year's crop.

3 The diagram shows how nitrogen-fixing bacteria add nitrate to soil.

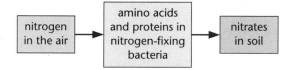

nitrogen in the air → amino acids and proteins in nitrogen-fixing bacteria → nitrates in soil

Some of these bacteria live in soil. Others live in the root nodules of leguminous plants such as peas or beans.

Denitrifying bacteria change nitrates in the soil back to nitrogen.

(a) Explain why organic farmers like to grow a leguminous crop every few years as part of their crop rotation.

(b) Copy the diagram and write the names of the bacteria in the correct boxes.

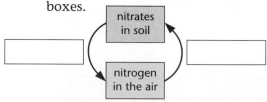

nitrates in soil

nitrogen in the air

(c) Lightning also changes nitrogen to nitrates. Show this on your diagram.

When fertilisers are pollutants

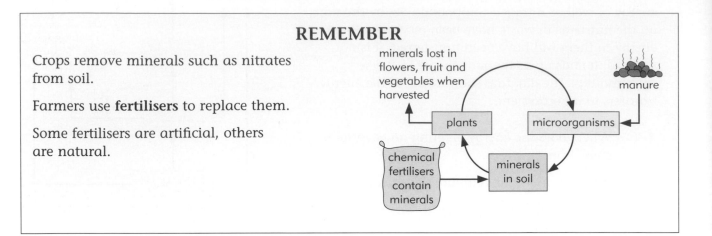

REMEMBER

Crops remove minerals such as nitrates from soil.

Farmers use **fertilisers** to replace them.

Some fertilisers are artificial, others are natural.

minerals lost in flowers, fruit and vegetables when harvested

manure

plants → microorganisms

chemical fertilisers contain minerals → minerals in soil

■ How do fertilisers get into rivers?

Some of the fertiliser that farmers add to soil gets washed out by rain. Natural fertilisers are broken down by microorganisms so the minerals are released into the soil a bit at a time. Artificial fertilisers dissolve in water straight away. So, they can be washed down through the soil more easily. We call this **leaching**.

These nitrates are fertilisers for the plants in the rivers too. These plants grow faster than usual. We call this type of excessive plant growth **eutrophication**.

rain

land drain

Fertilisers often leach into rivers and lakes.

1   Crops don't take in all the fertiliser that they are given. How does the excess fertiliser get into rivers and lakes?

2   The minerals in natural fertilisers are less likely to be leached than those in artificial fertilisers. Explain why.

3   (a) The water plants in the two photographs grew very rapidly. Why was this?

   (b) What do we call rapid plant growth in nutrient-rich water?

Fertilisers drained into this river. It is almost choked with plants.

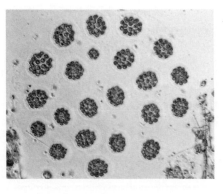

Under a microscope, the water was full of green algae.

How eutrophication leads to pollution

The flow chart shows what happens when the plants die.

Microorganisms feed on the dead plants.

↓

The number of microorganisms increases because there is more food.

↓

Microorganisms use oxygen to respire.

↓

There is less oxygen in the water.

↓

Fish and other animals can't get enough oxygen, so they die.

Microorganisms also feed on the organic material that is present in untreated **sewage**.

4 Eutrophication leads to an increase in the amount of dead plant material in the water. Explain how this happens.

5 Draw a flow chart, like the one above, to show how untreated sewage in a river can cause the death of fish.

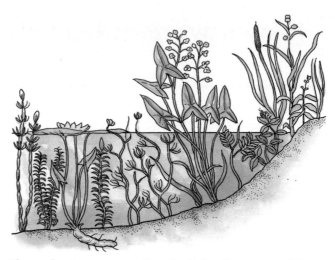

These plants are competing for light. So, many of them die sooner than they normally would and are decomposed by bacteria.

These fish competed for oxygen with bacteria in the water and lost.

Using your knowledge

1   Some students wanted to know if the amount of nitrates in the river water varied throughout the year. They knew that some of their drinking water came from the river and that too much nitrate is bad for your health.

Look at the chart of the students' results.

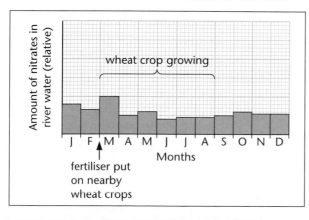

(a) Suggest reasons why the amount of nitrate in the river was higher in the winter than in the summer.

(b) Explain, as fully as you can, why the water had the most algae and other plants in it in September.

2(a) Plot the data on a bar chart.

Fish	Amount of oxygen needed for survival (mg/dm³)
Tench	0.7
Roach	0.8
Perch	1.2
Trout	3.7

(b) Which fish will survive best in water polluted with sewage? Explain your answer.

1 How a woman becomes pregnant

> A woman can become pregnant if one of her eggs is fertilised by a sperm.

About every 28 days:

- an egg ripens in one of a woman's ovaries and it is then released;

- a thick lining is prepared inside her womb.

The egg may be fertilised by a sperm as it travels down a tube called the egg duct, or oviduct. If it is fertilised it will settle into the thick lining of the womb and start to grow into a baby.

1 Copy and complete the following sentences.

An egg travels from the ovary to the womb through the _____ _____.

This is where it can join up with a sperm and become _____.

egg duct where an egg is fertilised

ovary where eggs ripen and are then released

lining of **womb**, where a fertilised egg grows into a baby.

■ How does everything happen at the right time?

The lining of the womb thickens at the same time as an egg is ripening. It is then ready for the egg if the egg is fertilised.

Chemical messengers make sure that everything happens at just the right time. We call these chemical messengers **hormones**.

2 Look at the diagram.
Then copy and complete the table.

Where the hormone is made	What the hormone does
	1 2
	1 2

3 Where in the woman's body is her pituitary gland?

4 How do hormones get from where they are made to where they make things happen?

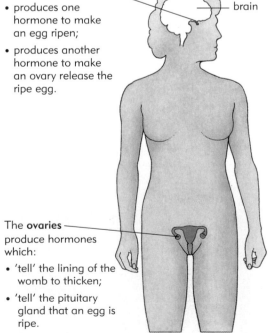

The **pituitary** gland:

- produces one hormone to make an egg ripen;

- produces another hormone to make an ovary release the ripe egg.

brain

The **ovaries** produce hormones which:

- 'tell' the lining of the womb to thicken;

- 'tell' the pituitary gland that an egg is ripe.

Hormones travel around the body in the blood.

■ What happens next?

What happens next depends on whether the egg has been fertilised.

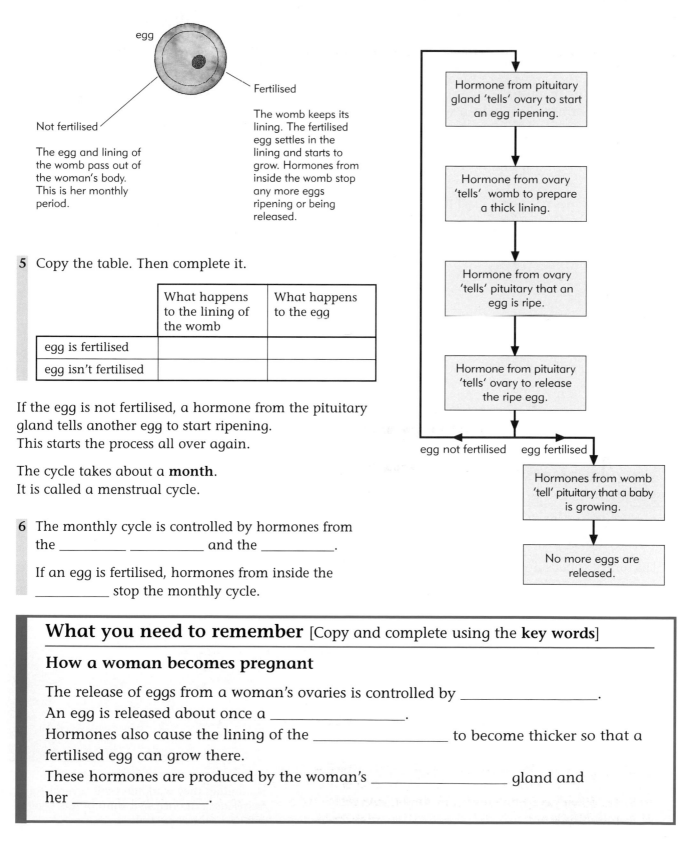

egg

Not fertilised

The egg and lining of the womb pass out of the woman's body. This is her monthly period.

Fertilised

The womb keeps its lining. The fertilised egg settles in the lining and starts to grow. Hormones from inside the womb stop any more eggs ripening or being released.

Hormone from pituitary gland 'tells' ovary to start an egg ripening.

Hormone from ovary 'tells' womb to prepare a thick lining.

Hormone from ovary 'tells' pituitary that an egg is ripe.

Hormone from pituitary 'tells' ovary to release the ripe egg.

egg not fertilised   egg fertilised

Hormones from womb 'tell' pituitary that a baby is growing.

No more eggs are released.

5 Copy the table. Then complete it.

	What happens to the lining of the womb	What happens to the egg
egg is fertilised		
egg isn't fertilised		

If the egg is not fertilised, a hormone from the pituitary gland tells another egg to start ripening.
This starts the process all over again.

The cycle takes about a **month**.
It is called a menstrual cycle.

6 The monthly cycle is controlled by hormones from the _____ _____ and the _____.

If an egg is fertilised, hormones from inside the _____ stop the monthly cycle.

What you need to remember [Copy and complete using the **key words**]

How a woman becomes pregnant

The release of eggs from a woman's ovaries is controlled by _____.
An egg is released about once a _____.
Hormones also cause the lining of the _____ to become thicker so that a fertilised egg can grow there.
These hormones are produced by the woman's _____ gland and her _____.

2

Using hormones to control pregnancy

Some women want to have a baby but can't become pregnant. Other women don't want to become pregnant. Both these problems can sometimes be solved using hormones.

> **1** Look at the diagram.
> Which hormones could be used:
>
> (a) to help a woman become pregnant?
>
> (b) to prevent a woman becoming pregnant?

These hormones are being used to control **fertility**.

REMEMBER

Hormones are chemical messengers.

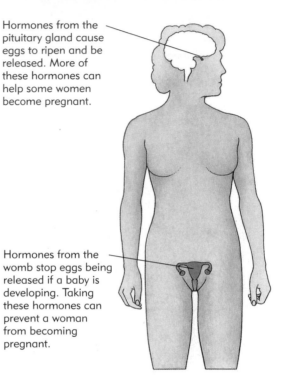

Hormones from the pituitary gland cause eggs to ripen and be released. More of these hormones can help some women become pregnant.

Hormones from the womb stop eggs being released if a baby is developing. Taking these hormones can prevent a woman from becoming pregnant.

■ Using hormones to help a woman become pregnant

Janet and Carl want a baby.
They have been trying for a year.

Doctors at Janet's hospital have found out that her ovaries do not release eggs. There isn't much chance of her becoming pregnant. She is infertile.

Janet can be treated by having a hormone regularly injected into her blood. The hormone makes her ovaries release **eggs**.

We call this fertility treatment. It has helped many women to have the babies they want.

> **2** Why is Janet not becoming pregnant?
>
> **3** What will her fertility treatment do to help?
>
> **4** Write down <u>two</u> problems there can be with fertility drugs.

Fertility drugs don't always work, and sometimes they work too well! Several eggs can be released at once so a woman has several babies at the same time.

■ What's the chance of having twins?

The pie charts show how fertility drugs affect the number of twins, triplets, etc. that women have. These are called multiple births.

5 Describe, as fully as you can, what the pie charts tell you.

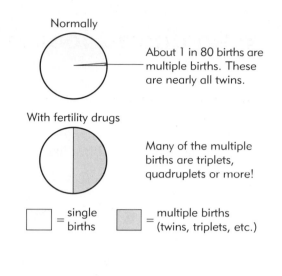

Normally

About 1 in 80 births are multiple births. These are nearly all twins.

With fertility drugs

Many of the multiple births are triplets, quadruplets or more!

☐ = single births   ▨ = multiple births (twins, triplets, etc.)

■ Using hormones to prevent pregnancy

Some couples want to have sexual intercourse but do not want the woman to become pregnant. The woman can take contraceptive pills. We call them oral **contraceptives**. These contain hormones which stop the ovaries from releasing eggs.

However, the pills can have side effects, such as sickness and headaches. In a very few women the pills can cause serious heart problems or even death. Also, the woman must remember to take the pills regularly. If she doesn't, they may not work.

6 Write down <u>two</u> reasons why a couple might not want the woman to become pregnant.

7 Some women who don't want to become pregnant don't want to use pills. Suggest <u>two</u> reasons why.

Couples may want to plan when they have their children.

Some couples already have children and do not want any more.

What you need to remember [Copy and complete using the **key words**]

Using hormones to control pregnancy

Some women use hormones to help them to become pregnant or to stop them from becoming pregnant.
We say they use hormones to control their _____.
Fertility drugs stimulate a woman's ovaries to release _____.
Pills that contain hormones which stop the release of eggs from the ovaries are called oral _____.

[You should be able to describe and explain some of the problems and benefits of using hormones to control fertility.]

These ideas are extended, for Higher Tier students, in Inheritance and selection H1 on pages 204–205.

Who do you look like?

Children look like their parents in many ways. We say they have many of the same **features** or characteristics. For example, the child in the picture has two eyes and five fingers on each hand just like her parents and most other people.

But people's eyes can be different colours. They can have green, grey, brown or blue eyes. The child has blue eyes just like her parents.

Young animals and plants also look like their parents.

1 Write down:

(a) <u>two</u> characteristics that the kitten shares with its parents and all other cats;

(b) <u>two</u> features that the kitten shares with its parents but does not share with all other cats.

The characteristics which are passed on from parents to children are called **inherited characteristics**.

■ How are characteristics inherited?

Gregor Mendel (1822–1884). Mendel was a monk in a monastery in what is now the Czech Republic.

This question was answered in the middle of the nineteenth century. Gregor Mendel worked out the inheritance pattern of several characteristics of peas. Peas are easy to grow and to cross-pollinate. Also, many features of peas have a fairly simple inheritance pattern. So, it was lucky that he chose peas.

In one experiment, Mendel cross-pollinated flowers of lots of tall pea plants with those of lots of dwarf plants. He grew more pea plants from the seeds. He called these the F1 generation. Then he cross-pollinated the F1 plants with each other to produce the F2 generation.

2 Look at the diagram.

   (a) Describe a plant from the F1 generation.

   (b) How did Mendel produce the F2 generation?

   (c) Describe the plants from the F2 generation.

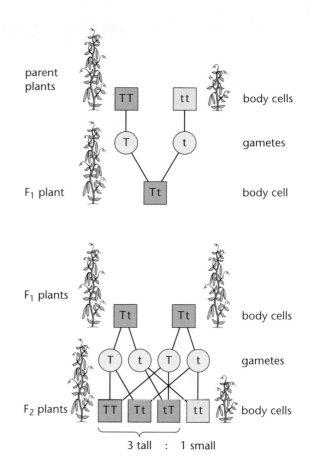

■ Explaining Mendel's results

Mendel explained his results in terms of what he called <u>inheritance factors</u>. He realised that these factors must come in pairs. The F1 plants shown in the diagram told him that the tallness factor was more powerful than the dwarfness factor. A pea plant only needs one tallness factor to make it tall. So we say that the tallness factor is **dominant**. A pea plant needs two dwarfness factors to make it dwarf. So we say that the dwarfness factor is **recessive**. Mendel called tallness, T, and dwarfness, t.

3 Copy and complete the table.

Inheritance factors	What the plant is like
TT	tall
Tt	
	dwarf

Mendel wrote up his work. Like other scientific papers, it was published in a scientific journal. The journal was the Archives of the Brno Natural History Society. It was published in 1865, but it was little known outside Brno. It was 1901 before scientists recognised the importance of Mendel's work.

4 Explain why the importance of Mendel's work was not recognised until after his death.

What you need to remember [Copy and complete using the **key words**]

Who do you look like?

Young plants and animals share many _____ with their parents.
We call these features _____ _____.
Mendel worked out some patterns of inheritance. He found that one factor could 'hide' another.
He called visible factors _____ and hidden factors _____.

[You need to be able to explain why Mendel suggested the idea of 'inheritance factors' and why the importance of his discoveries was not recognised until after his death.]

4

More about inheritance

Mendel discovered some of the patterns of inheritance in peas. Other scientists did experiments using other plants and animals. They found similar patterns. They also found out about human patterns of inheritance. They did this by looking at what happened in families.

We now call Mendel's 'inheritance factors' **genes**. Different forms of a gene can produce differences in a characteristic.

1 How do scientists investigate inheritance patterns in humans?

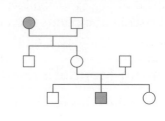

Family trees show how characteristics are passed on in humans.

■ How are genes passed on?

To produce a young animal, a **sex** cell from the father must join up with a sex cell from the mother. These sex cells are called **gametes**.

Plants can also produce young from sex cells.

The male sex cell of a plant is in a pollen grain. The female sex cell of a plant is in an ovule.

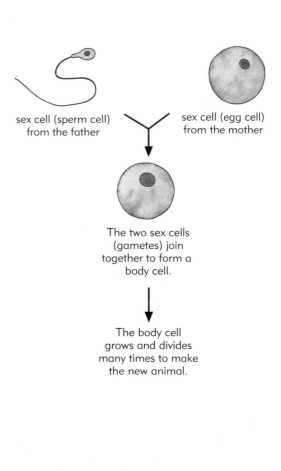

sex cell (sperm cell) from the father

sex cell (egg cell) from the mother

The two sex cells (gametes) join together to form a body cell.

The body cell grows and divides many times to make the new animal.

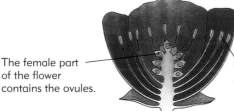

The female part of the flower contains the ovules.

The male part of the flower contains pollen.

2 Copy the table and complete it.

| | Sex cells (g_____) | |
	Male	Female
animals		
plants	in the	in the

■ Sex cells carry information

Sex cells from parents pass on information.
This information controls how the body cells of the
young animal or plant develop.

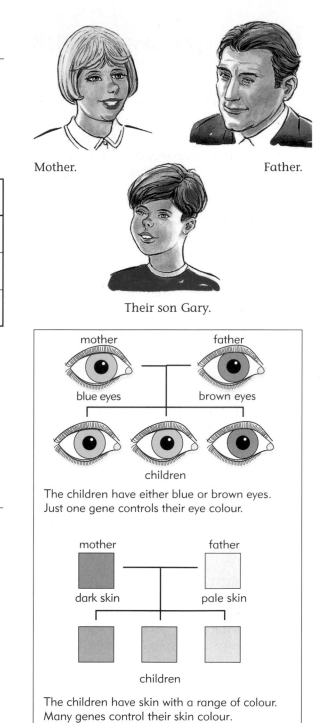

Mother.   Father.

Their son Gary.

3 Look carefully at the picture of a mother, father
   and son. Then copy and complete the table.

	Nose shape	Hair colour	Eye colour	Skin colour
mother			brown	
father	long and straight			
Gary				

4 Which characteristics have been controlled:

   (a) mainly by information from the egg?

   (b) mainly by information from the sperm?

   (c) by information from both egg and sperm?

■ Information is carried by genes

Information in cells is carried in units called genes.
Different genes control different **characteristics**.

5 Copy and complete:

   Some characteristics can be controlled by just one
   gene. An example of this is _____ colour.

   Most characteristics are controlled by _____
   genes. An example of this is _____ colour.

mother   father

blue eyes   brown eyes

children

The children have either blue or brown eyes.
Just one gene controls their eye colour.

mother   father

dark skin   pale skin

children

The children have skin with a range of colour.
Many genes control their skin colour.

What you need to remember [Copy and complete using the **key words**]

More about inheritance

Young plants and animals share many features with their parents.
This is because parents pass on information to their young in _____ cells.
These cells are also called _____.
The units of information in cells are called _____.
Different genes control different _____.

167

Why are we all different?

There are many different kinds of plants and animals. We call these <u>species</u>. Plants or animals of one species are the same as each other in many ways. They are also different in some ways.
The differences are called **variation**.

Steve and Paul are not related to each other. This means they have inherited many genes that are different from each other. So many of their characteristics are different.

1 Write down <u>three</u> differences that you can see between Steve and Paul.

2 Why do they have these different characteristics?

When variation is caused by different genes we say it has a **genetic** cause.

Steve and Paul are unrelated. They show lots of variation.

■ How can identical twins be different?

Sam and Jenny are identical twins. They have inherited exactly the same genes from their parents. Even so, Sam and Jenny are not exactly the same.

Sam has larger leg muscles than Jenny. Sam's body is different from Jenny's because different things have happened to it. Sam runs cross-country races, but Jenny doesn't. We say that the differences between them have **environmental** causes.

3 Look at the picture of Sam and Jenny.
Then copy and complete the table.

Difference between Sam and Jenny	Environmental cause of difference
Sam has larger leg muscles	

Sam and Jenny are identical twins. They show very little variation. Jenny cut her chin in a fall when she was small.

■ Genes and environment

Some differences have a **mixture** of genetic and environmental causes. For example, your genes control how tall you <u>can</u> grow. But if you don't get enough food as a child, you may not reach this height.

4 Ashfaq and David are not related. They are the same age. Ashfaq is 10 kilograms (kg) heavier. Give <u>two</u> possible reasons why you think they show this variation.

5 On average, people in Britain are a few centimetres taller than they were 50 years ago.
Why do you think this is?

The pictures show some variations between people.

6 Copy the following table headings. Then complete the table using the information from the pictures. One example has already been filled in for you.

Genetic cause	Environmental cause	Mixture of causes
		height

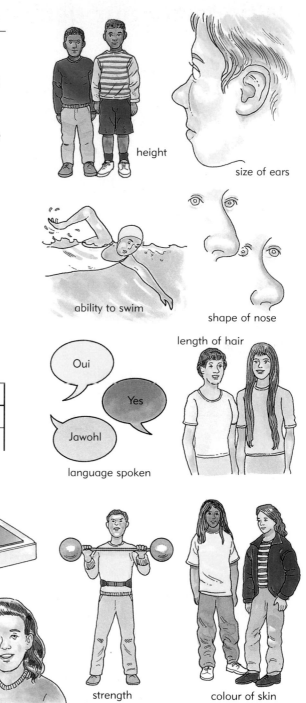

height

size of ears

ability to swim

shape of nose

length of hair

Oui

Yes

Jawohl

language spoken

eye colour

weight

strength

colour of skin

amount of tooth decay

natural hair colour

What you need to remember [Copy and complete using the **key words**]

Why are we all different?

Animals and plants of the same kind are not exactly the same as each other.
We call the differences between them _____.
These differences can have _____ causes or _____ causes.
Some differences are due to a _____ of both causes.

6

Where are our genes?

Our **cells** contain information which tells them how to develop. This information is in units called **genes**.

Our genes are on parts of our cells called **chromosomes**.

1 Copy the diagram of a cell.

2 Copy and complete the following sentences.

We find genes on _____.

These are inside the _____ of each cell.

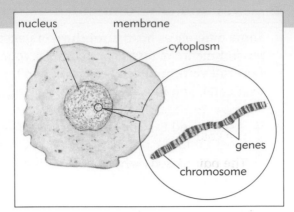

A human cheek cell.

A fruit fly chromosome.

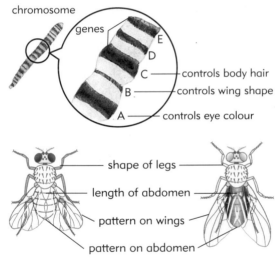

■ Looking at genes

The diagram shows some genes on the chromosome of a fruit fly.

3 Copy and complete the table.

Gene	What feature the gene controls
A	
B	
C	

4 Look at the different fruit flies.
What features could genes D and E control?

Fruit flies look different depending on their genes.

■ How many chromosomes?

The diagrams show the chromosomes in fruit fly cells and human cells.

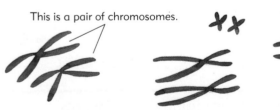

The chromosomes of a fruit fly.

5 Copy and complete the following sentences.

Chromosomes always come in _____.

Fruit fly cells have _____ pairs of chromosomes.

Human cells have _____ pairs of chromosomes.

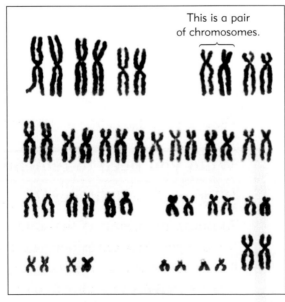

The pairs of chromosomes of a human female.

■ Pairs of genes

The diagram shows some of the genes in a pair of fruit fly chromosomes. Because chromosomes come in pairs, genes also come in **pairs**.

6 Copy and complete the following sentences.

Eye colour is controlled by the _____ of A genes.

The pair of B genes controls _____ _____.

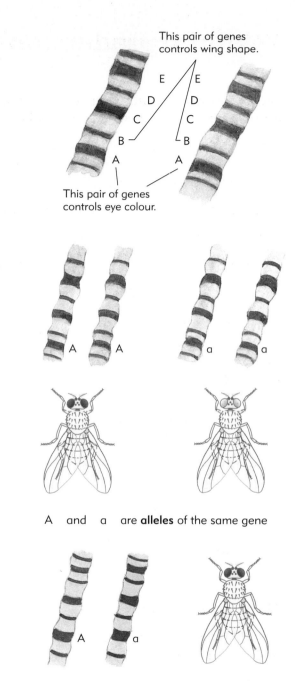

This pair of genes controls wing shape.

This pair of genes controls eye colour.

■ Different forms of the same gene

You can get different forms of the same gene. These are called **alleles**. Different alleles produce different **features**. Look at the diagrams.

7 Copy and complete the following sentences.

Two A alleles make the fruit fly have _____ eyes.

Two a alleles make the fruit fly have _____ eyes.

You can have one allele of a gene on one chromosome and a different allele on the other chromosome. Usually one of the alleles is stronger. This allele controls what happens. We say that it is <u>dominant</u>.

8 Is A or a the dominant allele of the gene for eye colour in the fruit fly? How do you know?

A and a are **alleles** of the same gene

What you need to remember [Copy and complete using the **key words**]

Where are our genes?

Living things are made of _____.

The nucleus of a cell contains many pairs of _____.

Each chromosome contains a large number of _____.

Because chromosomes come in pairs, genes also come in _____.

Different forms of a gene are called _____.

Different alleles produce different _____.

7

Sexual reproduction

A woman and a man produce a baby when the man's sperm joins with the woman's egg. We call this **sexual** reproduction.

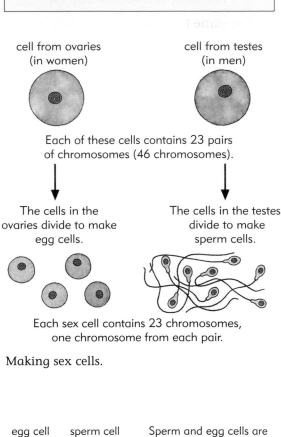

cell from ovaries (in women)   cell from testes (in men)

Each of these cells contains 23 pairs of chromosomes (46 chromosomes).

The cells in the ovaries divide to make egg cells.

The cells in the testes divide to make sperm cells.

Each sex cell contains 23 chromosomes, one chromosome from each pair.

Making sex cells.

> **REMEMBER**
>
> The nuclei inside cells have chromosomes.
>
> Chromosomes carry genes that control characteristics.

■ Sex cells

Look at the diagram on the right and then answer these questions.

1 (a) Where are sperm cells made?

(b) Where are egg cells made?

2 In humans, how many chromosomes are there in each sperm cell and in each egg cell?

■ Passing on life

The diagram shows what happens when a sperm cell and an egg cell join together.

3 Copy and complete the following sentences.

Another name for sperm and egg cells is _____.
These sex cells join to make one cell.

This cell grows into a baby by _____ many times. Each body cell in the baby contains _____ pairs of chromosomes.

One of the chromosomes in each pair comes from the _____. The other chromosome in each pair comes from the _____.

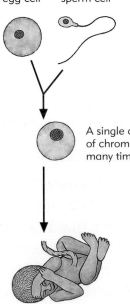

egg cell   sperm cell

Sperm and egg cells are called **gametes**.

There is one complete set of 23 chromosomes in each nucleus.

The sperm and egg join together.

A single cell is made with 23 pairs of chromosomes. The cell **divides** many times and grows into a baby.

Each body cell of the baby contains 23 pairs of chromosomes.

■ Mixing up the genes

All of the baby's cells have chromosomes from both parents. So they also have genes from both parents.

The parents may have different alleles of the same genes. So in their children these **alleles** can be mixed up in many different ways. This means that their children will be different from each other and from their parents.

The same thing happens with fruit flies.

4 Write down <u>three</u> features of the mother and father fruit flies which are different.

5 How many different types of young flies could they produce?

This shows that sexual reproduction produces a lot of **variation**. From two parents you can get a lot of different types of children with different features. This applies to plants as well as animals:

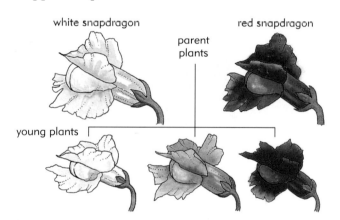

white snapdragon   red snapdragon

parent plants

young plants

6 Copy and complete the following sentence.

By breeding a white snapdragon with a red snapdragon you can get snapdragons which are _____, _____, or _____.

from this father and mother...

...you can get all these different fruit flies

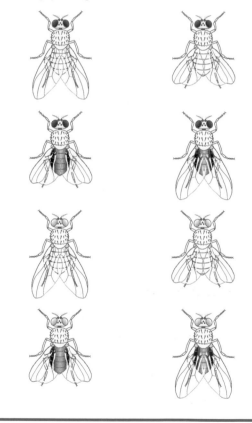

What you need to remember [Copy and complete using the **key words**]

Sexual reproduction

Another name for sperm and egg cells is _____.

When sperm and egg cells join, we call this _____ reproduction.

Sperm and egg cells join to make another cell.

This cell grows into a baby when it _____ many times.

In sexual reproduction, the _____ from the mother and father are mixed up.

This means that children show a lot of _____.

These ideas are extended, for Higher Tier students, in Inheritance and selection H2 on pages 206–207.

What makes you male or female?

Human body cells contain 23 pairs of chromosomes. They are in the nucleus of each cell.

Your 23 pairs of chromosomes look like this:

or like this:

1 Describe <u>one</u> difference between the two sets of chromosomes.

The last two chromosomes in each set carry the genes which make you male or female. We call them **sex** chromosomes. There are two different kinds of sex chromosome. They are called **X** and **Y** chromosomes.

2 Look at the photograph. What difference can you see between an X and a Y chromosome?

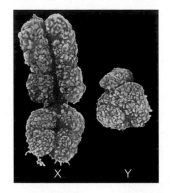
Sex chromosomes.

Each person has either one **X** and one Y or two X chromosomes.

3 Look at the pictures. What do you notice about the sex chromosomes of all the females?

4 What can you say about the sex chromosomes of all the males?

5 Look back at the two sets of chromosomes at the top of the page. Which set belongs to a female and which belongs to a male?

■ Chromosomes in sperm and eggs

Sex cells (**sperm** and **eggs**) have <u>one</u> chromosome from each pair of chromosomes.

6 Copy and complete the following sentences.

The sex chromosomes in the body cells of a woman are both ___ . So all her egg cells have one ___ sex chromosome.

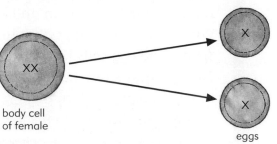

body cell
of female

eggs

7 In men, body cells have one ___ and one ___ sex chromosome. So half of a man's sperm contain an ___ and the other half a ___ sex chromosome.

A boy or a girl?

Whether a baby is a **girl** or a **boy** depends on which sperm fertilises an egg.

8 Copy and complete the table.
Use the diagrams to help you.

Egg	Sperm	Fertilised egg	Sex of child
X	X		
X	Y		

During the first few weeks inside the womb, boys and girls are exactly the same. Then part of the Y chromosome starts working in a boy. It makes the growing sex organs develop into testes instead of ovaries.

How many girls, how many boys?

9 We would expect equal numbers of baby girls and baby boys to be born. Explain why.

10 In fact, 105 boys are born for every 100 girls. Why do you think this is?

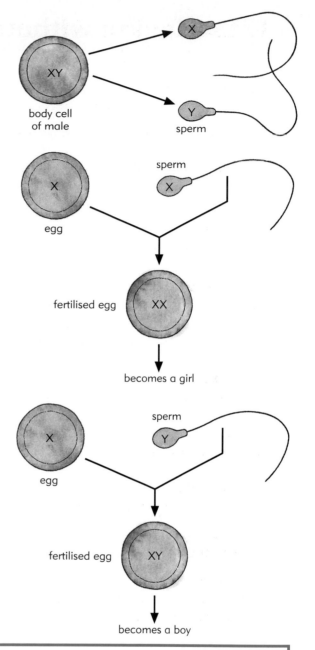

body cell of male — sperm

egg — sperm — fertilised egg XX — becomes a girl

egg — sperm — fertilised egg XY — becomes a boy

What you need to remember [Copy and complete using the **key words**]

What makes you male or female?

What sex you are depends on your _____ chromosomes.
In females both the sex chromosomes are the same; they are both _____.
In males one sex chromosome is an _____ and the other a
_____.

All the _____ cells of a woman contain an X chromosome.

_____ cells contain an X or a Y chromosome.

X egg cell + Y sperm cell ⟶ a baby _____
X egg cell + X sperm cell ⟶ a baby _____

175

Reproducing without sex

As you grow you need to make more cells. New cells are needed for **growth** and to **replace** damaged or dead cells. The diagram shows how new cells are made.

1 Write down <u>two</u> reasons why you need to keep making new cells.

2 How many pairs of chromosomes are there in the nucleus of each body cell?

3 Each chromosome makes a copy of itself before a cell divides. Explain why.

> **REMEMBER**
>
> In body cells the chromosomes are normally found in pairs. Your genes are on these chromosomes.

Making new body cells.

human body cell
(e.g. skin cell)

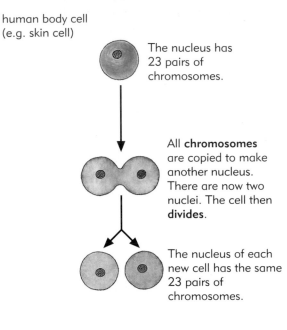

The nucleus has 23 pairs of chromosomes.

All **chromosomes** are copied to make another nucleus. There are now two nuclei. The cell then **divides**.

The nucleus of each new cell has the same 23 pairs of chromosomes.

■ A simple way to reproduce

An amoeba is a tiny animal which has just one body cell. This cell divides just like your body cells do. Then it splits into two to make two amoebas.

4 Copy and complete the following sentences.

An amoeba has _____ pairs of chromosomes in its _____. These copy themselves to give two _____.

The amoeba then _____ to make two amoebas. These amoebas are identical because they have exactly the same _____.

The amoeba does not use **sex** cells to reproduce. So we call this **asexual** reproduction. (<u>A</u>sexual means <u>non</u>-sexual). Only **one** parent is needed.

How an amoeba reproduces.

parent amoeba

The nucleus has 250 pairs of chromosomes.

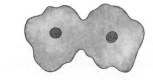

All chromosomes are copied to make another nucleus. There are now two nuclei.

■ Can bigger plants and animals reproduce without sex ?

Some plants and animals with many cells can also **reproduce** without using sex cells. Tiny new plants or animals may grow on the body of the parent. These then split off to make new plants or animals.

The amoeba divides.

Each new amoeba has some 250 chromosomes.

A plant called Bryophyllum can reproduce without sex cells.

5 (a) Where, on a Bryophyllum plant, do the new plants grow?

   (b) How do they become separate plants?

These new plants all have exactly the same **genes** as each other and exactly the same genes as the parent plant. We say they are **clones** of the parent plant.

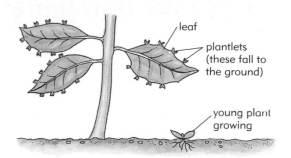

How a Bryophyllum plant reproduces.

How strawberry plants reproduce

New strawberry plants can grow from runners. The diagram shows how.

6 How many parents does a strawberry runner have?

7 Copy and complete the following sentences.

Strawberry plants grown from runners have exactly the same _____ as each other and the parent plant. They are all _____ of the parent plant.

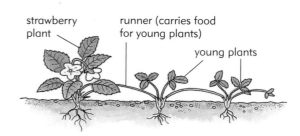

Strawberry plants can also be grown from seeds. They then have two parents.

8 Strawberry plants grown from seeds will all be slightly different from each other. Explain why.

9 Imagine you are a gardener. You have a strawberry plant which grows large and tasty strawberries. You want to grow more plants exactly like it. How would you grow them? Explain your answer.

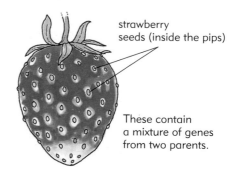

These contain a mixture of genes from two parents.

What you need to remember [Copy and complete using the **key words**]

Reproducing without sex

Body cells produce more cells. First, a cell copies its _____ and then it _____ in two.

We need more body cells for _____ and to _____ damaged or dead cells.

Some plants and animals can _____ by making new body cells.

They do not use _____ cells. We call this _____ reproduction.

Only _____ parent is needed for this kind of reproduction.

Plants and animals produced without using sex cells all have exactly the same _____. We call them _____.

These ideas are extended, for Higher Tier students, in Inheritance and selection H2 on pages 206–207.

10

Some human genes

■ Genes control many of your characteristics

Each of your 23 pairs of chromosomes is made of lots of genes. Chromosomes are made of long molecules of a substance called **DNA**. So each gene is a section of a DNA molecule.

1 Some people compare the genes on a chromosome to beads on a necklace. Explain why.

Chromosomes come in pairs, so genes come in pairs. Sometimes only one pair of genes controls a characteristic. But that gene may have more than one form. The DNA in each form is slightly different, so each produces a different effect.

One gene controls whether you can roll your tongue or not. It has two different forms or alleles. A recessive allele only shows up when the dominant allele is not present.

2 What do we call different forms of a gene?

3 Look at the pictures at the bottom of the page.
Is the allele for tongue-rolling dominant or recessive? Explain your answer.

4 Copy and complete the table.

Name	Alleles	Can roll his tongue (yes/no)
John	RR	
Carl	Rr	
Sam	rr	

> ### REMEMBER
>
> Genes come in different forms called **alleles**.
>
> The allele that controls what happens is called the dominant allele.

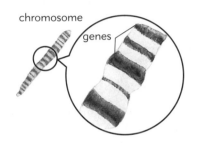

chromosome

genes

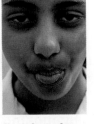

Mia has muscles that let her roll her tongue. She has an allele (R) for tongue rolling and an allele (r) for non-rolling.

Sara has the alleles rr.

Some human disorders are inherited

Some inherited disorders cause serious problems or disability. Others do not.

Huntington's disorder

Michael and his father both have a disease called Huntington's disorder. Michael did not <u>catch</u> the disorder from his father. He <u>inherited</u> it.

What is it like to have Huntington's disorder?

Huntington's disorder is a disease which damages your nervous system. The symptoms appear as you get older, usually when you are about 35 years old.

People with the disorder cannot control their muscles. Their bodies may jerk suddenly. As the disorder gets worse they cannot think clearly.

There is no cure for Huntington's disorder and people die from it in middle age.

5 Michael feels healthy now. How will the disorder affect him as he gets older?

h = normal allele
H = faulty allele for Huntingdon's disorder

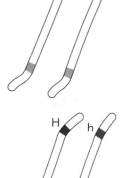

To be healthy you must have two normal alleles.

Even if you have just one faulty allele you will have the disorder.

How do people get Huntington's disorder?

A faulty allele causes Huntington's disorder. Just **one** faulty allele, from **one** of your parents, is enough to give you this disorder. We say that the allele is **dominant**.

6 Which parent passed on the faulty allele to Michael?

7 Why can't people be carriers of Huntington's disorder?

Some disorders are caused by recessive alleles.
You can find out more about this in the next spread.

What you need to remember [Copy and complete using the **key words**]

Some human genes

Genes are sections of _____ molecules on chromosomes.
Different forms of a gene are called _____.
The allele for Huntington's disorder is _____, so it shows up when it is
only _____ of a pair of genes. So, you get Huntington's disorder if you
have a faulty allele from only _____ of your parents.

These ideas are extended, for Higher Tier students, in Inheritance and selection H3 and H4 on pages 208–211.

Two disorders caused by recessive alleles

■ Cystic fibrosis

You can catch a cold or measles. Microorganisms cause these diseases. You cannot catch cystic fibrosis. It is caused by genes passed on to children by their parents. It is an **inherited** disorder.

1 Imagine you have cystic fibrosis. You are in hospital for a check-up. A friend is worried about coming to see you. Write her a note explaining why she cannot catch the disorder from you.

■ What is it like to have cystic fibrosis?

Laura has cystic fibrosis. It is a disorder of cell membranes, so it affects Laura in many ways. She has to have physiotherapy every day to help her get rid of the very thick and sticky mucus that blocks the tubes to her lungs.

This mucus affects her breathing. Also her lungs are easily infected as microorganisms are trapped in this mucus.

Another problem is that Laura's digestive glands, such as her pancreas, do not work properly. She has to take enzymes every time she has a meal. These enzymes help her to digest her food. If she forgets to take them, she cannot digest her food very well.

2 Laura cannot play sports. Why is this?

3 Laura is smaller than most other girls of her age. Write down one possible reason for this.

■ How do people get cystic fibrosis?

Faulty alleles cause cystic fibrosis. You can get cystic fibrosis only if you get a faulty allele from **both** parents.

4 Explain why you need a faulty allele from both parents to get cystic fibrosis.

People who have one faulty allele but don't have the disorder are called **carriers**.

5 A person with two healthy parents could still get cystic fibrosis. Explain why.

> ### REMEMBER
> Alleles are different forms of the same gene.

Laura needs physiotherapy every day.

If you have two normal alleles you are healthy.

If you have one normal allele and one faulty allele you are healthy.

If you have two faulty alleles you have the disorder.

■ Sickle cell anaemia?

Jomo has **sickle cell** disorder. Sometimes he feels well. At other times he feels tired. He catches infections easily. His red blood cells can go out of shape and block capillaries causing painful swellings. Sometimes he has to go into hospital.

6 Describe two differences between the red blood cells of people with sickle cell and normal alleles.

7 Explain why Jomo feels tired more often than he should.

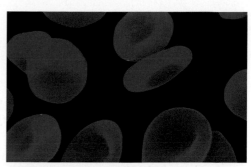
Normal red blood cells.

■ How is sickle cell disorder inherited?

The sickle cell allele must be present in both of Jomo's parents, just like the allele for cystic fibrosis. The normal allele is dominant so that one recessive sickle cell allele produces no symptoms. We call people with one recessive allele carriers. Even when both parents are carriers they don't always pass on the disease.

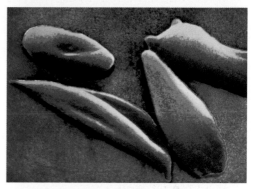
Jomo's red blood cells. Sickle cells don't carry oxygen as well as normal cells.

■ The sickle cell allele can be useful

Doctors think that people with one sickle cell allele hardly ever catch malaria.

8 The maps support this idea. Explain how.

9 (a) Why can it be useful to have one sickle cell allele?

 (b) Why is it harmful to have two copies?

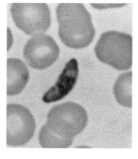
Malaria is a disease caused by a parasite that lives in red blood cells. (The parasite is in the crescent-shaped cell.)

Distribution of sickle cell disease.

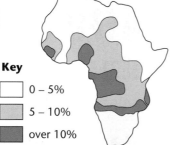

Key

☐ 0 – 5%
☐ 5 – 10%
☐ over 10%

Distribution of malaria.

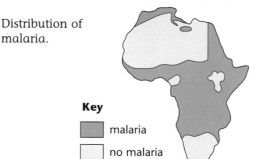

Key
☐ malaria
☐ no malaria

What you need to remember [Copy and complete using the **key words**]

Two disorders caused by recessive alleles

Some disorders are passed on by genes. We say they are _____ .

To get cystic fibrosis you must have a faulty allele from _____ of your parents. You inherit _____ _____ anaemia in the same way.

Healthy parents can pass on the faulty allele; we say they are _____ .

These ideas are extended, for Higher Tier students, in Inheritance and selection H3 on pages 208–209.

12

Mutation and change

Do you ever make a mistake when you copy a sentence?
A small mistake can make a big difference.

1 Sentence b is a copy a student made of sentence a.
How many letters were copied wrongly?

2 What difference did it make to the reindeer?

Before it divides, a nucleus makes a new copy of its
chromosomes. Sometimes there are mistakes in these
copies. We call these mistakes **mutations**.
They are often harmful.

> ## REMEMBER
> The genes that control your features
> are on your chromosomes. Different
> forms of the same gene are called
> alleles.

a Your nose is not red. **b** Your nose is now red.

■ Sometimes alleles are faulty

Joanna has inherited the same faulty allele from each of
her parents. She has sickle cell disease.

3 Look at the diagram then copy and complete the
sentences:

A change in just one _____ causes sickle cell
disease. In this disease one _____ acid in the
haemoglobin is different from the one in normal
_____. This can make the red blood cells
_____ shaped.

1 changed gene
⬇
1 different amino acid in Joanna's haemoglobin
⬇
Red blood cells become sickle-shaped when Joanna doesn't get enough oxygen

When Joanna's blood cells go out of shape they block
tiny blood vessels. This makes her joints, hands and feet
swell up and hurt. She also gets pains in her stomach
and back. Sometimes she has to go into hospital.

■ Chromosomes can also be faulty

Look at the pictures of the chromosomes of two brothers.
Mark has Down's syndrome. He has mental and
physical problems.

4 Write down <u>one</u> difference between the chromosomes
of the two boys.

This one difference caused Mark's problems.

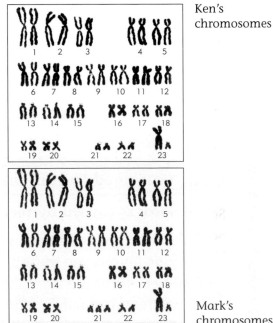

Ken's chromosomes

Mark's chromosomes

What causes mutations?

Mutations happen by chance. However, some things **increase** the chance of mutation. One of these is radiation from **radioactive** substances. We call this **ionising** radiation.

The more radiation you receive, the more chance there is of mutations.

5   What is the biggest source of the radiation each of us receives?

6   What percentage of radiation we receive comes from fallout from weapons tests?

7   How much radiation does a person receive, on average, for medical reasons?

X-rays, **ultra-violet** rays and some chemicals, e.g. mustard gas, also increase mutation rates.

8   Write down why it is against the Geneva Convention to use mustard gas as a weapon.

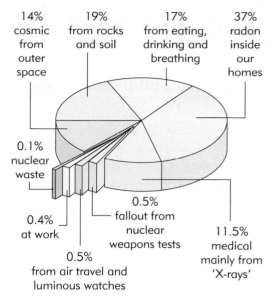

Where the radiation that we receive comes from.

Not all mutations are harmful

Scientists use radiation to cause mutations in seeds such as wheat. They see the effects when they grow the seeds. The picture shows some of these effects.

9   The scientists are very pleased with plant C. Why is this?

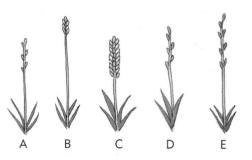

What you need to remember [Copy and complete using the **key words**]

Mutation and change

Sometimes genes change to produce new forms. We call these changes _____.
Some chemicals and some forms of radiation, for example _____ light,
X-rays and _____ radiation from _____ substances,
all _____ the chances of mutation.
The more radiation a cell receives, the greater the chance of mutation.

These ideas are extended, for Higher Tier students, in Inheritance and selection H5 on page 213.

Selective breeding

■ Making useful plants even more useful

People have been collecting useful plants from the wild for thousands of years. Wheat was one of the first wild plants to be grown as a crop. However, the wheat we grow today is a lot different from wild wheat. Farmers choose the biggest ears from each crop. They use these seeds to grow the next crop. So the ears of wheat gradually get bigger. This is called <u>selective breeding</u>.

Look at the photograph showing the original wild wheat and a new modern <u>variety</u> (type of plant).

1 Write down the differences between wild and modern wheat.

2 Copy and complete the boxes and sentence.

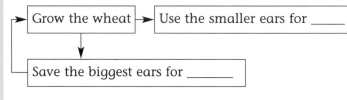

So each year the ears of wheat get _____ .

Wild wheat.

This is called an ear of wheat. It contains many wheat seeds. We grind the seeds into flour to make bread.

Modern wheat gives us <u>more</u> food on each plant. We say it has a higher <u>yield</u>.

■ Why do hens lay so many eggs ?

A few thousand years ago, hens laid a few eggs each year, just like other birds.

3 How many eggs can a hen now lay in a year?

4 Copy and complete the following sentence.

To breed the next lot of hens, farmers choose the hens that lay the _____ eggs.

Today's hens have been produced by selective breeding over and over again for many years.

Different breeds of hens:

■ lay different numbers of eggs
■ lay eggs of different sizes
■ need different amounts of food.

5 When breeding hens for laying eggs the number of eggs they lay isn't the only thing that matters. What other features of the hens are also important?

Most birds lay a few eggs once a year.

One hen can lay all these eggs in one year

Farmers today keep many different kinds of cattle. We call them different breeds. All these breeds of cattle have come from wild cattle which lived thousands of years ago.

Egyptian cattle from 3400 years ago. These were very like wild cattle.

■ Breeding the next generation

Farmers need new young cattle all the time.

6 Look at the diagram. Then copy and complete the following sentence.

To produce a new young calf, sperm from a _____ must join up with an egg from a _____.

Choosing the best bulls and cows for breeding is a good example of selective breeding.

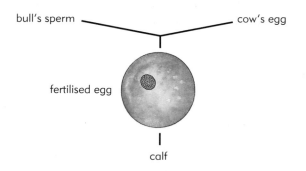
bull's sperm   cow's egg

fertilised egg

calf

The calf gets its genes from both its parents. These genes control what the calf is like.

■ Breeding the cattle we want

Different breeds of cattle are good for different things. We keep dairy cattle for their milk, but we keep beef cattle for their meat.

7 (a) Which two breeds of cattle do farmers keep mainly for milk?

(b) Which two breeds of cattle are used mainly for meat?

8 Why are Friesians the most common dairy cow in this country?

9 Meat from Aberdeen Angus cattle is expensive. Why do you think this is?

10 A farmer keeps cattle for meat. What features should she look for in the cattle she is going to breed from?

11 Another farmer keeps Friesians for milk. What features should he look for in the cattle he is going to breed from?

12 Copy and complete the sentences.
Farmers want plants and animals which will produce _____ food. We say they want increased _____.

They choose the _____ plants and animals for breeding. We call this _____ _____.

Friesians give the highest yields of milk.

Jerseys give less milk. The milk contains a lot of cream.

Charolais cattle are used for beef. They grow quickly.

Aberdeen Angus cattle don't grow very fast. People who eat beef like their meat.

185

Choosing the best of the bunch

People often set out to breed plants or animals with certain features. At other times, a new feature of a living thing suddenly appears.

In the 18th century, a farmer noticed that one of his lambs was born with short legs. He decided to breed from this lamb to produce more short-legged sheep.

1 Why did the farmer decide that short legs are useful?

We call breeding living things in this way **selective** breeding. Another name for this is **artificial** selection.

■ Our best friend

A dog may be our best friend, but sometimes we are not very friendly to dogs. We have bred many different kinds of dogs. But some of the features we have selected cause problems for the dogs.

2 Write down the names of <u>three</u> different breeds of dog.

3 (a) Write down <u>two</u> features which people selected when they bred basset hounds.

(b) What problems do these features cause?

Droopy eyelids – they often get eye infections.   Long ears – they sometimes trip up over them.

very long back

Basset hound

Basset hounds often have back problems.

4 Why is a basset hound more likely to have back problems than a Yorkshire terrier?

Other breeds of dog have other problems.

Yorkshire terrier

5 Dogs with short noses have breathing problems. Which breed of dog might find it hard to breathe?

Narrow hips – this makes it harder for females to give birth to their pups.

Bulldogs have narrow hips.

6 What problem does this cause for female bulldogs?

7 Some people think that we should change some of the features of pedigree dogs that we select for. Why do you think this is?

French bulldog

■ Breeding the dog we want

The diagram shows how the cocker spaniel breed was produced.

8 Copy and complete the boxes and sentences.

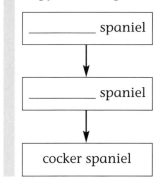

You choose the _____ you want and then use them for _____.

Italian spaniels

They chose the dogs with the longest ears and longest backs for breeding.

↓

Norfolk spaniels

↓

They chose the dogs with the shortest tails and shortest legs for breeding.

↓

cocker spaniels

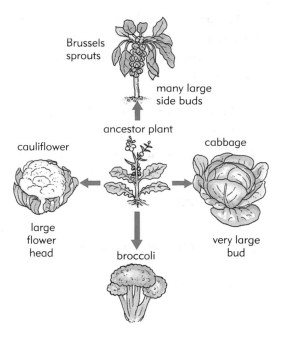

Breeding a cocker spaniel.

■ When is a cauliflower not a cabbage?

Cabbages, cauliflowers, Brussels sprouts and broccoli were all bred from the same ancestor plant. Farmers bred cauliflowers by choosing plants with the largest flower heads. They then used these plants to produce the next lot of seeds. They did this again and again for many years. Eventually they produced cauliflowers.

Brussels sprouts are large side buds.

9 Tell the story of how Brussels sprouts were produced from the ancestor plant.

What you need to remember [Copy and complete using the **key words**]

Choosing the best of the bunch

We breed living things to grow the way we want. This is called _____ breeding. We choose the animals or plants which have the features we want and breed from them. We also call this _____ selection.

14

More about clones

New plants don't always grow from sex cells. They sometimes grow from the ordinary cells of plants. New plants sometimes grow this way by themselves. If they don't do this, we can produce more plants from parts of older plants. We call these parts **cuttings**.

When we grow plants from seeds, we do not know what the plants will be like. Cuttings, on the other hand, have the same characteristics as the plant we take them from.

1 Why do plants from cuttings look exactly like the plant they came from?

2 Making new plants from cuttings is called asexual reproduction. Explain why.

■ Taking cuttings from plant shoots

Dawn wants to take cuttings from a geranium plant. The diagram shows what she needs to do.

Cuttings from the same plant have exactly the same **genes**. We say they are **genetically** identical. We call them **clones**.

3 Write down the following stages in the right order. Use the diagram to help you.

- Plant the cutting in compost.
- Dip the cut end of the shoot into rooting hormone.
- Cut a young shoot from the parent plant.
- Cover the cutting with a polythene bag. Cuttings need to be in a **damp** atmosphere until the roots grow.
- Take off some of the lower leaves.

4 What does rooting hormone do?

5 What <u>two</u> things should Dawn do so the plant loses less water?

Plants will wilt and may die if they don't have enough water.

REMEMBER

Plants are made up of cells.
Cells contain genes.
Genes control what plants look like.
Cells from the <u>same</u> plant contain the <u>same</u> genes.
Reproduction which doesn't use sex cells is called asexual reproduction.

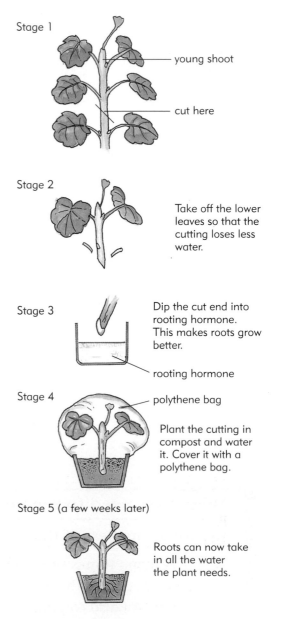

Stage 1
young shoot
cut here

Stage 2
Take off the lower leaves so that the cutting loses less water.

Stage 3
Dip the cut end into rooting hormone. This makes roots grow better.
rooting hormone

Stage 4
polythene bag
Plant the cutting in compost and water it. Cover it with a polythene bag.

Stage 5 (a few weeks later)
Roots can now take in all the water the plant needs.

Taking geranium shoot cuttings.

■ Using other parts of a plant for cuttings

We take cuttings because it helps us to produce many plants **quickly** and **cheaply**. We can also take cuttings from leaves and roots.

African violet

The leaf cutting is dipped in hormone and planted.

polythene bag

new plant

Taking a leaf cutting.

African violets are usually grown from leaf cuttings.

6 Write down <u>three</u> reasons why plant nurseries usually grow African violets from cuttings rather than sowing seeds?

The diagrams show how you can make new rhubarb plants.

7 (a) Which part of the rhubarb plant is used to make cuttings?

  (b) When is the best time to take these cuttings?

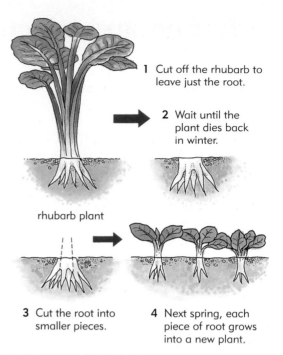

1 Cut off the rhubarb to leave just the root.

2 Wait until the plant dies back in winter.

rhubarb plant

3 Cut the root into smaller pieces.

4 Next spring, each piece of root grows into a new plant.

Making new rhubarb plants.

■ Reappearing dandelions

Cuttings can sometimes grow where you do not want them to. When you dig up dandelions from a flower bed or lawn they often grow again.

8 Look at the diagrams. Why did the dandelions reappear after two weeks?

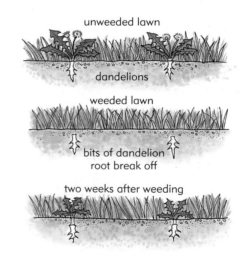

unweeded lawn

dandelions

weeded lawn

bits of dandelion root break off

two weeks after weeding

What you need to remember [Copy and complete using the **key words**]

More about clones

We can grow more plants from parts of older plants. We call them _____.

Cuttings from the same plant all have exactly the same _____.

Plants with exactly the same genes are _____ identical.

Living things that are genetically identical are called _____.

Taking cuttings helps us to produce many plants _____ and _____.

We grow cuttings in a _____ atmosphere until roots develop.

15

Cloning and selective breeding

■ New varieties of potatoes

The parts of potato plants that we eat are underground stems called tubers. They are produced by asexual reproduction, so they are clones. It is these clones that a farmer plants to grow more potatoes. So, if he plants a type of potato called Desiree, his whole crop will be Desiree potatoes.

1 Look at the picture. Write down <u>two</u> advantages of growing a potato crop by cloning.

Potato plants also have flowers which produce seeds. So, scientists produce <u>new</u> types called varieties of potatoes by sexual reproduction. They breed from plants with the characteristics they want. They grow new plants from the seeds and choose the best plants to breed from. This is called **selective breeding** or artificial selection. When they find a useful variety, they clone it to produce potato tubers for the farmers to plant.

2 Copy and complete the sentence.
Breeders produce new types of potatoes called varieties by _____ selection.
They grow plants from _____ and choose the plants which have the _____ that they want.

■ Another way of cloning plants

A way of growing a large number of identical plants even more quickly is by using **tissue culture**. Scientists can sterilise the surface of cells without damaging them. Then they grow the cells on sterile jelly called agar so that there aren't any bacteria or fungi.
The cells divide to produce a mass of identical cells. These can be divided to produce lots of new plants.

3 Write down <u>two</u> reasons why bacteria and fungi don't grow in the culture tube.

4 Scientists add different chemicals to the agar at each stage. What do they add and why?

> **REMEMBER**
>
> ■ In asexual reproduction, a parent and its offspring have exactly the same alleles. They are clones.
>
> ■ In sexual reproduction, the alleles from the parents are mixed up. So the offspring show a lot of variation.

Cloning produces a large number of genetically identical tubers fairly quickly.

The agar that was used at first contained nutrients and hormones that made shoots grow.

Then the plant was grown on agar with nutrients and hormones that made roots grow.

Animals can be cloned too

Angora goats produce valuable wool. So, they are expensive. If a breeder buys only a few goats, it will be a long time before he has bred a big herd. The diagram shows how scientists can use ordinary goats as the 'mothers' of Angora goats.

5 (a) Describe <u>one</u> way of cloning an animal.

(b) Explain why cloning is useful.

Cloning produces genetically identical animals or plants. So, in a population of cloned organisms, the genetic variation decreases. The number of <u>different</u> **alleles** in the population falls.

Problems with cloning

If conditions change, plants and animals that we have selected for farming may not grow as well as they did. Different alleles may make them better able to **survive** in the new conditions. But, if these alleles have been bred out of the population, they are lost forever. This is why scientists save seeds from old or wild varieties of plants and why some farmers keep rare breeds of farm animals.

6 (a) Explain why it is useful to have a lot of different alleles in a population.

(b) Wild potato plants produce poor crops of tiny potatoes. Explain, as fully as you can, why plant breeders are interested in them.

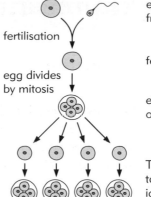

egg and sperm from Angora goats

fertilisation

fertilised egg

egg divides by mitosis

early embryo – a ball of unspecialised cells

The embryo is divided to produce four identical embryos.

Each **embryo** is transplanted into the womb (uterus) of an ordinary goat.

Angora kid.

Ordinary nanny goat.

What you need to remember [Copy and complete using the **key words**]

Cloning and selective breeding

Modern cloning techniques include:

- _____ **culture**,
- _____ transplants.

We have reduced the number of different _____ in some populations of animals and plants by:

- _____ **breeding** or artificial selection
- _____ .

We may have lost the alleles needed for selective breeding to allow a species to _____ changed conditions.

16 Genetic engineering

■ Finding and transferring genes

All your body cell nuclei contain 23 pairs of chromosomes. Each chromosome is made of a large number of genes. Scientists have made chromosome maps to show where all the human genes are. This is the Human Genome Project. It should help scientists to detect and treat some inherited diseases.

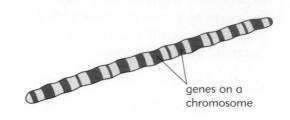

genes on a chromosome

1 (a) Where exactly are genes?

  (b) What are they made of?

  (c) What does a gene do?

2 Why did scientists want to map human chromosomes?

Chromosomes are made of long molecules of DNA. A gene is a section of this DNA. It is a code that controls the order of amino acids in a protein.

When scientists find out where a gene is, they can 'cut' it out and make copies. They use **enzymes** to make the 'cuts'. They use different enzymes to make the copies. They can then transfer the genes into the cells of other living things. These cells may then make proteins that they wouldn't normally make. We call this **genetic engineering**. Making copies of genes is called gene cloning.

The hormone **insulin** is a protein. Scientists have transferred the human insulin gene to bacteria. Now, many people with diabetes use this 'human' insulin. In the past, they used insulin from pigs or cattle.

3 Look at the diagram, then copy and complete the sentences.

  Scientists 'cut out' the human insulin _____.
  They transferred it to _____.
  We call this _____ _____.
  The gene continued to make _____ in the bacterial cells. Scientists grew large numbers of bacteria to produce lots of insulin.

4 Some people think that it is wrong to use insulin from animals. Think of some reasons for this and write them down.

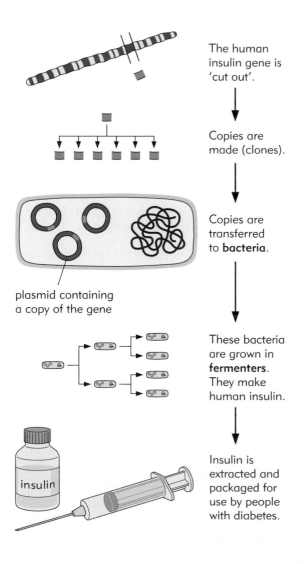

The human insulin gene is 'cut out'.

Copies are made (clones).

Copies are transferred to **bacteria**.

plasmid containing a copy of the gene

These bacteria are grown in **fermenters**. They make human insulin.

Insulin is extracted and packaged for use by people with diabetes.

More gene transfers

Some scientists have transferred genes for different proteins into fertilised sheep eggs. These cells make copies of the gene when their nuclei divide. So, all the new nuclei of the embryo contain the new gene. Examples of human genes transferred to sheep are those producing:

- human insulin,
- a protein needed to treat emphysema,
- factor IX, a protein needed for blood clotting.

Doctors hope to find a way to transfer genes into human cells. For example, if normal genes could be transferred into enough cells of cystic fibrosis patients, they could live healthy lives. We call this gene therapy.

Genes can be transferred into **plant** cells too. For example, scientists transferred a gene for herbicide resistance from a bacterium into sugar beet.

5 Describe <u>one</u> example of gene transfer in an animal and <u>one</u> in a plant.

6 Many farmers save money by planting seeds from a previous year's crop. Some charities think that herbicide resistant crops are bad for farmers in poor countries. Why is this?

Scientists hope that this sheep will secrete human factor IX in its milk.

This sugar beet will not be killed when the farmer sprays the field with herbicide (weedkiller). But the farmer has to buy new seed and the matching weedkiller each year. Saved seeds do not grow.

What you need to remember [Copy and complete using the **key words**]

Genetic engineering

Genes control the production of proteins such as the hormone _____ in cells.

We can make use of some genes. Scientists can:
- find a useful gene,
- 'cut' it out using _____,
- make copies of the gene,
- transfer the copies to _____.

This is _____ **engineering**.

The genetically engineered bacteria are grown in _____ to produce large amounts of the useful protein.

Scientists can also transfer genes into animal and _____ cells.

[You may be asked to consider economic, social and ethical issues concerning cloning and genetic engineering.]

Evolution

In nature, plants and animals usually produce more offspring than there is space or food for. So, only a few of the offspring survive long enough to **breed**.

1 (a) Describe the two forms of moth in the picture.

   (b) Which one is the more likely to die before it can breed? Explain your answer.

So, the moths that breed are the ones that are best suited to that particular **environment**. They pass on the alleles. It <u>looks as if</u> the environment has 'selected' moths with the useful characteristics. So we call it **natural selection**.

2 (a) What changes did the Industrial Revolution cause in the moths' environment?

   (b) In what way did the changes affect the moth population?

■ A more worrying change

We use antibiotics to kill the bacteria that cause disease. Sometimes mutations in bacteria stop an antibiotic killing them. We say the bacteria have become antibiotic resistant.

In 1972, there was an epidemic of typhoid in Mexico. Normally an antibiotic called chloramphenicol cured it. This time it didn't work. Over 14 000 people died. Eventually they found an antibiotic that worked.

3 Explain, as fully as you can, why chloramphenicol didn't control this epidemic.

■ Explaining change

In the nineteenth century, Charles Darwin collected a lot of evidence about changes in plants and animals. He was not the first scientist to suggest the idea of change or **evolution**. But he and Alfred Russel Wallace were the first to explain <u>how</u> it could happen. They called it evolution by natural selection. Many people mocked the idea. It was not what they had been taught and it went against what the Bible said. Now many people do accept it, but not everyone.

4 Why did it take so long for Darwin's idea to be accepted?

REMEMBER

We use artificial selection to produce plants and animals with the characteristics we want. Many don't survive long enough to breed.
So they don't pass on their genes to the next generation.

Peppered moths rest on tree trunks during the day. Only the best camouflaged moths escape being eaten by birds.

Before the Industrial Revolution, tree trunks were light coloured and covered in lichen. Most peppered moths were light then.
Once the Industrial Revolution started, many trees had no lichen and their bark was covered in soot. Most peppered moths were then dark.

Chloramphenicol was used in people without prescription or supervision. It was <u>over-used</u>.

↓

A few bacteria developed resistance to chloramphenicol. They were mutants.

↓

The mutant forms multiplied.

↓

Only mutant forms survived. Chloramphenicol was no use against them.

■ Causes of natural selection

You have seen that some animals are better at avoiding predators than others.

5 Write down <u>two</u> other reasons why some plants and animals are better able to survive than others.

Thousands of years ago, the animals that evolved into giraffes were not as tall as giraffes are now. Over a long period of time, the legs and necks of giraffes got longer and longer. They could reach leaves high in the trees, as well as reaching down for water.

6 Copy and complete the diagram below.

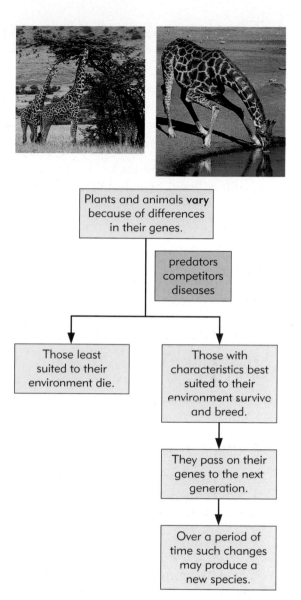

Giraffes ancestors varied because of differences in their _____

Some were better at reaching _____ than others

Some starved

The tallest ones survived and _____

They passed on the alleles for long _____ and _____

Over a period of time giraffes got _____

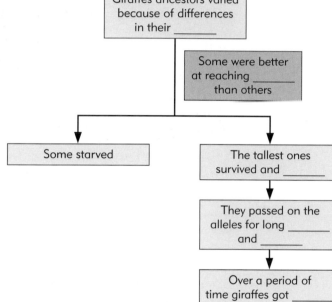

Plants and animals **vary** because of differences in their genes.

predators
competitors
diseases

Those least suited to their environment die.

Those with characteristics best suited to their environment survive and breed.

They pass on their genes to the next generation.

Over a period of time such changes may produce a new species.

How natural selection can produce a new species. (Darwin's idea of natural selection was very similar, except that he didn't know about genes.)

Fossils also give us evidence for change. The next few pages tell you more about this.

What you need to remember [Copy and complete using the **key words**]

Evolution

Individuals in a species _____ because of differences in their genes.
They compete for food and try to avoid predators and disease. Many die.
Those which survive and _____ are the ones with the characteristics best
suited to their _____.
Their genes have enabled them to survive. They pass these on to the next generation.
Over a period of time a species changes. This is _____ by
_____ _____.

These ideas are extended, for Higher Tier students, in Inheritance and selection H5 on pages 212–213.

The mystery of fossils

The fossils in the picture were found near Whitby on the Yorkshire coast. The people of Whitby used to say that an ammonite was a snake turned into stone by St Hilda. They called another fossil a devil's toenail.

Fossils are found in **rocks**. That is why cliffs at the seaside are good places to look for them.

ammonite

devil's toenail (gryphaea)

Quarrying.

Road cutting.

1 (a) Write down <u>two</u> other places where you could look for fossils.

   (b) What is similar about these two places?

■ What do scientists think fossils are?

Scientists think that fossils are the remains of dead **plants** and **animals** from millions of years ago. The devil's toenail and the ammonite both lived in the sea more than 180 million years ago.

The diagram shows how ammonites became fossils.

2 How long ago did ammonites live?

3 Write down the following sentences in the right order. Use the diagrams to help you.

   ■ Ammonite fossils were then surrounded by rock.

   ■ Layers of sand and mud covered the ammonites.

   ■ Ammonites died and fell to the bottom of the sea.

   ■ The sand and mud turned into rock.

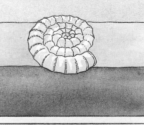

Ammonites lived in the sea about 180 million years ago.

When they died they fell to the bottom and were covered with sand and mud.

The sand and mud slowly changed into rock.

fossil ammonite

■ What sort of remains are found?

Some parts of plants and animals are more likely to become fossils than other parts.

4 What is similar about the parts of plants and animals which are common fossils?

Soft parts of dead animals and plants may be eaten by animals. They also rot or **decay** easily. They do not last long enough to become fossils. Most fossils are formed from **hard** parts, which do not **decay** very quickly. Sometimes only traces remain. We may find signs of plant rootlets or animal burrows and footprints.

The photograph shows a dinosaur's footprint. The diagrams show how this footprint has lasted for millions of years.

5 Explain how the dinosaur's footprint came to be in the rock.

Common fossils are from hard parts of living things, for example shells and bones.

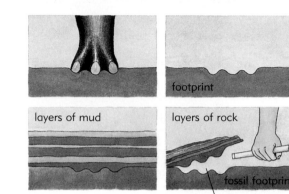

layers of mud

footprint

layers of rock

fossil footprint

■ Where did the plants and animals live?

About 90 per cent of all fossils found are the remains of sea creatures. They were buried in the mud or sand on the sea bed.

6 Why are the remains of land animals and plants uncommon?

Ammonites are similar to a sea creature called a pearly nautilus which still lives in tropical seas.
Look at its tentacles.

7 The fossil ammonite has no tentacles. Write down <u>two</u> things which could have happened to them.

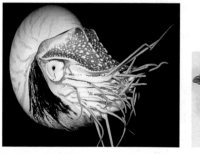

Pearly nautilus.   Ammonite.

What you need to remember [Copy and complete using the **key words**]

The mystery of fossils

Fossils are found in _____.
They are the preserved traces and 'remains' of dead _____ and
_____ from many years ago.
Soft parts of plants and animals usually _____ too fast to form fossils.
Fossils are usually formed from _____ parts of plants and animals.
These parts do not _____ quickly.

Some special fossils

All **fossils** are the remains of dead animals and plants. Most fossils are made from the hard parts of animals and plants. Often these hard parts stay the same.

A shell is made of a mineral called calcite. The diagrams show what happens when a shell is buried in bits of other shells.

1 Copy and complete the following sentences.

The shell becomes a _____.

It is made of _____.

The bits of shell form a rock called _____.

Sometimes the hard parts of the plants or animals don't stay the same. They can be turned into stone.

When they are turned to stone we say they are petrified.

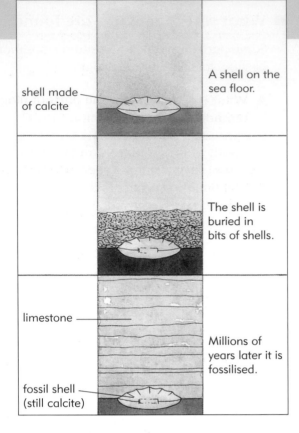

shell made of calcite — A shell on the sea floor.

The shell is buried in bits of shells.

limestone

Millions of years later it is fossilised.

fossil shell (still calcite)

■ How do fossils get turned into stone?

Sometimes a shell is buried in layers of sand. Sand contains a mineral called silica.

The diagram shows what can then happen.

2 Copy and complete the following sentences.

A mineral called _____ replaces the _____ in the shell. It does this a tiny bit at a time.

This turns the shell into a _____.

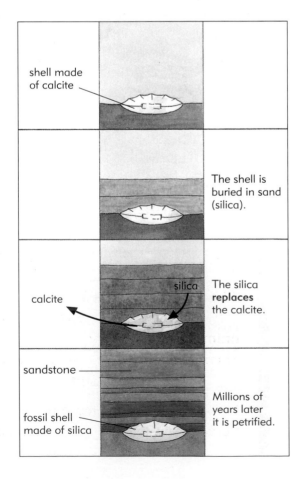

shell made of calcite

The shell is buried in sand (silica).

calcite   silica — The silica **replaces** the calcite.

sandstone

Millions of years later it is petrified.

fossil shell made of silica

The picture shows a slice across a fossil tree.
The wood has been turned into stone.

3 How do we know the fossil was once a tree?

4 You can still see the detail of what the wood was like. Explain why.

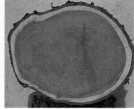

Silica has replaced the wood a bit at a time.

This is a slice of a tree which has just been cut down.

■ Are soft parts of plants and animals ever preserved?

Soft parts of plants and animals usually decay quite quickly. This is because microorganisms feed on them. Microorganisms need **oxygen**, **moisture** and **warmth** to feed and grow.

Without all of these conditions, microorganisms cannot cause **decay**. The plants and animals are preserved.

We often find fossil insects in amber. Sometimes soft parts of plants and animals can be preserved for long enough in other ways to form fossils.

5 The animals in the pictures were preserved because one of the conditions for decay was missing. In each case, give one reason why the animal did not decay.

6 The photograph below shows a fossil leaf. How could it have been preserved for long enough to form a fossil?

This mummified animal was found in the desert.

This baby mammoth was found frozen in ice.

Spider in amber. Resin from a tree set hard around this spider. Oxygen could not get to it.

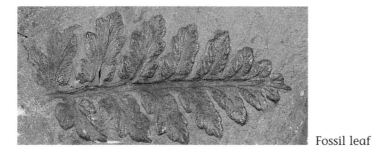

Fossil leaf

What you need to remember [Copy and complete using the **key words**]

Some special fossils

Some fossils are formed when another material _____ parts of a plant or animal a bit at a time.

Microorganisms cause decay. They do this fastest when they have _____, _____ and _____.

Sometimes soft parts do not _____ because one or more of these conditions for decay are absent. These soft parts can then form _____.

20

Three billion years of life

Scientists think that the Earth was formed about 4600 million years ago. They think that life on Earth began over 3000 million (**three billion**) years ago.

1 For about what fraction of its history has there been life on Earth? Choose from:

(a) half

(b) more than half

(c) less than half

Rocks that are more than about 600 million years old contain very few fossils. But this does not mean that there weren't many living things before then.

2 Look at the picture of a fossil which has been found in rocks more than 600 million years old.
Explain why this type of fossil is rare.

■ New forms of life

Fossils can also tell us how life on Earth has changed. Most scientists think that all species of living things on Earth today came from earlier, simpler species. We say that living things have **evolved**.

3 Where do scientists think that life began?

4 Copy and complete the following sentences.

Simple forms of life _____ into plants and animals. These then evolved into bigger and more _____ plants and animals.

■ Some ancient species

We know from fossils that some plants and animals are very like their ancestors. They have changed very **little**.

5 Show which fossils were the ancestors of the modern plants and animals in the diagram.
For example:
A ⟶ ginkgo

This shows a fossilised jellyfish. Jellyfish have no hard parts.

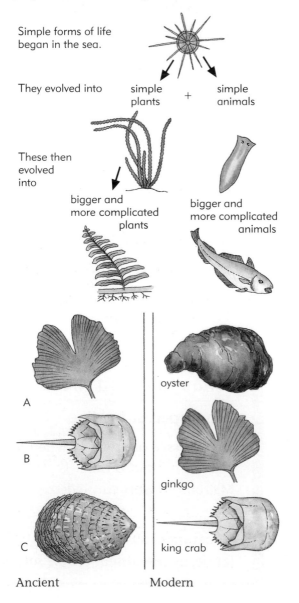

Simple forms of life began in the sea.

They evolved into simple plants + simple animals

These then evolved into bigger and more complicated plants

bigger and more complicated animals

A

B

C

oyster

ginkgo

king crab

Ancient   Modern

■ Which plants and animals lived when?

Scientists can use fossils to tell them which plants and animals lived when. The diagram shows some of the things scientists have found out.

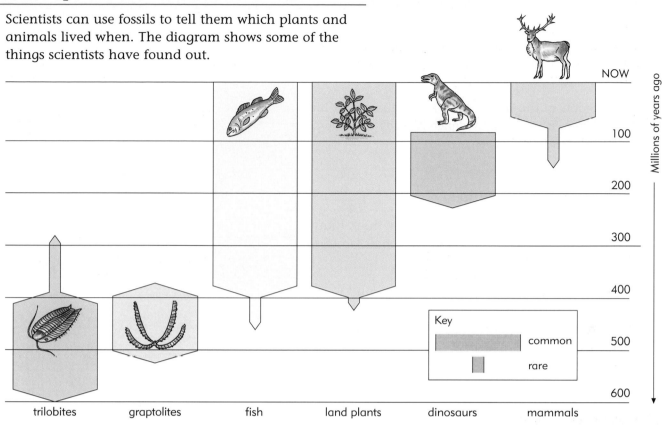

You can see from the diagram that graptolites were very common between 400 and 500 million years ago.
Then they died out. We say they became **extinct**.

6 When did trilobites first appear?

7 When did trilobites become extinct?

8 Which group of animals first appeared about 220 million years ago?

9 Name a group of animals which became common between 300 and 400 million years ago.

10 How long ago did the first mammals appear?

What you need to remember [Copy and complete using the **key words**]

Three billion years of life

All species of plants and animals which exist today _____ from simple life forms. These first developed more than _____ _____ years ago. Some have changed a lot. Others have changed very _____.

Many plants and animals have died out or become _____.

21

Fossil detective stories

Fossils can tell us a lot about living things in the past and how they changed. They tell us how living things **evolved**.

There are lots of things we don't know about past life because there is no fossil evidence. We say that there are <u>gaps</u> in the fossil record.

■ Some changes were big

Scientists have studied fossil horses. They think that today's horses evolved from small mammals which ate soft leaves from bushes.

The fossils in older rocks showed that the animals were small and had teeth with few ridges. In younger rocks the animals were bigger and had longer teeth. The teeth had strong ridges for grinding tough grass.

1 Copy and complete the table to show how horses changed.

Older fossils	Younger fossils
small animals	_____ animals
_____ teeth	longer teeth
teeth with _____ ridges	teeth with _____ ridges

2 Write down how the toes changed:

(a) between horses 1 and 2

(b) between horses 2 and 3

(c) between horses 3 and 4.

Scientists think that these changes took place because the environment changed. They think that grassy plains took the place of trees and bushes.

The horses which were best at chewing tough grass and at running fast survived. They bred and passed on their genes, so the young horses they produced were also good at running and chewing tough grass.

3 Why is speed more important on grassy plains than where there are bushes?

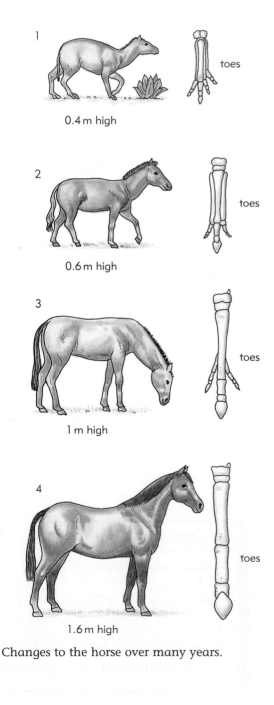

1
toes
0.4 m high

2
toes
0.6 m high

3
toes
1 m high

4
toes
1.6 m high

Changes to the horse over many years.

Other changes were smaller

A scientist worked out how an oyster called Ostrea evolved into a different oyster called Gryphaea. The chart shows what he found.

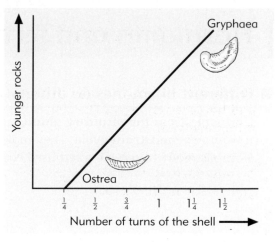

4 The Gryphaea shell has more _____ than the Ostrea shell.

5 About how many turns has

(a) the oldest shell, and

(b) the youngest shell?

The most curved modern oysters live in the muddiest seas. The curve keeps the opening of the oyster above the sea bed. This stops the shell filling up with mud.

6 Ostrea probably evolved into Gryphaea because of a change in the environment 180 million years ago. What could this change have been?

Why did dinosaurs become extinct?

If the environment changes quickly but an animal or plant cannot change quickly, it will die out. It will become **extinct**. Dinosaurs became extinct about 65 million years ago. Scientists argue about the reason. Look at some of their ideas.

7 Choose one of the ideas which you think is <u>not</u> very sensible. Explain why you think it is probably wrong. (Use the 'Information box' to help you.)

8 Explain, as fully as you can, how a meteorite could have made dinosaurs extinct.

Ideas that could explain the extinction of dinosaurs

- New **predators** killed them.

- A very big meteorite hit the Earth. Dust blocked out the sun.

- A new **disease** killed them.

- New **competitors** took over their food.

Information to help you

- Plants cannot grow without the Sun.

- The biggest dinosaurs were bigger than other animals at that time.

- Most dinosaurs ate plants.

- Dinosaurs probably couldn't survive very cold weather.

What you need to remember [Copy and complete using the **key words**]

Fossil detective stories

We can learn from _____ how animals and plants have changed or _____ since life began on Earth. Species may become _____ if the environment which they need to survive changes.

Extinction can happen because of new _____, new _____ or new _____.

[You should be able to explain how fossil evidence supports the theory of evolution like you have done on these pages.]

Hormones and fertility

■ Different hormones do different jobs

Hormones from the **pituitary gland** and **ovaries** control a woman's **menstrual cycle**. They make sure that the womb is ready to receive a fertilised egg.

Some women use manufactured hormones to help them to become pregnant. Other women use different hormones to prevent pregnancy.

> **REMEMBER**
>
> **Hormones** control the menstrual cycle.
>
> Manufactured hormones can be used to increase or to reduce fertility.

The pituitary gland produces:
■ **FSH** – to make an egg mature in an ovary.
　　　 – to make the ovaries secrete oestrogens.
■ **LH** – to make an ovary release an egg in the middle of the menstrual cycle.

1 Look at the picture.
  Then copy and complete the diagram.

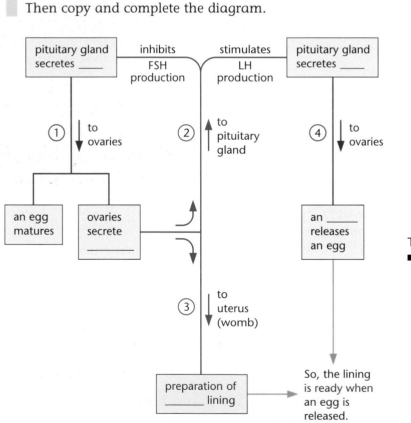

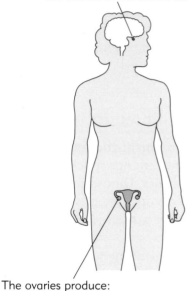

The ovaries produce:
■ **oestrogen** – to inhibit FSH production.
　　　　　　 – to stimulate LH production.
　　　　　　 – to stimulate preparation of the womb lining.

■ Fertility drugs

Janet can't become pregnant. The doctor thinks that this is because she doesn't make enough FSH. So, eggs don't develop in her ovaries. Her doctor can give her injections of FSH to make eggs mature. If her egg tubes and her partner's sperm are normal, she can then become pregnant.

If Janet's egg tubes are blocked, she will not become pregnant. Doctors can still help. They can take mature eggs from her ovaries and fertilise them in a dish. Then, they can transplant the embryos into her womb.

2 (a) Why is FSH called a 'fertility drug'?

(b) Explain how a 'fertility drug' works.

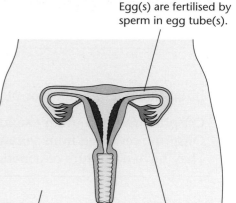

Egg(s) are fertilised by sperm in egg tube(s).

Fertility drug (FSH) is injected into the blood.

Eggs mature in the ovaries.

■ Oral contraceptives

Some women use hormones to prevent pregnancy. They use **contraceptive** pills. There are lots of different kinds, but most contain oestrogen. This hormone prevents FSH production by the pituitary. As a result, eggs do not mature in the ovaries so the woman cannot become pregnant.

3 Copy and complete the sentences.

Most oral contraceptives contain _____. This stops the pituitary gland producing _____. So, no eggs mature in the _____.

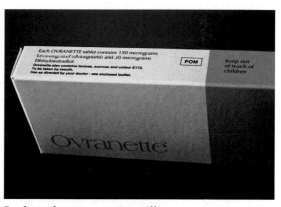

Packet of contraceptive pills.
Ethinyloestradiol is one form of oestrogen.

Using your knowledge

1 Ovaries make a hormone called oestrogen. After an ovary releases an egg they make another hormone called progesterone. This hormone prevents breakdown of the lining of the womb.

Look at the graph.

(a) Why is it important to prevent breakdown of the womb lining after ovulation?

(b) Which line, A or B, is the line for progesterone?

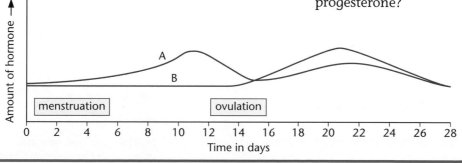

H2   This extends *Inheritance and selection* 7 and 9 for Higher Tier students

What happens when nuclei and cells divide?

REMEMBER

In an individual animal or plant, all the body cell nuclei are genetically identical.

Offspring resulting from **asexual reproduction** are genetically identical. We call them **clones**.
Offspring resulting from **sexual reproduction** vary.
They have a mixture of genetic information from two parents.

■ Producing genetically identical cells

The genetic information in a cell is in strands of material called **chromosomes**. These are in the **nucleus** of a cell. Each human body cell nucleus has 23 pairs of chromosomes. One chromosome in each pair came from the mother and the other from the father.

Before a body cell divides, each chromosome makes a copy of itself to produce two strands of genetic information that are attached to each other. The two copies of each chromosome then separate and move apart. So, two new nuclei are produced. Each nucleus has 23 pairs of chromosomes exactly like those in the nucleus of the original cell. We call this type of division **mitosis**.

1 Copy and complete the sentences.

> Before a cell divides by mitosis, each chromosome makes a copy of itself. So, the nuclei of the two new cells contain exactly the same _____ information. This happens when:
>
> ■ new _____ cells are made;
> ■ clones are produced by _____ reproduction.

■ Producing sex cells

A different kind of division takes place in organs of sexual reproduction such as testes and ovaries. These organs make sex cells or **gametes**. Gametes have only <u>half</u> the usual number of chromosomes. So, in humans, gametes have 23 chromosomes, one from each pair. The chromosomes make copies of themselves in this kind of division too. But the cell then divides <u>twice</u> to produce four gametes. This is called **meiosis**.

2 What are the differences between mitosis and meiosis?

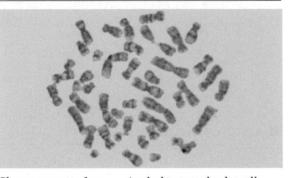

Chromosomes from a single human body cell. (These have been coloured to show banding more clearly.)

23 pairs of chromosomes.

Each chromosome copies itself.

Copies of chromosomes separate to form two sets of 23 pairs.

The cell divides.

MITOSIS for: ■ making new body cells
■ asexual reproduction

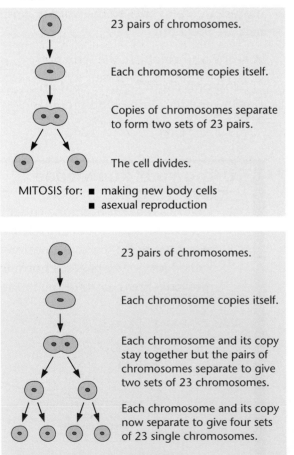

23 pairs of chromosomes.

Each chromosome copies itself.

Each chromosome and its copy stay together but the pairs of chromosomes separate to give two sets of 23 chromosomes.

Each chromosome and its copy now separate to give four sets of 23 single chromosomes.

MEIOSIS produces new cells with a single set of chromosomes (gametes).

When sex cells join

When two sex cells or gametes join, we call the process **fertilisation**. The new cell gets half of its chromosomes from each parent.

3 (a) Copy and complete the diagram.

(b) Explain why the new cell divides by mitosis.

Why do babies of the same parents vary?

A baby gets half of its chromosomes from each parent. Lots of different combinations of chromosomes are possible.

The diagrams show how four different eggs can be made from a cell with only two pairs of chromosomes. Then, how sixteen different offspring can be produced if these eggs join at random with four different sperm.

The information carried at a particular position on a chromosome is called a **gene**. Chromosomes come in pairs, so genes are also in pairs. One of each pair of genes in a baby comes from each parent.

The two members of a pair of genes can have different forms. They are called alleles. So, the gene for eye colour could be in the form of an allele for blue eyes or an allele for brown eyes. A baby may get different alleles from each parent. Different combinations of alleles produce different characteristics.

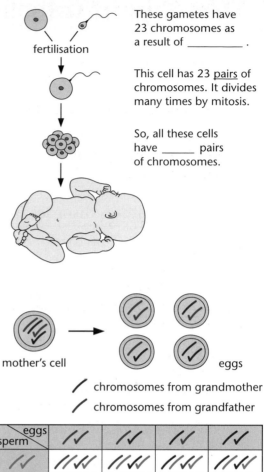

These gametes have 23 chromosomes as a result of _____ .

This cell has 23 pairs of chromosomes. It divides many times by mitosis.

So, all these cells have _____ pairs of chromosomes.

mother's cell → eggs

/ chromosomes from grandmother
/ chromosomes from grandfather

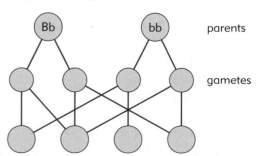

Using your knowledge

1 The diagram shows the chromosomes in a sperm-producing cell. Draw diagrams of the chromosomes in the sperm it could produce.

2 Copy the diagram.

Bb ... bb   parents

gametes

B is the allele for brown eyes and b is for blue eyes. Fill in the missing alleles on your diagram.

More about inherited diseases

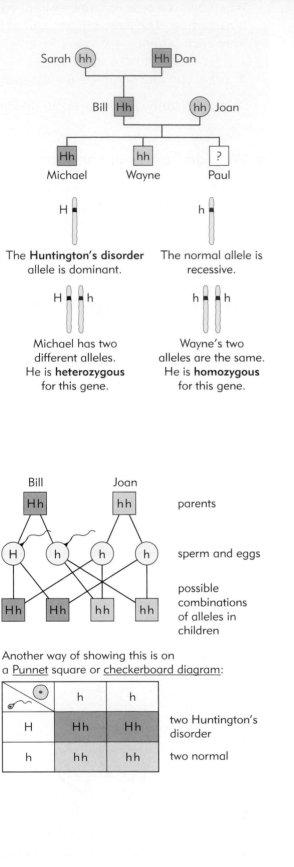

The **Huntington's disorder**
allele is dominant.

The normal allele is
recessive.

Michael has two
different alleles.
He is **heterozygous**
for this gene.

Wayne's two
alleles are the same.
He is **homozygous**
for this gene.

REMEMBER

A **dominant** allele can produce its effect even
when a recessive allele is also present. So, it takes
two recessive alleles to have an effect.

■ How Huntington's disorder is inherited

The allele that causes this condition is dominant.
Everyone who has this allele develops the disorder.
But, it doesn't develop until a person is 30 to 40 years old.
So, the allele may already have been passed on
to children.

Look at Michael's family tree. Michael has the disorder.
His brother, Wayne has had a test. He has only normal
alleles. Paul, aged 21, can't decide whether to have the
test or not.

1 Why does everyone with the Huntington's disorder
allele always develop symptoms?

2 The diagram shows the allele combinations possible
in Bill and Joan's children. What is the probability
that Paul has only normal alleles?

3 For Paul, write down the advantages and
disadvantages of having a test.

4 Copy and complete the sentences.

Chromosomes and genes are in _____.
Sometimes the two alleles in a pair of genes are the
same. We say that the individual is _____ for
that gene. Sometimes the two alleles are different so
the individual is _____ for the gene. We call the
one which shows up, the _____ allele.
A _____ allele shows up only when it is present
on both chromosomes.

Another way of showing this is on
a <u>Punnet</u> square or <u>checkerboard diagram</u>:

	h	h	
H	Hh	Hh	two Huntington's disorder
h	hh	hh	two normal

■ Sickle cell disorder

The allele for **sickle cell disorder** is **recessive**.

5 Look at the diagrams. Then copy and complete the sentence.

If both parents are _____ of sickle cell disorder there is a 1 in _____ chance of a child having the disease.

6 Complete diagrams, similar to the one below and on the right, for an nn mother and an Nn father.

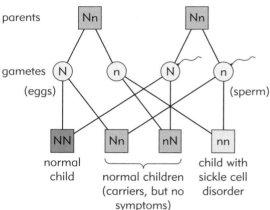

sperm \ eggs	N	n
N	NN normal	Nn carrier
n	nN carrier	nn sickle cell disorder

OR

■ The allele for cystic fibrosis is also recessive

One in 20 people carries the **cystic fibrosis** allele. Until Laura was born, her parents had no idea that they were carriers of cystic fibrosis. They were worried about the risk of having another child with the disorder. Their doctor sent them to a genetic counsellor.

7 Look at the counsellor's charts.

   (a) Write down the alleles of Laura and her parents.

   (b) Why do we call her parents carriers?

   (c) Imagine that you are the counsellor. Explain why there is a probability of 1 in 4 of Laura's parents having another affected child.

8 Some people think that anyone wanting to start a family should have a test for cystic fibrosis. Explain why.

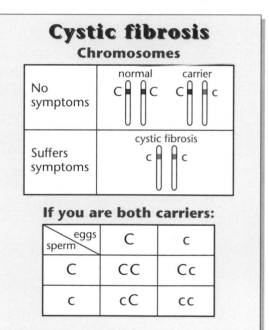

Using your knowledge

1 There is a clue in this family tree that the characteristic shown in green is caused by a recessive allele. What is the clue?

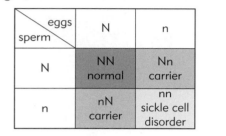

2 Parent 1   red hair   bb
   Parent 2   brown hair   Bb

The probability of these parents having a red-haired child is 1 in 2. Draw a diagram to show this. Indicate the hair colour of the offspring.

[You need to be able to construct genetic diagrams and to predict and explain the results of crosses just like you have done on these pages.]

DNA and the genetic code

■ Discoveries about DNA

In 1859 a scientist called Friedrich Miescher was able to separate **DNA** from the cell nucleus. He called it nuclein. Then, in 1944, other scientists showed that this nuclein is our genetic material and that it controls what we are like. In 1953 Francis Crick and James Watson worked out the chemical structure of DNA. They based their work on discoveries made by chemists, physicists, biologists and mathematicians.

Information box

Chargaff found a pattern in the amounts of the 4 bases in the DNA molecule.

amount of base A = amount of base T
amount of base C = amount of base G

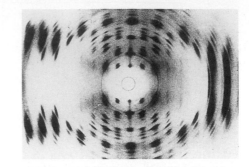

Maurice Wilkins and Rosalind Franklin found that there was a repeating pattern in the structure of DNA.

1 Look at the information box. Write down <u>two</u> patterns that helped Crick and Watson to work out the structure and build a model of DNA.

Think of a DNA molecule as a bit like a ladder. The base pairs are like the rungs of the ladder. They are either A–T or C–G.

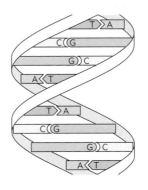

The shape of the DNA molecule turned out to be a double helix. So think of the ladder twisted into a spiral.

2 DNA is made of two strands linked together.

(a) What is the shape of the molecule?

(b) What links the two strands together?

There was still the problem of how DNA did its job. No one knew how DNA coded for the genetic information.

3 What discoveries did the people in the photographs make about DNA?

(a) Wilkins and Franklin.

(b) Crick and Watson.

Crick   Watson   Wilkins   Franklin

Finding the structure of DNA was such an important discovery that Wilkins, Crick and Watson were awarded a Nobel Prize in 1962. Franklin didn't share it because she died in 1958.

■ Cracking the genetic code

There are over 20 different **amino acids**. Cells combine them in different numbers and different orders to make different **proteins**. So we can make lots of different proteins. Our cells make proteins in tiny structures in the cytoplasm. They get their instructions in code from the DNA in the nucleus. Scientists know that one gene codes for one protein. What they needed to find out was the codes for the amino acids which make up proteins.

In 1961, Crick worked out the code.

4 It is possible to make hundreds of different proteins from just 20 amino acids. Explain why.

■ How does the code work?

- If <u>one</u> base codes for <u>one</u> amino acid, four bases (A,T,C,G) can only code for four amino acids.

- If <u>two</u> bases code for <u>one</u> amino acid, 16 different amino acid codes are possible.

- But there are more than 20 different amino acids.

- So a <u>three</u>-base code is needed. Each group of <u>three</u> bases is the code for <u>one</u> amino acid.

5 The diagram shows only 10 three-base codes. Work out at least 10 more for yourself.

If you wanted to, you could work out 64 different codes.

The order of these bases on the DNA molecule controls the sequence in which the amino acids are joined to make a protein. A change in the order of bases causes a change in the protein produced. This is a **mutation**.

6 This is the code for a small part of a protein molecule.

GTT ATG TGG TTT GTT

Write down the sequence of amino acids that this codes for.

If one base codes for one amino acid, four bases can only code for four amino acids.

If two bases code for each amino acid, sixteen different amino acid codes are possible.

	A	T	G	C
A	AA	AT	AG	AC
T	TA	TT	TG	TC
G	GA	GT	GG	GC
C	CA	CT	CG	CC

If three bases code for each amino acid, there are more possible codes than there are amino acids.

GCA   GCG   GTA   CAT   ATA

AAT   TAG   TTT   CAA   AAG

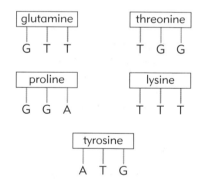

These are the codes for five amino acids. You do not need to remember them. You do need to remember that three bases code for one amino acid.

Using your knowledge

1 (a) Write down the sequence of amino acids for this DNA: GTT/TGG/ATG/G

   (b) One letter is lost. So it is now: TTT/GGA/TGG. Write down the new sequence of amino acids.

   (c) What do we call this sort of change in our DNA?

[You do not need to remember this story. You do need to remember that DNA contains <u>four</u> different bases.]

More about evolution and mutation

■ Ideas about evolution

In the eighteenth and nineteenth centuries scientists found out more and more about **fossils**. Many accepted that fossils were the remains of ancient plants and animals. So they wanted to know why some new ones appeared and why some became **extinct**. The Church taught that species did not change.

An eighteenth-century French naturalist called Georges Louis de Buffon thought that the Earth was much older than the Bible suggested and that species had changed. The Church forced him to say that he was wrong.

1 (a) What was Cuvier's explanation of new species and extinctions?

   (b) Why weren't people willing to suggest other explanations at the time?

Lamarck thought that an organ would change when it was necessary. He would have said that giraffes developed long necks because they needed them to reach up into the trees for food. He also thought that characteristics which an animal developed during its life, such as stronger muscles, would be passed on to its offspring. This is not true. So it was easy to challenge his other ideas.

A French scientist called Georges Cuvier suggested that a series of Noah's floods and creations explained the fossil record.

Darwin and Wallace's explanation for change was harder to challenge. This was **evolution** by **natural selection**. Another name for it is 'the survival of the fittest'.

2 Lamarck and Darwin both suggested theories of evolution, but they explained how it happened in different ways. Write down the differences in their explanations.

3 (a) Why do you think that so many people had ideas about evolution in the eighteenth and nineteenth centuries?

   (b) Why were people's ideas different?

Another French scientist called Chevalier de Lamarck observed artificial selection. He thought that something similar might happen in nature.

Darwin thought that the animals or plants best suited to their environments would survive, breed and pass on their characteristics.

■ Ideas about mutation

Darwin knew about **variation** but not the causes. He didn't know about genes, alleles and mutations. Mutations produce new **alleles**. A few of these new alleles are useful, most are harmful and others seem to make no difference. But they do add to the range of alleles (the **gene pool**). They increase the number of variations on which natural selection can act. They may turn out to be useful if the environment changes. Useful mutations are ones that increase the chances of survival.

4 (a) Describe <u>two</u> examples of harmful effects of mutations in reproductive cells.

 (b) Explain why a neutral mutation might become useful.

Mutations of genes in body cells can also be harmful. Some of our genes control cell division. Some are like 'on' switches and make a cell start to divide. Others are like 'off' switches and stop cell division. Factors in the environment such as cigarette smoke and radiation can affect these switch genes. If the switch stays on, cells do not stop dividing when they should. They are out of control. This is **cancer**.

5 (a) Write down <u>one</u> difference between division of cancer cells and normal cells.

 (b) What do we call the change that makes a normal cell change into a cancer cell?

> **REMEMBER**
>
> **Mutations** are changes in genes and chromosomes. Most mutations are harmful. For example, a mutation produces the sickle cell allele.

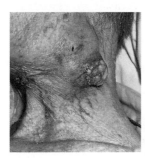

A mutation in a body cell caused this cancer. The new cell grew out of control and cells spread to other parts of the body.

This fetus died because it was abnormal. A mutation in a reproductive cell caused this abnormality.

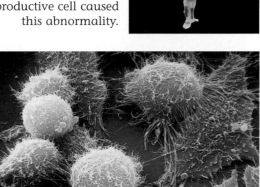

Cancer cells.

Using your knowledge

1 Dan had a bacterial infection. The doctor gave him a week's supply of penicillin. This kills most of the bacteria within a few days and only the more resistant bacteria remain. After a few days, Dan felt better and stopped taking the penicillin. However, he passed the infection on to Paula. She got some penicillin too. But it did not cure her.

The doctor said that there had been a mutation in the bacteria. The bacteria were now penicillin resistant. Paula had to have a different antibiotic.

Explain why you should always take the full course of antibiotics.

[You need to be able to identify differences between different theories of evolution and to suggest reasons for different theories.]

213

Handling data

In tests and examinations you will be asked to interpret scientific data. This data may be represented in several different ways, for example pie charts, bar charts, graphs and Sankey diagrams.

■ Pie charts

What's in a meal?
The pie chart shows what the food in a meal is made up of:

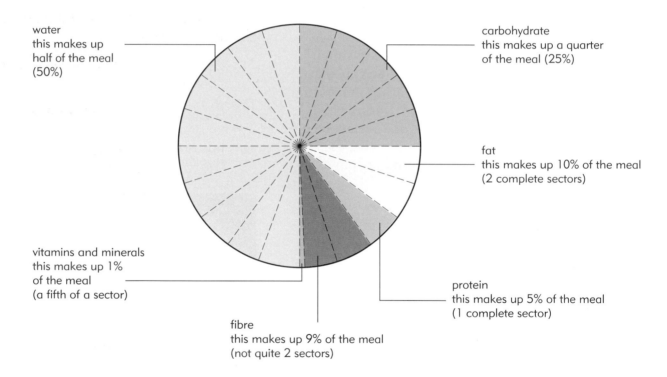

water
this makes up
half of the meal
(50%)

carbohydrate
this makes up a quarter
of the meal (25%)

fat
this makes up 10% of the meal
(2 complete sectors)

vitamins and minerals
this makes up 1%
of the meal
(a fifth of a sector)

protein
this makes up 5% of the meal
(1 complete sector)

fibre
this makes up 9% of the meal
(not quite 2 sectors)

You may be asked to read the data from a pie chart and put it into a table like this:

water	50%
carbohydrate	25%
fat	10%
protein	5%
fibre	9%
vitamins and minerals	1%

↑
These should add up to 100%.

You may be asked to complete a pie chart. Draw thin, straight lines. Remember to add all the labels, or provide a key like this:

water	
carbohydrate	
fat	
protein	
fibre	
vitamins and minerals	

■ Bar charts

Your heart rate
The bar chart shows a person's heart rate before and after exercise.

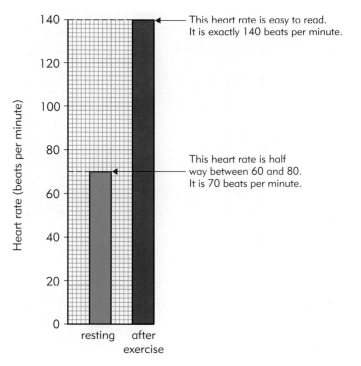

This heart rate is easy to read. It is exactly 140 beats per minute.

This heart rate is half way between 60 and 80. It is 70 beats per minute.

You may be asked to **compare** the bars on a bar chart.

You could say that the heart rate is **faster** after exercise.

A better answer is to say that the heart rate is **twice as fast** after exercise.

You may be asked to draw bars on a bar chart. Remember:

■ to look carefully at the scale;

■ to draw the bars the same thickness and equally spaced out;

■ to draw the top of each bar with a thin straight line;

■ to label each bar, or draw a key like this:

resting	
after exercise	

■ Sankey diagrams

What happens to the energy?
The diagram shows what happens to each 100 J of energy in the food a young rabbit eats:

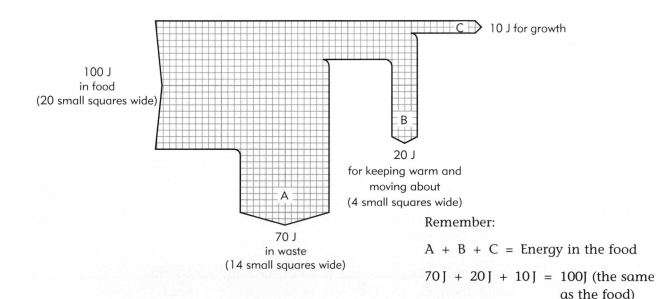

C ⊳ 10 J for growth

100 J
in food
(20 small squares wide)

B

20 J
for keeping warm and
moving about
(4 small squares wide)

A

70 J
in waste
(14 small squares wide)

Remember:

A + B + C = Energy in the food

70 J + 20 J + 10 J = 100 J (the same as the food)

■ Interpreting line graphs

When you are reading off values from a graph make sure you do the following:

- Check the scales on the axes so that you know what each small square on the grid represents.
- Remember to quote units in your answer.
  [You can find these on the axis where you read off your answer. You can still quote the correct units even if you don't understand what they mean!]
- Be as precise and accurate as you can:
  - when describing trends or patterns [in the example, if you're asked what happens to the rate of water loss between 8 a.m. and 9 a.m. '*increases steadily*' is a better answer than '*increases*'.]
  - when specifying key points [in the example: water loss does not start to increase until 7 a.m. water loss starts to level off after 10 a.m. water loss doesn't increase any more after 11 a.m. maximum rate of water loss is 32 g/hour.]
  - when making comparisons [in the example, if you're asked how the rate of water loss at 8 a.m. compares with the rate at 9 a.m. '*it's twice as big*' or '*it's double the size*' is a better answer than '*it's bigger*'.]

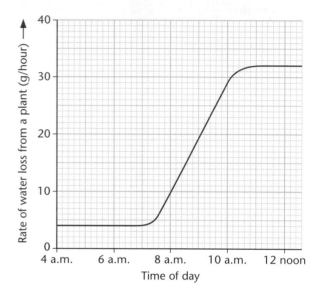

Get plenty of practice interpreting graphs, etc. as indicated above until you do it perfectly with as little effort as possible.

■ Drawing line graphs

- Choose sensible scales for the axes.
  [You should use <u>more than half</u> of the available squares along each axis.]
- Label the axes [e.g. *Rate of water loss (g/hr)*].
- Mark all the points neatly and accurately
  like this   or like this

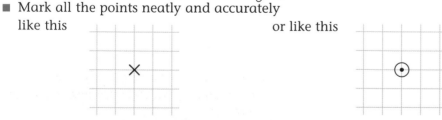

- If the points are close to being a straight line or smooth curve, then draw the 'best fit' straight line or smooth curve. Use a pencil so you can rub your line out if you don't get it right first time. If there's an <u>obviously</u> wrong point, <u>ignore</u> it and indicate that you've done so.

Get plenty of practice doing these things so that you'll do the right thing even if you're nervous in an examination.

Revising for tests and examinations

Stage 1

See if you know which words go into the **'What you need to remember'** boxes for the pages you are revising.

Try to do this *without* looking at the text or diagrams on the pages. Then, if there is anything you can't do, read the text and look at the diagrams to find the answer.

Remember:

- the key words are printed like this:
  These bacteria and fungi feed on **waste** such as dead plants and animal droppings.

- you can check your answers at the back of the book (pages 221–228).

If you are taking the Higher Tier tests or examinations, you will also need to make sure that you can answer the questions that occur at various points in the text of the extension pages.

But you don't just have to *remember* the scientific ideas, you also need to be able to *use* these ideas. You may be asked to do this in a situation you haven't met before.

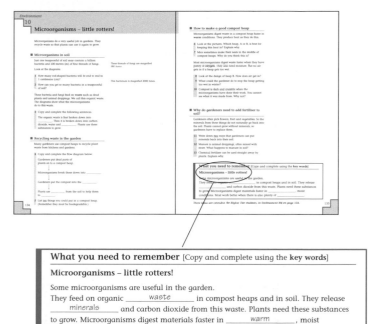

What you need to remember [Copy and complete using the **key words**]

Microorganisms – little rotters!

Some microorganisms are useful in the garden.
They feed on organic _____waste_____ in compost heaps and in soil. They release _____minerals_____ and carbon dioxide from this waste. Plants need these substances to grow. Microorganisms digest materials faster in _____warm_____, moist conditions. Most work better when there is also plenty of _____oxygen_____.

Example of a question

> When microorganisms feed and grow they produce waste. If you add the right microorganisms to warm milk in a vacuum flask they produce a waste acid. This turns the milk into yoghurt in less than a day.
>
> Write down <u>two</u> reasons why this happens quickly.

Answer to the question

The two simplest answers are that the milk contains water and that it is warm. Oxygen probably *isn't* the reason because it happens in a sealed container. You could also say:

- the milk contains plenty of food for the microorganisms;

- the microbes reproduce quickly (like microorganisms which cause diseases inside your body).

Stage 2

See if you can *use* the ideas you have revised. There are lots of questions in the text which ask you to do this. Higher Tier students will find questions of this type at the ends of the extension pages. Your teacher should also be able to give you some extra questions. Some of these questions may have been used in examinations in previous years.

How to write good answers in GCSE Science examinations

■ Short answer questions

Here is an example of this type of question:

> Three hormones control the maturing of an egg in an ovary and then its release. Which of the three hormones directly stimulates the <u>release</u> of an egg in the middle of the menstrual cycle?

If you're not sure of the answer to this type of question, you might be tempted to write down <u>several</u> answers in the hope that one of them is right. This is a bad idea. In most cases you'll automatically get <u>no</u> marks.

If you wrote FSH or LH as your answer to the above question you would score 0 marks even though LH is the correct answer.

> You must make up your mind what you think is the most likely answer. If you change your mind later, you can cross out the old answer and write the new one.

■ Questions that require longer answers

It's easy to tell when you are expected to give a longer answer to a question. There will be lots of space for your answer and the question paper will indicate that you can score more than one or two marks for your answer. For example:

> Explain why deforestation in tropical areas can lead to an increase in concentration of carbon dioxide in the atmosphere.
>
> This tells you the number of marks available ────→ (4)
> ────→ or (4 marks)

When answering these questions, don't just write down the first thing you think of and then leave it at that. You should include <u>all</u> the relevant ideas that you can remember. But you should be sure that the ideas you write down really are relevant.

<u>Don't</u> write down things that you just hope might possibly be relevant. That's a sure way to lose marks because, if they're not relevant, it tells the person marking your answer that you don't really understand the question.
This means that you will probably lose marks.

When answering the above question about deforestation, for example, you should <u>not</u> mention anything about why the trees are chopped down or about global warming. The question relates only to the process by which carbon dioxide is added to, or removed from, the atmosphere.

You should also try to <u>organise</u> your answer. This means putting all your ideas into a sensible order and then linking them together in a way that shows you really understand what's going on.

A few words like this in your answer:

First of all ... then ... because ... This means that ... So, on balance, ...

can help a lot.

Don't rush into writing down your longer answers.

Decide what the relevant ideas are and jot them down in pencil.

Then decide what order to write them down in and how you are going to link them together.

GCSE Science consists mainly of many separate ideas which, once you've understood them, you'll probably remember. But there are also some longer scientific 'stories' that you're also expected to remember, for example:

- describing the various stages in the carbon cycle;
- explaining why pollution of river water by fertilisers can cause the death of fish;
- explaining the recovery of a wilting plant after it is watered;
- explaining evolution in terms of natural selection.

And for Higher Tier students;

- describing the various stages in the nitrogen cycle;
- describing how urine is made in the kidneys;
- analysing a reflex action in terms of
  stimulus → receptor → coordinator → effector → response.

Very few candidates can <u>correctly</u> remember <u>all</u> the details of these stories that GCSE syllabuses require them to know.

Try setting out the stories in different ways, for example as a list of points in the correct order or in the form of a flow diagram. You will then find out which is the best way for you to remember them.

Finally, <u>practise</u> remembering the stories until you can remember them accurately.

How to write good answers in GCSE Science examinations (continued)

■ Diagrams

You do not need to be an artist to draw the types of diagrams used in science.
You just have to follow a few simple rules.

In science, your drawings need to be:
- large;
- simple;
- clear;
- accurate.

So, you need to use a sharp pencil and to draw thin, clear lines. There is no need for artistic shading. Use shading <u>only</u> to help to distinguish one structure from another, for example the nucleus from the chloroplasts in a plant cell.

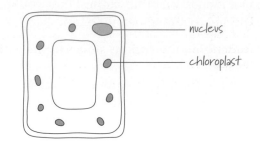

Labelling lines should touch exactly the part to be labelled and one labelling line should not cross another.

Wherever possible the labels should be well away from the diagram itself.

Labels on, or too near a diagram, can hide detail or make a diagram harder to understand.

■ Calculations

GCSE questions in Biology don't normally include calculations except for percentages.

Even if you get the wrong answer to a percentage calculation, you can still get quite a lot of marks. To gain these marks, you must have gone about the calculation in the right way. But the person marking your answer can only see that you've done this if you write down your working neatly and set it out tidily so it's quite clear what you have done.

Example

A potato has a mass of 150 grams. All of the water in the potato is evaporated in a cool oven. The dry matter in the potato has a mass of 7.5 grams.
What is the percentage of water in the potato?

There is $150 - 7.5 = 142.5$ g of water in the potato

So the potato is $\frac{142.5}{150}$ water

i.e. $\frac{142.5}{150} \times 100\%$ water

$= 95\%$ water

You gain marks for these steps even if you make a mistake.

<u>Always</u> set out your classwork and homework calculations as in the example above so that you get into good habits. Then you'll still do calculations in the right way even under the pressure of examinations.

Humans as organisms

1 What are cells like?

Most human cells are made up of the same basic parts. Cells have a **nucleus** that controls everything that happens in the cell. Most of the chemical reactions of the cell take place in the **cytoplasm**. It is the cell **membrane** that controls which substances pass in and out of the cell. Cells that do a particular job are called **specialised** cells.

[You should be able to match special cells to the jobs that they do in tissues, organs or the whole organism when you are given information about the structure of the cells.]

2 Why do we need to digest our food?

Starch (a carbohydrate), proteins and fats are made of large **molecules**. They cannot dissolve so we say they are **insoluble**. They are broken down into **soluble** molecules. Then they can pass into the bloodstream in the wall of the **small intestine**. Starch is broken down into **glucose**. Protein is broken down into **amino acid** molecules. Fat is broken down into **fatty acid** and **glycerol** molecules. Breaking down large food molecules is called **digestion**. **Fibre** cannot be digested by humans. It makes up most of the undigested waste that we call **faeces**. This leaves the body via the **anus**.

3 How do we digest our food?

The breakdown of large food molecules into smaller ones is speeded up by **enzymes**. An enzyme is a **catalyst**. It is not used up. Enzymes that break down starch into sugars are called **amylases**. Enzymes that break down proteins into amino acids are called **proteases**. Enzymes that break down fats into fatty acids and glycerol are called **lipases**.

4 Your digestive system: what happens where?

Enzymes are produced by **glandular** tissue. **Muscle** tissue moves food along the gullet and intestines and churns it up in the stomach. **Hydrochloric** acid in the stomach kills **bacteria**. The acid also makes the **enzymes** in the stomach work better.

Type of food	Where it is digested	What makes the enzymes
starch	**mouth** and small intestine	salivary **glands**, **pancreas** and small intestine
protein	**stomach** and small intestine	stomach, pancreas and small intestine
fat	**small intestine**	pancreas and small intestine

5 More about your digestive system

The liver makes **bile**.

In the small intestine, bile:

- neutralises **acid**. It provides the conditions that the enzymes need.
- **emulsifies** fats. This increases the surface area for enzymes to work on.

Small, soluble food molecules pass through the lining and into the **bloodstream** in the wall of the **small intestine**. We call this **absorption**. The large intestine absorbs **water** from the digested food.

6 Why do you need energy?

Your muscles contract so that you can **move**. To do this, muscles need **energy**. Some of the energy from food is used to keep your body at the same **temperature**. Cells are mainly built of **proteins**. Proteins themselves are built up of **amino acids**. This building up process also needs **energy**.

7 How you get the oxygen you need

You breathe air in and out of your lungs. This is **ventilation**. Gases pass from where they are in **high** concentration to where they are in **low** concentration. We call this **diffusion**. So we say that oxygen diffuses into your **blood** and carbon dioxide diffuses out. This exchange of gases takes place in your **alveoli**. Blood carries oxygen to your cells.

8 Two types of respiration

Living cells release **energy** from the sugar **glucose**. Normally, **oxygen** is used to do this. This process is called aerobic **respiration**. It can be shown like this:

glucose + oxygen → carbon dioxide + **water** + energy

If cells don't get enough oxygen, they carry out **anaerobic** respiration. It can be shown like this:

glucose → **lactic acid** + energy

The amount of oxygen that a cell uses to get rid of the lactic acid is called the **oxygen debt**.

9 Exchange surfaces and diffusion

Particles of a gas or a dissolved substance move in all directions. There is a net movement from a **higher** concentration to a **lower** concentration. This is called **diffusion**. A bigger difference in concentration makes diffusion **faster**. Organs which are specialised for exchanging materials are alike in many ways. They have:

- an enormous **surface area**
- thin walls
- a **moist** lining
- a rich supply of blood **capillaries**.

10 The heart – a pump for blood

Your heart wall is mainly **muscle** fibres. When the atria contract, blood passes into the **ventricles**. When the ventricles contract, blood is forced into **arteries**. The heart has **valves** to stop the blood from flowing in the wrong direction.

11 Know your blood vessels – you could save a life!

Blood is carried away from the heart by **arteries** and back to the heart by **veins**. Small blood vessels called **capillaries** join arteries and veins. Arteries have thick walls of **muscle** and **elastic** fibres. Veins have thinner walls and contain **valves** which prevent the blood from flowing backwards. Capillaries are so small that their walls are only one **cell** thick. To travel all round your body, your blood must go through your heart **twice**.

12 Your body's transport system

Waste carbon dioxide leaves the blood and **oxygen** enters the blood in the **lungs**. Blood picks up dissolved food in the **small intestine**. The cells in the organs and muscles receive **oxygen** and dissolved **food** from the blood. They give out **carbon dioxide** and other waste. All of these substances pass in and out of very narrow blood vessels called **capillaries**.

13 Dracula's dinner

Blood is made of a liquid called **plasma**. Blood also contains **red** cells, **white** cells and small bits of cells called **platelets**. Red blood cells transport **oxygen** from the lungs to other parts of the body.
Blood plasma carries many things around your body:

- carbon dioxide from body cells to the **lungs**;
- digested foods from the **small intestine** to the body cells;
- urea from the **liver** to the **kidneys**.

White blood cells help to **defend** the body against disease. They do this by **destroying** bacteria or by producing **antibodies** which destroy bacteria. Platelets are bits of cells and have no nucleus. They help the blood to **clot** at the site of a wound.

14 Invading microorganisms

Microorganisms such as **bacteria** and **viruses** can get into your body and cause **disease**. The cells of bacteria have cytoplasm, cell membranes and cell walls, but the genes are not in a **nucleus**. **Viruses** are even smaller than bacteria. They have a few **genes** in a **protein** coat. They can only **reproduce** inside living cells. This **damages** the cells.

15 What happens when microorganisms get into your body?

It takes large numbers of **microorganisms** to make you ill. They get into your body when you are in contact with an **infected** person. Microorganisms reproduce rapidly inside your body. They make poisons (**toxins**) which make you ill. Large numbers of microorganisms are present in dirty or **unhygienic** conditions. People living in **overcrowded** conditions are also more likely to take in microorganisms which cause infection.

[You need to be able to use evidence to explain how the conditions people live in, and the way they behave affect the spread of disease.]

16 The spread of infection

Your body has several ways of stopping microorganisms getting in. Your **skin** acts as a barrier. Blood **clots** to seal cuts. The linings of the passages to the lungs make **mucus**. This is a sticky liquid which **traps** microorganisms.

17 Humans against microorganisms

White blood cells help to defend the body against the **microorganisms** which cause disease. Some white cells take the microorganisms into their cells and digest them. We say they **ingest** them. Some white cells destroy bacteria or viruses by making **antibodies**. Poisons or **toxins** made by microorganisms also have to be made harmless. Some white cells make **antitoxins** to do this. Once they have made antibodies against a particular microbe, white cells can quickly do this again. That is why a person who has the disease or who has been **vaccinated** against it does not become ill. We say that the person is **immune** to the disease.

Maintenance of life

1 How are plants built?

All plants and animals are made up of small parts called **cells**. Most plant cells and animal cells have a **cell membrane**, **cytoplasm** and a **nucleus**. Plant cells also have cell walls to make them **stronger**. Plant cells often have other parts such as chloroplasts. The **chlorophyll** in chloroplasts gives leaves their green colour. Plant cells often have spaces called vacuoles. These are filled with a liquid called **sap**.

2 The cell for the job!

A group of cells with the same shape and job is called a **tissue**. Leaves, stems and roots are called **organs**; they are made of more than one kind of tissue. Tissue called **xylem** transports water and **minerals** from **roots** to stems and leaves. Tissue called phloem carries **sugar** from leaves to growing points, **storage organs** and other parts of plants. Different plant cells do different jobs. We say they are **specialised**.

[Remember that you should be able to look at a cell and work out what it's job is.]

3 How do plants get their food?

Green **plants** make their own food. They produce a sugar called **glucose**. Plants use some of the sugar for **respiration** to release energy. Some of the sugar is changed into **starch**. The starch is stored. Starch is a good storage substance because it is **insoluble**.

4 Food factories – the leaves

Green plants use **light** energy to make food. This process is called **photosynthesis**. A green substance called **chlorophyll** absorbs the light energy. Chlorophyll is found in the parts of cells called **chloroplasts**. These are mainly in the **leaves** of plants.

5 What do plants make sugar from?

Plants make their own food by **photosynthesis**.

Things needed for photosynthesis	Things made by photosynthesis
chlorophyll	oxygen
light	sugar
water	
carbon dioxide	

6 Limits to plant growth

Plants need light, carbon dioxide, water and suitable temperature so they can make food.
We call this **photosynthesis**.
The rate of photosynthesis can be limited by:

- low **light** intensity
- low **carbon dioxide** concentration, or
- low **temperature**.

Plants also need minerals for healthy growth. For example they need **nitrates** to make proteins.

7 Water that plant!

The loss of water vapour from leaves is called **transpiration**. Most leaves have a **waxy** layer to reduce this loss. Most of the water is lost through tiny pores called **stomata**. **Guard** cells can close the stomata when a plant loses water faster than it takes it in. This means the plant does not **wilt**. Transpiration is fastest when it is hot, dry and windy.

8 How do plants get the water they need?

Most of the water which goes into a plant is absorbed by the **root hair** cells. Root hairs increase the surface area for **absorption**. Water diffuses from a **dilute** solution to a more **concentrated** solution through a **partially permeable** membrane. We call this process **osmosis**. A partially permeable membrane is one that lets water molecules through, but not large solute molecules or ions.

9 How do plants get the carbon dioxide they need?

Carbon dioxide goes in and out of leaves by **diffusion**. It spreads from where there is a higher **concentration** outside the leaves to where there is a lower concentration inside the leaves. We say that it **diffuses**. Supplies of water and mineral ions reach leaves in **xylem** tissue. The tissue which carries nutrients such as sugars out of a leaf is called **phloem**.

10 How do plants know which way to grow?

Plants are **sensitive** to gravity and water. They can also sense **light**. Shoots grow towards the **light** and away from the direction of the force of **gravity**. **Roots** grow in the direction of the force of gravity and also towards **water**.

11 Controlling the way plants grow

Hormones control the way plants **grow**. Treating fruits with hormones helps us to **ripen** them. We can also use **hormones** to kill weeds. We can make new plants from small parts of older plants by taking **cuttings**.

12 Making sense – the nervous system

We use sense organs to detect **stimuli** from the world around us. Sense organs contain special cells called **receptors**. We can taste things because there are receptors on our **tongue**. Receptors in our **nose** help us to smell things. Our skin contains receptors sensitive to changes in temperature and **pressure**. Our eyes contain receptors which detect **light**. Our ears contain receptors sensitive to the movement of our heads that help us keep our **balance**. Our ears also contain receptors sensitive to **sounds**.

13 Eyes – your windows on the world

A tough layer called the **sclera** surrounds the eye. The transparent part at the front is called the **cornea**. The lens is held in place by **suspensory** ligaments and ciliary **muscles**. The muscular iris controls the size of the **pupil**. This affects the amount of light reaching the retina. The **retina** contains receptor cells which are sensitive to light. Light from an object enters the eye through the pupil. The cornea and lens produce an image on the retina. Impulses are sent to the brain along sensory neurones in the **optic** nerve.

[You need to able to label the following on a diagram of the eye: optic nerve, lens, cornea, ciliary muscles, iris, suspensory ligaments, sclera, retina, pupil.]

14 Making decisions – coordination

Your **nervous** system allows you to react to your surroundings. Information from receptors passes along **sensory** neurones to your spinal cord and brain. Your brain sends impulses along **motor** neurones to your muscles. We say that your brain **coordinates** your responses to stimuli. In **reflex** actions your response is fast and automatic. Impulses pass along sensory neurones to your **spinal cord** then along motor neurones to muscles or glands. The muscles or glands bring about the response.

15 Keeping things the same inside your body

For your body to work properly everything inside your body must be kept at a **constant** level. Your body controls these things **automatically**. You do not have to 'think' about it. Your **skin** helps control your body temperature. Sweating helps to **cool** your body. You need to replace the water that you lose when you sweat. Your body must be at 37°C so that **enzymes** can work properly.

16 Keeping your blood glucose concentration constant

Your blood glucose concentration must be kept **constant**. If there is too much glucose, your pancreas releases the hormone **insulin**. If there is too little glucose, your pancreas releases the hormone **glucagon**. Diabetics cannot make enough **insulin** so the concentration of glucose in their blood rises too high. They need injections of insulin and have to be careful how much carbohydrate (sugar and starch) they eat.

17 Cleaning blood and balancing water – your kidneys

A poisonous waste substance called **urea** is made in the liver from broken down **amino acids**. The **kidneys** remove urea from the blood. The kidneys also control the amount of **water** and salts (ions) in the body. Urine is stored temporarily in the **bladder**.

18 People and drugs

A substance that can change the way your body works is called a **drug**. There are many different types of drugs. These include **solvents**, **alcohol** and the chemicals in **tobacco** smoke. Some people become dependent on a drug. They have **withdrawal** symptoms when they cannot get it. We say they are **addicted**.

19 The dangers of sniffing solvents

Products like glue, aerosol sprays and petrol contain **solvents**. Solvents cause damage to your **brain**, **lungs** and **liver** and also affect your **behaviour**. There is a high chance that people will **die** if they sniff solvents.

20 What's your poison – alcohol?

Alcohol can damage the **brain** and **liver**, as well as many other parts of the body. It also slows down your **reactions**. If people drink too much, they can lose self-control. They can become unconscious and even go into a **coma**. People can become dependent on alcohol. We say that they are **addicted** to it.

21 Legal but harmful – tobacco

Smoking can cause diseases of the lungs like **bronchitis**, **emphysema** and **cancer**. Smoking also affects your heart and can increase your chance of having a **heart attack**. In a pregnant woman the fetus can be deprived of **oxygen** so the baby has a low **birth mass**.

22 Smoking and lung cancer

[Remember that you need to be able to interpret information that you are given about smoking and lung cancer.]

Environment

1 Surviving in different places

Organisms live, grow and reproduce in places where **conditions** are suitable for them. We say that they are **adapted** to their conditions.

You need to be able to explain how adaptations of plants to dry conditions are related to how well they take in **water** and keep it in. You also need to be able to explain how adaptations of animals to desert and Arctic conditions are related to

- body size and **surface area**;
- amount of insulating **fur** and **fat**;
- camouflage.

2 Surviving in water and on land

To survive, animals must be **adapted** to the conditions in which they live.

[You should be able to look at a picture of an animal and say how it is adapted to its surroundings.]

3 Different places, different plants

Plants and animals live in places where **conditions** are suitable. A plant is **adapted** to survive in its **habitat**. That is why different plants live in different places.

[You need to be able to explain why particular plants or animals live where they do.]

4 Why weed the garden?

Plants need the right conditions to grow well. They need:

- **water** and **nutrients** from the soil;
- **carbon dioxide** from the air;
- and plenty of **light**.

When plants grow close together they **compete** with each other for these things. If plants have plenty of **space** they get all the things they need more easily.

[You should be able to suggest what plants are competing for if you are given information about a particular habitat.]

5 Competition between animals

Animals of one species often **compete** with each other. They also compete with members of other **species**. They may compete for **food**, **water** or **space**.

[You should be able to suggest what animals are competing for if you are given information about a particular habitat.]

6 Predators and their prey

Animals which kill other animals for food are called **predators**. The animals they eat are called their **prey**. The number of animals of a species is called its **population**. This is usually limited by the amount of **food** available. If the population of prey increases, predators have more **food** so the number of **predators** also increases. The size of a population can also be affected by **disease**.

7 Kill and be killed

The populations of different species in the same place are called a **community**. In a community the number of animals of a particular species depends on the amount of **food** available. If the number of predators goes up (**increases**), they need more food. This means that the population of their **prey** goes down (decreases).

8 Energy for life

Plants capture **light** energy from the Sun and store the energy in **food**. When animals eat plants they only use a part of this food to **grow**. A lot of the energy in the food is used to **move** and to keep **warm**. This energy is lost to the surroundings as **heat** so less energy is passed to the next stage of a food chain. This means there is less biomass to pass along a food chain. We can show this by drawing a **pyramid** of biomass. We can improve the efficiency of food production for humans if we **reduce** the number of stages in the food chain.

[You need to be able to draw and interpret pyramids of biomass]

9 Recycling minerals

Dead parts of plants and animals **decay**. They break down into simple **chemicals** like carbon dioxide and water. Waste which can be broken down by microorganisms is called **biodegradable** waste. The decay also produces **minerals** which can then be used again by plants to grow. So the same minerals are used over and over again. We say that the minerals are **recycled**.

10 Microorganisms – little rotters!

Some microorganisms are useful in the garden. They feed on organic **waste** in compost heaps and in soil. They release **minerals** and carbon dioxide from this waste. Plants need these substances to grow. Microorganisms digest materials faster in **warm**, moist conditions. Most work better when there is also plenty of **oxygen**.

11 Down the drain

Watery waste from homes, factories and gutters is called **sewage**. Microorganisms are used at sewage works to break down the waste in sewage. The microorganisms used to treat the watery waste are more active when there is plenty of **oxygen**. Sludge can also be digested using different **microorganisms**. These microbes do not need **oxygen**.

12 The carbon cycle

Carbon dioxide is taken from the **air** by plants. They use it to make **carbohydrates, fats** and **proteins** These **carbon** compounds are used by animals and microorganisms to provide energy. This is called **respiration** and releases **carbon dioxide** into the air. In nature the amount of carbon dioxide released into the atmosphere in respiration and the amount taken out for photosynthesis **balance**. The constant recycling of carbon is called the carbon **cycle**.

[You should be able to show all of these things on a diagram of the carbon cycle.]

13 Sustainable development

[Remember that you need to be able to form judgments about **environmental issues**, including the importance of **sustainable development**.]

14 More people, more problems

The human **population** keeps on increasing. Many people have a high **standard** of living. This means that the **raw** materials we need to make things are being used up faster. It also means that we produce more waste and **pollute** the air and water a lot more.

15 How humans have changed the landscape

Humans often change the land around them. They do this by:

- cutting down **trees** and using the land for **farming**;
- taking stone from **quarries** and using it to make **roads** and **buildings**;
- dumping waste in **landfill** sites.

All these things can destroy the **habitats** of many plants and animals.

[You need to be able to describe the effects of humans on landscapes when you are given information about them.]

16 How humans affect water

Humans can pollute water in many ways:

- with untreated **sewage**;
- with chemicals like **pesticides** and **herbicides** which farmers use to protect their crops, or **fertilisers** which they use to make crops grow better;
- by causing acid rain which can make the water in lakes **acidic**.

17 How humans affect the air

Coal, oil and gas are all **fuels**. Burning fuels produces waste gases which pollute the **air**.

These gases include:

sulphur dioxide and **nitrogen oxides**   — These gases dissolve in rain and make it **acidic**.

carbon dioxide   — This may cause **global** warming.

18 Are we changing the climate?

The amounts of **carbon dioxide** and **methane** in the Earth's atmosphere are increasing. This may increase the **greenhouse effect** and cause **global warming**. Global warming may cause **climate** change and a rise in **sea level**. Some causes of the increase in the amounts of greenhouse gases are **deforestation**, burning **fuel**, keeping cattle and growing rice.

[You need to be able to consider evidence about environmental issues such as global warming.]

Inheritance and selection

1 How a woman becomes pregnant

The release of eggs from a woman's ovaries is controlled by **hormones**. An egg is released about once a **month**. Hormones also cause the lining of the **womb** to become thicker so that a fertilised egg can grow there. These hormones are produced by the woman's **pituitary** gland and her **ovaries**.

2 Using hormones to control pregnancy

Some women use hormones to help them to become pregnant or to stop them from becoming pregnant. We say they use hormones to control their **fertility**. Fertility drugs stimulate a woman's ovaries to release **eggs**. Pills that contain hormones which stop the release of eggs from the ovaries are called oral **contraceptives**.

[You should be able to describe and explain some of the problems and benefits of using hormones to control fertility.]

3 Who do you look like?

Young plants and animals share many **features** with their parents. We call these features **inherited characteristics**. Mendel worked out some patterns of inheritance. He found that one factor could 'hide' another. He called the visible factors **dominant** and the hidden factors **recessive**.

[You need to be able to explain why Mendel suggested the idea of 'inheritance factors' and why the importance of his discoveries was not recognised until after his death.]

4 More about inheritance

Young plants and animals share many features with their parents. This is because parents pass on information to their young in **sex** cells. These cells are also called **gametes**. The units of information in cells are called **genes**. Different genes control different **characteristics**.

5 Why are we all different?

Animals and plants of the same kind are not exactly the same as each other. We call the differences between them **variation**. These differences can have **genetic** causes or **environmental** causes. Some differences are due to a **mixture** of both causes.

6 Where are our genes?

Living things are made of **cells**. The nucleus of a cell contains many pairs of **chromosomes**. Each chromosome contains a large number of **genes**. Because chromosomes come in pairs, genes also come in **pairs**. Different forms of a gene are called **alleles**. Different alleles produce different **features**.

7 Sexual reproduction

Another name for sperm and egg cells is **gametes**. When sperm and egg cells join, we call this **sexual** reproduction. Sperm and egg cells join to make another cell. This cell grows into a baby when it **divides** many times. In sexual reproduction, the **alleles** from the mother and father are mixed up. This means that children show a lot of **variation**.

8 What makes you male or female?

What sex you are depends on your **sex** chromosomes. In females both the sex chromosomes are the same; they are both **X**. In males one sex chromosome is an **X** and the other a **Y**. All the eggs of a woman contain an X chromosome. **Sperm** cells contain an X or a Y chromosome.

X egg cell + Y sperm cell → a baby **boy**

X egg cell + X sperm cell → a baby **girl**.

9 Reproducing without sex

Body cells produce more cells. First, a cell copies its **chromosomes** and then it **divides** in two. We need more body cells for **growth** and to **replace** damaged or dead cells. Some plants and animals can **reproduce** by making new body cells. They do not use **sex** cells. We call this **asexual** reproduction. Only **one** parent is needed for this kind of reproduction. Plants and animals produced without using sex cells all have exactly the same **genes**. We call them **clones**.

10 Some human genes

Genes are sections of **DNA** molecules on chromosomes. Different forms of a gene are called **alleles**. The allele for Huntington's disorder is **dominant**, so it shows up when it is only **one** of a pair of genes. So, you get Huntington's disorder if you have a faulty allele from only **one** of your parents.

11 Two disorders caused by recessive alleles

Some disorders are passed on by genes. We say they are **inherited**. To get cystic fibrosis you must have a faulty allele from **both** of your parents. You inherit **sickle cell** anaemia in the same way. Healthy parents can pass on the faulty allele; we say they are **carriers**.

12 Mutation and change

Sometimes genes change to produce new forms. We call these changes **mutations**. Some chemicals and some forms of radiation, for example **ultra-violet** light, X-rays and **ionising** radiation from **radioactive** substances, all **increase** the chances of mutation. The more radiation a cell receives, the greater the chance of mutation.

13 Choosing the best of the bunch

We breed living things to grow the way we want. This is called **selective** breeding. We choose the animals or plants which have the features we want and breed from them. We also call this **artificial** selection.

14 More about clones

We can grow more plants from parts of older plants. We call them **cuttings**. Cuttings from the same plant all have exactly the same **genes**. Plants with exactly the same genes are **genetically** identical. Living things that are genetically identical are called **clones**. Taking cuttings helps us to produce many plants **quickly** and **cheaply**. We grow cuttings in a **damp** atmosphere until the roots develop.

15 Cloning and selective breeding

Modern cloning techniques include:

- **tissue culture**,
- **embryo** transplants.

We have reduced the number of different **alleles** in some populations of animals and plants by

- **selective breeding** or artificial selection,
- **cloning**.

We may have lost the alleles needed for selective breeding to allow a species to **survive** changed conditions.

16 Genetic engineering

Genes control the production of proteins such as the hormone **insulin** in cells. We can make use of some genes. Scientists can:

- find a useful gene,
- 'cut' it out using **enzymes**,

- make copies of the gene,
- transfer the copies to **bacteria**.

This is **genetic engineering**.
The genetically engineered bacteria are grown in **fermenters** to produce large amounts of the useful protein. Scientists can also transfer genes into animal and **plant** cells.

[You need to be able to consider economic, social and ethical issues concerning cloning and genetic engineering.]

17 Evolution

Individuals in a species **vary** because of differences in their genes. They compete for food and try to avoid predators and disease. Many die. Those which survive and **breed** are the ones with the characteristics best suited to their **environment**. Their genes have enabled them to survive. They pass these on to the next generation. Over a period of time a species changes. This is **evolution** by **natural selection**.

18 The mystery of fossils

Fossils are found in **rocks**. They are the 'remains' of dead **plants** and **animals** from many years ago. Soft parts of plants and animals usually **decay** too fast to form fossils. Fossils are usually formed from **hard** parts of plants and animals. These parts do not **decay** quickly.

19 Some special fossils

Some fossils are formed when another material **replaces** parts of a plant or animal a bit at a time. Microorganisms cause decay. They do this fastest when they have **oxygen**, **moisture** and **warmth**. Sometimes soft parts do not **decay** because one or more of these conditions for decay are absent. These soft parts can then form **fossils**.

20 Three billion years of life

All species of plants and animals which exist today **evolved** from simple life forms. These first developed more than **three billion** years ago. Some have changed a lot. Others have changed very **little**. Many plants and animals have died out or become **extinct**.

21 Fossil detective stories

We can learn from **fossils** how animals and plants have changed or **evolved** since life began on Earth. Species may become **extinct** if the environment which they need to survive changes. Extinction can happen because of new **predators**, new **diseases** or new **competitors**.

[You should be able to explain how fossil evidence supports the theory of evolution.]

Glossary/index

[Notes Some words are used on lots of pages. Only the main examples are shown. Words that are also in the Glossary/index are shown in *italics*.]

A

abdomen: the part of your body containing most of the *organs* of your *digestive system*   23, 48

absorb, absorption: when *cells* or blood take in dissolved food or *oxygen*   9, 13, 16, 21, 30, 70–71

acid rain: rain made acid by dissolved *sulphur dioxide* and *nitrogen oxides*   143, 148

active transport/uptake: when cells use energy from respiration to take in substances more quickly or to take them in against a *concentration gradient*   50, 54, 102–103, 110

adapted, adaptation: when plants or animals have features which make them suitable for where they live   114–119

addicted: when a person can't do without a *drug*   91, 95

ADH: a hormone secreted by the *pituitary gland* which causes the reabsorption of water by the *kidney* tubules   111

aerobic respiration: using *oxygen* to break food down to release energy   22, 28–29, 50–51

alcohol: a chemical which can be used as a *drug*   90, 94–95

allele: form of a *gene*, e.g. there is an allele for blue eyes   171, 173, 178–182, 190–191, 207–209, 213

alveoli: small air sacs in the lungs; one is called an alveolus   23, 26–27, 30–31, 37, 49, 97

amino acids: carbon compounds that *proteins* are built from   17, 20, 25, 30, 36, 38, 100–101, 110, 182, 192, 211

amylase: enzyme that *digests starch*; it changes starch to maltose   17–18

anaerobic respiration: release of energy from food without the use of *oxygen*; less energy is released than in *aerobic respiration*   29, 50–51

antibiotics: chemicals that kill bacteria in your body   90, 194, 213

antibody: chemical made by *white blood cells* to destroy *bacteria* and other *microorganisms*   39, 46–47

antitoxin: chemical made by *white blood cells* to neutralise *toxins* (poisons)   46

anus: opening at the end of the *digestive system*   13, 15–16, 20

arteries: blood vessels which carry blood away from the *heart*   32–35, 37

artificial selection: breeding only from the plants or animals which have the characteristics we want; also called *selective breeding*   186, 190–191, 194

asexual reproduction: reproduction without sex, that is by a single animal or plant, resulting in the production of *clones*   176–177, 188–191, 206

atria: upper chambers of the *heart*; one is called an atrium   32–33

B

bacteria: *microorganisms* made of *cells* with a *chromosome* which is not in a *nucleus*; one is called a bacterium   19, 39, 47, 90, 112, 134, 192

bile: a substance secreted by the *liver*. It neutralises acid and *emulsifies fats* in the *small intestine*   20

biodegradable: made of material which *microorganisms* can break down or *decay*   133

biomass: the material plants and animals are made of   131

bladder: a stretchy bag which stores *urine*   38, 110

breathing: taking air in and out of the *lungs*   22–23, 26–27, 48

bronchi: air tubes between the *windpipe* and the *lungs*; one is called a bronchus   23, 45, 97

bronchioles: tubes which branch from *bronchi* into each *lung*   23, 49

C

cancer: a disorder in which *cells grow* out of control   96–99, 213

capillary: narrow blood vessel with walls only one *cell* thick   10, 26–28, 30–31, 34–35, 37, 49, 53–54, 108, 110

carbohydrates: carbon compounds used by living things as food e.g. *starch* and sugars   12, 15, 18, 87

carbon cycle: the recycling of carbon in nature   138–139

carbon dioxide: a gas in the air used by plants in *photosynthesis* and made in *respiration*   22, 27–29, 31, 33, 36–37, 50–51, 54, 64–77, 84, 100, 102–103, 105, 138–139, 150, 155

carbon monoxide: a poisonous gas   96, 105

cardiac muscle: *heart* muscle   32

carriers: people who have a *recessive allele* of a *gene* for a *disorder* and can pass it on to their children but who do not have the *disorder* themselves   180–181, 209

catalyst: a substance which speeds up a chemical reaction and which can be used over and over again   16, 20

cell: the building block of plants and animals   8–12, 22, 25, 27–28, 30–31, 40–41, 56–59, 68–73

cell membrane: *partially permeable* outer layer of the living part of a *cell*   10–12, 56, 70–71, 73, 102, 180

cellulose: the *carbohydrate* which makes up plant *cell walls* and the *fibre* in your diet   56, 100

cell wall: outer permeable layer of a plant *cell* made of *cellulose*   56, 71, 100

central nervous system: made of the brain and spinal cord, it is the part of the nervous system that coordinates activity   107

chlorophyll: the green substance in *chloroplasts* which traps light energy   57, 63, 65, 100–101

chloroplasts: the parts of plant *cells* which contain *chlorophyll*; in leaves they are found in the largest numbers in palisade cells   56–59, 62–63

chromosomes: structures made of *genes* found in the *nucleus* of a *cell*   170–176, 192, 206–207

cilia: hair-like fringes on some *cells* which beat to make a current or to move a cell   45

ciliary muscle: muscle in the eye which relaxes and contracts to change the shape of the *lens*   80–81, 106

clones: groups of genetically identical living things produced in *asexual reproduction*   177, 188, 190–191, 206

community: a collection of *species* living in one particular place   126

compete, competition: when several plants or animals are all trying to get the same things   120–123, 195, 203

concentration gradient: difference in concentration that allows materials to *diffuse*   102, 110

consumer: an animal which cannot make its own food but gets it from plants or other animals   128

contraceptive: a device or a *drug* to prevent pregnancy   163, 205

contract: in the case of a muscle, to become shorter and fatter   8, 24–25, 32, 48, 106

core temperature: inner body temperature; in humans it is about 37°C   108

cornea: transparent layer at the front of the eye which plays a part in focussing   80–81, 106

cuttings: parts of plants cut off an older plant and grown into new plants; *clones*   77, 158–159

cystic fibrosis: an *inherited disorder* of *cell membranes* caused by a *recessive allele*   180, 193, 209

cytoplasm: the contents of a *cell* excluding the *nucleus*; the place where most chemical reactions happen   10–11, 56, 59

D

Darwin, Charles: 76, 194–195, 212–213

decay: rot or break down 132, 197, 199

decomposers: *microorganisms* which cause *decay* 132–133, 138–139

denitrifying bacteria: *bacteria* that change nitrates to nitrogen 157

diabetic: person with diabetes, a *disorder* caused by shortage of the *hormone insulin* 86–87, 192

diaphragm: a sheet of muscle separating your *thorax* (chest) from your *abdomen* and used in *breathing* 20, 23, 26, 48

diffuse, diffusion: the spreading of liquids and gases from where the concentration is high to where it is low along a *concentration gradient* 26–27, 30–31, 49–50, 54, 70–73, 102–103

digestion: breakdown of large insoluble food molecules into small, soluble molecules which can be *absorbed* 13–21

digestive system: all the *organs* which are concerned with the *digestion* of food 9, 13–21

disease, disorder: when some part of a plant or animal isn't working properly 39, 43–47, 125, 173–181, 194, 203, 208–209

DNA: the chemical that *genes* and *chromosomes* are made of 178, 192, 210–211

Doll, Richard: 98–99

dominant: an *allele* that can hide the effect of another *(recessive)* allele 165, 171, 178–179, 181, 208

Down's syndrome: an *inherited disorder* caused by an extra *chromosome* 182

drug: a substance which can change the way your body works 90–99

E

ecosystem: all the living and non-living things in an area 156

effector: a part of the body which brings about a response, such as a muscle or a gland 107

emulsify: break down fat into tiny droplets 20

environmental: related to the environment 168–169, 140–142

enzymes: *protein* substances made in cells which speed up chemical reactions. They are *catalysts* 16–20, 85, 180, 192

eutrophication: excessive growth of microscopic plants in water as a result of excess nutrients (minerals) in the water 158–159

evolve, evolution: the changes in a plant or animal *species* over a long period of time 194–195, 201–203, 212

extinct: no longer existing 200, 203, 212

F

F1 generation: first generation offspring 164–165

F2 generation: offspring resulting from a cross between two individuals from the *F1 generation* 164–165

faeces: undigested waste which passes out through the *anus* 15, 89, 152

fat: part of our food which we use for energy and for making *cell membranes* 12, 14–15, 17–20

fatty acids: one of the building blocks of *fats* 14–17, 20

fertilise, fertilisation: when a male sex cell joins with a female sex cell to start a new plant or animal. It forms a single cell which gets half its *chromosomes* from each parent 11, 160–161, 204–205, 207

fertilisers: you add these to soil to provide the minerals plants need to grow; some are natural, e.g. manure, others are artificial, e.g. potassium nitrate 135, 142, 147, 158–159

food chain: diagram showing what animals eat 128–131, 152–153

food web: diagram showing what eats what in a *habitat* 129

fossil: remains of plants and animals from a long time ago 139, 196–203, 212

FSH: a hormone made in the *pituitary gland* that makes eggs mature in *ovaries* and makes ovaries secrete *oestrogens*   204–205

fungi: plants which do not make their own food but break down dead bodies of plants and animals and other waste; one is called a fungus   134

G

gametes: another name for sex cells, cells with half the usual number of *chromosomes* for a *species*   165–166, 172, 206–209

genes: these control the characteristics of plants and animals; they are passed on by parents in chromosomes; they are made of DNA   40–41, 166–174, 176–183, 188–189, 194–195, 207, 213

gene cloning: making copies of *genes*   192

gene therapy: transfer of *genes* into the cells of those affected by a genetic disorder in order to make them healthy   193

genetic: related to *genes*   168–169, 206, 210–211

genetic engineering: transferring *genes* from the cells of one living organism into the cells of a different organism   154, 192–193

glandular tissue: groups of *cells* which produce useful juices, e.g. digestive juices, *hormones*   9, 19

global warming: increase in the average temperature on Earth   149–151, 155

glucagon: a *hormone* made in the *pancreas* which makes *liver cells* change *glycogen* to *glucose*   86–87, 109

glucose: a *carbohydrate* with a small, *soluble molecule* (a sugar)   14–15, 17, 20, 22, 28–30, 50, 60–62, 86–87, 100, 102, 109

glycerol: one of the building blocks of *fats*   14–17, 20

glycogen: a *carbohydrate* with large, insoluble molecules that is stored in animal cells   109

greenhouse gases: gases such as methane and *carbon dioxide* that stop some of the thermal energy escaping from the atmosphere   150–151, 155

guard cells: cells around *stomata* (pores) in the skin of a leaf   58, 68–69, 103–104

gullet: tube from mouth to *stomach*; another name for the *oesophagus*   13, 16, 18, 20

H

habitat: the place where a plant or animal lives   116, 118, 145

haemoglobin: chemical in *red blood cells* that carries *oxygen*   52–53, 105, 182

heart: an *organ* which pumps blood   32–35, 50, 53, 94

herbicide: weedkiller   142, 146–147, 193

heterozygous: when an individual has two different alleles of a *gene*   208

Hill, Bradford: 98–99

homeostasis: keeping the internal environment of an organism constant, for example by controlling temperature or salt content   108–111

homozygous: when the two *alleles* of a *gene* in an individual are the same   208

hormones: chemicals secreted in small amounts which coordinate the growth and activities of living things   76–77, 86–87, 109, 111, 154, 160–163, 188–190, 204–205

Huntington's disorder: an *inherited disorder* of the *nervous system* caused by a *dominant allele*   179, 208

hypothermia: when your body temperature falls below 35°C   24–25

I

immune, immunity: when your body stops you catching a particular *infection*   47

infected, infection: when *microorganisms* get into your body and cause a *disease*   42–47, 213

inherited: passed on in the *genes* from parents   164–166, 179–181

insulin: a *hormone* secreted by the *pancreas* that helps in the control of blood *glucose* concentration and prevents *diabetes*; many diabetics need injections of animal insulin or of human insulin from *genetically engineered* bacteria   86–87, 109, 192–193

iris: part of your eye which controls the size of your *pupil*   80–81

K

kidneys: organs of excretion and *homeostasis*, they excrete waste *urea* in your *urine* and regulate the water and salt content of your body   36, 84, 88–89, 94

L

lactic acid: a chemical produced in *anaerobic respiration* in muscles and one of the causes of *muscle fatigue*   29, 50–51

large intestine: wide part of intestine between *small intestine* and *anus*   9, 16, 20–21

lens: part of the eye which changes shape to focus light on the *retina*   80–81, 106

LH: a hormone made in the *pituitary gland* that stimulates the release of female sex cells (eggs)   204

lipase: *enzyme* which digests *fat*   17–20

lipids: another word for fats and oils   100

liver: large organ in the *abdomen* which makes *bile* and works with your *pancreas* to keep the right amount of *glucose* in your blood   13, 16, 20–21, 36, 87–9, 92, 94 109–110

lungs: *organs* which provide a large surface area for the exchange of gases between the blood and the air   22–23, 26–28, 30, 32, 35–37, 45, 48–49, 53, 84, 92, 98–99, 116–117, 180

M

meiosis: the type of nuclear division for *gamete* formation in which the *chromosome* number is halved   206

Mendel, Gregor: 164–166

menstrual cycle: monthly cycle controlled by *hormones* in the human female reproductive system   161, 204–205

mitosis: the type of nuclear division for body cell formation in which the *chromosome* number is the same in the parent and daughter cells 206–207

microorganisms: microscopic living things 40–47, 132–139, 154, 156–159, 199

mitochondria: structures in the *cytoplasm* where *aerobic respiration* happens; one is a mitochondrion   50

motor neurones: nerve cells which carry impulses from the brain and spinal cord to muscles 82–83, 107

mucus: sticky fluid made by some *cells*, e.g. in the *bronchi* to trap *microbes* and dirt   45, 180

muscle fatigue: when muscles are tired, ache and don't work as well as usual after respiring anaerobically   51

muscular tissue: group of muscle *cells* which *contract* to do work   8–9, 19

mutation: a change in a *chromosome* or a *gene* 182–183, 194, 211–213

N

natural selection: the survival of the organisms best suited to the environment   194–195, 212

nervous system: *organ system* which co–ordinates the activities of the body   78–79, 82–83, 107, 179

neurones: nerve cells   81–83, 107

nitrifying bacteria: *bacteria* which change ammonium compounds to nitrites, and nitrites to nitrates   156

nitrogen cycle: the circulation of nitrogen in nature   156–157

nitrogen–fixing bacteria: *bacteria* which use nitrogen from the air to make their *proteins*; they add nitrate to soil   157

nitrogen oxides: gases which *pollute* the air and are one of the causes of *acid rain*   143, 148

non-biodegradable: made of materials which *microorganisms* cannot break down   133

nucleus: the part of a *cell* that controls what happens in the cell; it contains the *chromosomes*   10–11, 39–41, 52, 56, 58

nutrients: foods needed by animals or minerals needed by plants   54, 100, 120–121

O

oesophagus: another word for *gullet*   16, 18

oestrogens: hormones made in the *ovaries*   204–205

optic nerve: the nerve which carries impulses between your eye and your brain   80–81

organ: structure in a plant or animal made of several different *tissues*   9, 58

organ system: a group of *organs* which work together to do a particular job   9

osmosis: *diffusion* of water through a *partially permeable membrane*   70–71, 103–104, 110

ovaries: where female *gametes* and the *hormones* oestrogen and progesterone are made   11, 160–163, 204–206

oviduct: egg tube where *fertilisation* happens   11, 160

oxygen: a gas in the air used in *aerobic respiration* and produced in *photosynthesis*   10, 22–23, 26–29, 31, 33, 36–37, 39–40, 49–54, 61, 64–66, 97, 105, 116, 146, 159

oxygen debt: the extra oxygen needed to get rid of the *lactic acid* produced in *anaerobic respiration*   29, 51

oxyhaemoglobin: chemical formed when *oxygen* joins with *haemoglobin* in *red blood cells*   52–53, 105

P

pancreas: *organ* which makes pancreatic juice and *insulin*   9, 13, 16, 19–20, 84, 86–87, 109, 180

partially permeable membrane: a membrane which allows the passage of some substances but not others   70–71

pesticide: chemical which kills pests   142, 146–147

phloem: *tissue* which transports sugars in plants   58–59, 73

photosynthesis: process in which plants use light energy to make *glucose* from *carbon dioxide* and water   59, 62–68, 72, 100–101, 138

pituitary gland: gland in the base of the brain that produces *hormones* including *ADH, FSH* and *LH*   111, 160–162, 204–205

plasma: the liquid part of blood   38–39

platelets: bits of *cells* needed for clotting blood   38–39, 52

pollute, pollution: to contaminate the environment with undesirable materials or energy   136–137, 142–143

population: all the plants or animals of one *species* which live in a particular place   124–127

predator: an animal which eats other animals   124–127, 195, 203

prey: an animal which is eaten by another animal   124–127

producer: an organism (usually a green plant) which makes its own food   128

progesterone: a hormone produced in the *ovaries* after the release of an egg; it prevents the breakdown of the lining of the *uterus (womb)*   205

protease: an *enzyme* which *digests* proteins   17–20

protein: part of your food which you need for growth and repair; *genes* control the order of the *amino acids* which make up proteins   12, 14–15, 17–20, 25, 66–67, 88, 192, 211

pulse: the stretching of an *artery* each time your *heart* beats   34

pupil: an opening in the *iris* of your eye which lets light reach your *retina*   80–81, 92

pyramid of energy: pyramid-shaped diagram showing the decrease in energy as you go up a *food chain*   152–153

pyramid of number: pyramid-shaped diagram showing how the numbers of organisms change as you go up a *food chain*   129, 131, 153

pyramid of biomass: pyramid-shaped diagram showing the decrease in *biomass* as you go up a *food chain*   131, 152

R

receptors: sensory cells, cells which detect *stimuli*   78–83, 107

recessive: an *allele* that does not show up if the *dominant allele* is present   178–179, 181, 208

recycling: using materials over and over again   133, 136, 138–9, 156–157

red blood cells: *cells* in blood which carry *oxygen* as oxyhaemoglobin   10, 38–39, 52–53, 105, 181–182

reflex action: a quick automatic response to a *stimulus*; no thought is needed   83, 107

relax: in the case of a muscle, become longer and thinner; the opposite of *contract*   24, 48, 106

relay neurone: a connector *neurone* in the *central nervous system*   107

reproduce, reproduction: to breed or make offspring   41, 176–177

respiration: the breakdown of food to release energy in living *cells*   28–29, 61, 89, 100–101, 138, 152

retina: layer of light sensitive *cells* lining the eye   80–81, 106

root hairs: the tiny hairs just behind root tips; they increase the surface area for absorption of water and minerals   70–71, 103

rooting hormone: plant *hormone* which stimulates root growth in a *cutting*   77, 188–189

S

salivary glands: glands in the mouth which produce a digestive juice called *saliva*   18, 107

sclera: the tough white outer coat of the eye   80–81

selective breeding: breeding only from the plants or animals which have the characteristics we want; also called *artificial selection*   154, 184–187, 190–191

sense organ: *organ* which detects *stimuli*, e.g. the eye   78–82

sensory neurones: nerve *cells* which connect *receptors* to the brain and spinal cord   81–83, 107

sewage: watery waste containing organic material which goes into the sewers   136–137, 146, 159

sex cells: cells which join to form new plants or animals (also called *gametes*)   166–167

sexual reproduction: reproduction in which two *gametes* join to form a new cell; the offspring produced vary   172–173, 190, 206

sickle cell disorder: an *inherited disorder* of the *red blood cells* caused by a *recessive* allele   181–182, 209

small intestine: the narrow part of intestine between *stomach* and *large intestine* where *digestion* finishes and *absorption* takes place; *villi* increase its surface area for absorption   9, 13–16, 19–21, 30, 36, 54

solute: the name for a substance that dissolves in a liquid   70–71

solvent: a chemical in which other substances will dissolve, some are *drugs*   90–93

specialised: particularly suited or *adapted* to do a particular job   10–11

species: we say that plants or animals which can breed with each other belong to the same species. Members of a species vary because they inherit different combinations of **alleles**   123, 126, 168, 212

sperm: male *gamete* (sex cell)   11, 160, 167, 172–175, 207

starch: a *carbohydrate* made from large insoluble molecules   14–15, 17, 19–20, 59, 61–62, 66, 100

stimuli: changes in the surroundings to which living things respond; one is called a stimulus   78, 82–83, 107

stomach: an *organ* in the *digestive system*   9, 13, 16, 18–20

stomata: pores in the skin of a leaf   68–69, 103–104

sulphur dioxide: a poisonous gas that pollutes the air and is one of the causes of *acid rain*   143, 148

suspensory ligament: ligament involved in changing the shape of the *lens* of the eye   80–81, 106

sustainable development: development in a way that won't damage the Earth and will let development keep going   140–141

sweat glands: glands in the skin that produce sweat; this evaporates to cool the body   9, 84, 108

synapse: a tiny gap between one *neurone* and the next   107

T

taste buds: groups of cells on the tongue sensitive to some chemicals   79

thermoregulatory centre: part of the brain that monitors the temperature of the blood   108

thorax: the chest; the part of the body that contains the *heart* and *lungs*   23, 26, 48

tissue: a group of *cells* with the same shape and job   8–9, 58–59

toxins: substances which are poisonous (toxic)   42, 46, 146

trachea: another word for *windpipe*   23, 45

transpiration: the loss of water vapour from plants through leaf pores (*stomata*)   68–69

turgor: the firmness of a plant cell resulting from pressure of the contents on its *cell wall*   103

U

urea: poisonous waste made when the *liver* breaks down excess *amino acids*   36, 38–39, 84, 88–89, 110–111

ureter: a tube that carries urine from a *kidney* to the *bladder*   88, 110–111

urine: the liquid containing water, salts and *urea* excreted by the *kidneys*   88–89, 110–111, 115

uterus: where a baby develops before birth; also called the *womb*   11

V

vaccinated: injected with a weakened *disease* organism to make a person *immune* to that disease   47

vacuole: space filled with cell sap in the *cytoplasm* of a plant cell   56

vagina: opening of human female reproductive system   11

valves: these stop blood flowing the wrong way   32–33

variations: differences   168–169, 173, 191, 213

veins: blood vessels which carry blood towards the *heart*   34–35, 37

ventilate, ventilation: causing a flow of air, e.g. into and out of the *lungs*   26, 48

ventricles: the two thick–walled lower chambers of the *heart*   32–33

villi: microscopic folds in the lining of the *small intestine* that increase its surface area   30, 55

viruses: *microorganisms* which can only live inside other *cells*   40–41, 44, 46

vitamins: substances in food which we need in small amounts to cell stay healthy   12, 15

voluntary action: an action that you decide to do   107

W

white blood cells: *cells* in blood which help to destroy *microorganisms* and the *toxins* they produce   38–39, 42, 46–47

wilting: drooping of the leaves and stems of a plant as a result of water loss and loss of *turgor*   68, 104, 188

windpipe: the tube between your throat and your *bronchi*; also called the *trachea*   23

womb: another word for *uterus*   11, 160–162, 191

X

X chromosome: human sex *chromosome*; males
have one, females have two   174–175

xylem: a *tissue* in plants which transports water
and minerals   58–59, 71, 73

Y

Y chromosome: human sex *chromosome* causing
maleness   174–175

yield: how much food a plant crop or farm animal
can produce   100, 184